Ultrasound Unwrapped

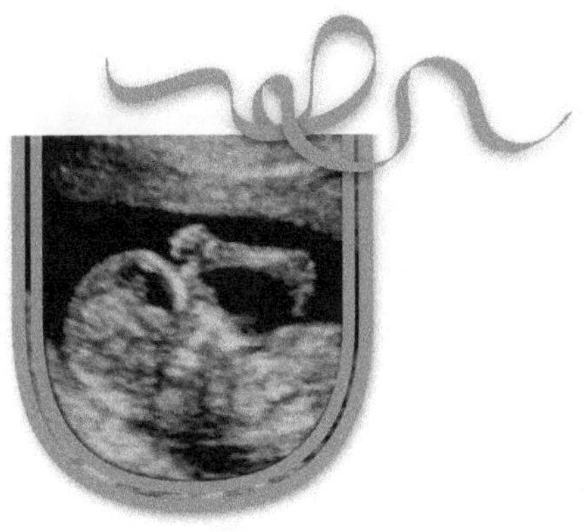

Ultrasound Unwrapped

A Week-by-Week
Pregnancy Image Guide

Sandra M. Minck, RDMS

Published by Parta Arts LLC, Sarasota, Florida

Library of Congress Cataloging-in-Publication Data is available:

Ultrasound Unwrapped: A Week-by-Week Pregnancy Image Guide / by Sandra M. Minck.
    p. cm.

ISBN 978-163821933-0 (paperback)

E-Pub ISBN: 978-163821936-1

To Her & Her ~

You have made motherhood worth every ache & labor pain.

To Him ~

Your love, encouragement & support have been invaluable.

Oh, yeah, & your patience…definitely that.
Thank you for all your patience as I pushed out this baby,
a labor about as long as the gestation period of an elephant.

Okay, two.
Two elephants.

Contents

Part Two ~ First Trimester Growth
Week 4 through Week 13

Part Three ~ Gender Identification
Week 14 through Week 38

Preface

My greatest love of ultrasound lies with teaching, whether it's expectant parents, gynecology patients, students, or my daughters' friends. I'm happy to help anyone who expresses a genuine interest in understanding the shifting clouds of gray on the monitor. My patients' topics of interest were:

- How we do what we do,
- How in the *world* we see anything, and
- How long did it take *me* to understand "The Art of Ultrasound."

My greatest concerns are the misconceptions and myths surrounding OB ultrasound. My patients voiced the same questions over the years, on a weekly basis. Despite an age of technology at our fingertips, they still didn't understand ultrasound or what to expect from their examinations. Whether excited for a peek at their fetus, anxious for results, or skeptical about what they can't read on the monitor, many demonstrated a fascination for how ultrasound works and a curiosity to understand it better.

All my years of baby-bump scanning and parent unease sent me to my computer. It was time I consulted Dr. Google, myself, as so many patients do, to obtain a first-hand look at what my patients were finding. The results were astonishing, to say the least. With all the fearful and contradictory material proliferated by the Internet and social media, it's no wonder expectant parents are either confused, or disappointed, by their exams!

- "Why can't you determine my baby's sex?"
- "Machines are so sophisticated these days; how does anyone get the gender wrong?"
- "I've read ultrasound isn't safe."
- "What should you see at this week in pregnancy?"

- "How can you tell how far along I am?"
- "Why can't you give me results?"

These are just a few of the many concerns posed by my patients. Expectant moms worry about enough, right? Information is power; but the wrong information can prove harmful, feeding the anxiety we all feel when we can't comprehend the present or anticipate the future. Medical articles are too complicated for the majority to pick apart. Many in the "natural pregnancy" camp push slanted views with no credible or factual basis of truth, improperly influencing those who are unfamiliar. Often, expectant parents turn to family and friends or hundreds of strangers in a community forum to gain insight into an ultrasound finding. Unfortunately, these contributors grow the problem, often leaving the anxious parent with more questions.

I've scanned more women than I can recall who came in for their sonograms, afraid by what they were told or something they read. Unfortunately, despite the desperate search for answers, only your physician can answer questions about *your* specific case. However, so much general ultrasound information exists that can and should be shared with you, the parents-to-be.

Fetal sonography is one of *the* most anticipated events between the home pregnancy test and delivery. But I don't have to tell *you* that, do I! I want this book to leave you with the information you crave, the knowledge you seek, and the awareness you need.

Ultrasound today plays a major role in your pregnancy. I hope I'm successful in enlightening you about this ever-important technology—a vehicle to a healthier mom and baby and safer delivery.

Best wishes for a happy and healthy pregnancy!

Sandra M. Minck, RDMS

Sarasota, Florida
April 2021

Acknowledgements

The creation and publication of this book became the closest thing to labor I've experienced since my pregnancies with my own two babies many moons ago. And delivery, nearly as sweet. Very similar to raising children, it requires a learning curve, necessitates help from professionals when we don't have all the answers, and takes a village of support. I couldn't have completed this without my fellow villagers. Otherwise, the idea might still be sitting quietly on the back burner of life, waiting for an opportunity to bloom. Without further ado, I'd like to extend a heart-filled thanks to some honeybees who helped me grow this concept to become the print and digital creation I hoped it could be.

I might not very well have a book, or a decent one, if not for Lisa and Lee, the truly ingenious book crafters with a world of knowledge who generously extended their expertise and guidance in formatting and design. Lisa, a million thanks for the million emails and my never-ending list of questions. My deepest gratitude for not only your willingness to help me create the most polished version of my book but too for the vast amount of precious time and consideration invested. I will be forever indebted.

Thanks to Dianne, who allowed me to use the images of her Sweet Peas for the creation of this book, which would not have been the same without them.

Thank you to my family and friends who gave up a bit of prized personal time to provide outside perspective for improvements to this work. Your support means the world. You know how much I love you.

A warm thanks to Alex, for sharing her long journey to motherhood and her creative contribution to my book and website's title, Ultrasound Unwrapped. A perfect fit!

I must also express sincere thanks to some very special co-workers and physicians who have taught me much on this journey called my career. I have learned volumes through your own work, your direction and instruction, the caring relationships you developed with your patients, your constructive feedback, and respect for my work. It fueled my motivation to keep learning and scanning. You *all* made me a better sonographer.

To the many patients who touched my heart and inspired me to share what I've learned…they promoted a desire in me to teach others but taught me empathy, which is what we all need in healthcare to be better providers. Most importantly, they've helped me to be a better, more caring person. Thank you.

To every expectant mom or dad who allowed images for use on my site or in this book—thank you for sharing and trusting me with your questions. They may very well have helped others with your same concerns.

S.M.M.

Introduction

Congratulations! The results are in, and you've got the positive pregnancy test to prove it. Now what?

Welcome to one of the most incredible and surreal experiences of your life. Early pregnancy has your heart racing and your mind reeling with so many thoughts and questions. How far along am I? When can I see a heartbeat? And how *do* we first see that heartbeat which fosters the bond with your baby through the eyes of ultrasound? The excitement is overwhelming but seeing your doctor for the first visit may be weeks away. You want to soak in as much about your new world as your brain will absorb. What else is a curious new mom expected to do but dive head-first into the sea of Internet obstetrics?

Well, you're not alone and surfing through hundreds of mysterious ultrasound images from popular sites to subjective forums may leave you more confused than ever.

Most newly expectant parents ponder the same things. Do all babies look the same this early? When will I have my first ultrasound? When can Baby's sex be seen? How big is Baby now, and how much growth will take place next week and the week after? How will Baby change, and what should I expect to see at Week 5, 7, or 11?

I am a certified sonographer, having specialized in the field of OB/GYN with experience in all weeks of pregnancy. With a career spanning more than 25 years, I answer all these questions, and more, in this book where an expectant parent can follow Baby's amazing transformation in the First Trimester via the modern-day technology of ultrasound. Part One of this book provides interesting facts about how ultrasound works and what you can expect from your ultrasound examination.

Part Two of this book provides captivating weekly images and measurements from the First Trimester, beginning at Week 4 through Week 13. You can explore Baby's evolution from the first signs of pregnancy to a fully formed fetus.

E-book readers can enjoy a fun little video clip of movement at Week 9, and all readers can follow the intriguing journey of weekly change in the First Trimester, when the greatest changes take place.

As an added bonus, all in one place, Part Three shows you images of both male and female genders from the Second and Third Trimesters. From Week 14 and almost every week after, you can explore the differences between male and female genitalia on ultrasound and how different one image can appear from the next. Each image is annotated with a full explanation, taking out the guesswork and providing a bit of insight. By the end of this book, you will have a clearer understanding of ultrasound and some of the images taken during your own sonogram.

Based on my blog, UltrasoundUnwrapped.com, this book addresses in more detail some of the very same concerns readers have in common with parents-to-be who've emailed with similar questions from all over the world. This book will not only guide you through ultrasound growth and gender differences but will educate, inform, and entertain the expectant mother, couple-in-waiting, or even the curious-at-heart. Patients are always astounded by Baby's metamorphosis, and you will be, too.

Read what these moms have to say about my blog:

I just wanted to let you know that your blog has been a complete savior to me and my sanity over the past few nights. It is brilliant and informative and just what I needed in my hormonal state.

Oh my gosh, this is so funny, interesting, and highly informative. I've been searching for information about sonography to get the real point of view, and yours is the best I've seen. I am so happy to have found your blog!!

Yes! Finally, something about week-by-week pregnancy! At last, someone who can explain this topic clearly in a manner somebody like me can understand.

Are you craving more information about what you can expect to see when it comes time for your first ultrasound examination? Are you curious about Baby's weekly changes and growth via ultrasound in the First Trimester? Would you love to learn a little more about how to decipher between male and female genders on ultrasound? If so, read on!

Part One ~

Unpacking the Facts

Chapter 1

Unwrapping Ultrasound

You're pregnant! What a thrilling time in your life and that of your family. If this is your first experience with pregnancy, a whole new world is opening to you, and you want to learn as much as you can about this new life inside you. Whether this is your first or fifth pregnancy, each is a new universe in and of itself.

After 25 years in the practice of obstetrical ultrasound, it seems that as many perplexities about ultrasound still exist today for expectant parents as when I began in the field. However, most everyone with access to modern medicine is familiar in some way with a fetal sonogram. It has become one of the most anticipated events of a pregnancy. In fact, most people do not consider their ultrasound the medical examination it really is, but instead, an exciting event that allows all branches of the family tree to meet the new addition.

In my years of performing literally tens of thousands of ultrasound examinations, the early pregnancy scan can truly be one of the happiest and most fulfilling experiences for both patient and operator, but also the most heart-wrenching. I always felt overwhelmed with emotion when I could show an overjoyed couple the first flutters of their baby's heartbeat. If they cried, I had to choke back the tears, too. As a healthcare provider, I always felt so very honored to witness such a special moment in the lives of others.

When all was good, it was very good. Holding hands. Tears of happiness. I would hear them quietly (or exuberantly) congratulate one another with "I love you!" or cheers of "We did it!" This became my most favorite experience of all over the years. The occasion was especially sweet for those patients who had tried for a baby for so long, either undergoing tiresome fertility treatments or otherwise suffering traumatic recurrent pregnancy losses. Both scenarios create such anxiety, but success is so beautiful! I even thought to myself on occasion how sentimental it was for these people, wishing I could vanish for a while so they could savor the moment together. Yet, I was the one holding the probe. So, instead, I would simply give them a minute to relish the elation and on I'd go, happily narrating the big show on the monitor. It's about the only time, I believe, that a patient *doesn't* mind the endovaginal examination.

When all was not good, I was reminded of the important roles of ultrasound and sonographer. What it meant to a heart-broken parent. To witness and experience the first news of loss with a couple. To guide them through a very difficult, emotional, and sometimes traumatic examination. Unfortunately, a sonogram is not always the celebratory event to which many equate it.

Even though ultrasound is generally considered a fun and exciting event because it allows visibility of the unborn child, to count little fingers and look for gender, the technology is foremost a very important diagnostic tool for the obstetrician or other healthcare professional. These examinations assist in managing the mother's pregnancy, health, and Baby's health. During your amazing belly transformation, you might find yourself swimming in a foreign sea of obstetrics and technology. And there is absolutely no shortage of material on the subject, is there? It's enough to make a new parent's head swim with what to read first.

> *I'll take the opportunity here, as I've expressed in my blog, to reinforce that I am not a physician, nor do I act as one in this book. I am not providing medical advice but, instead, simply sharing knowledge I've gained in the field and extending the same general information to you that I have shared with past patients or blog and social media followers. I do not overstep the boundaries of my title. It is essential to understand that the information presented here may not be representative of your pregnancy or experience. Any concerns regarding your ultrasound examination or prenatal health should be directed to your healthcare professional.*

No matter what people look like on the outside, we are all the same on the inside...including our growing, unborn babies. We all start out the same way! The goal of this first chapter is to address the questions I was asked most often and to help you better understand the use of ultrasound, its purpose and limitations, and the curious role of sonographer. Let's dive right in!

1.1 A Little Ultrasound History

Many patients over the years have asked when ultrasound started and you might be surprised just how far back it dates. You may already know it is used for other parts of the body, beginning in the 1930s. However, the application to obstetrics for the care of mother and baby is credited to a U.K. obstetrician, Dr. Ian Donald, for his work in Glasgow, Scotland in the late 1950s. In 1958, he co-authored a medical article which published the very first images of a fetus [1]. Of course, vast improvements in the technology developed over the ensuing years with better and better visualization of fetal and maternal organs until it became the integral tool it is today.

Ultrasound has become a vital instrument for obstetricians and other providers caring for you, the patient. It plays an imperative role in the management of mother and fetus and, in the most knowledgeable hands, remains a tool which can diagnose volumes of pregnancy-related problems and fetal malformations. The information we can obtain with sonography has saved the lives of mothers and babies by removing some of the guesswork for the clinician. This is especially true for the patient who presents with a particular history, such as ectopic pregnancy, or abnormal symptoms such as pain or bleeding in early pregnancy.

When ultrasound sheds light on a potentially life-threatening or life-limiting abnormality, it enables your doctor to more safely and effectively manage your pregnancy and delivery. Moreover, these discoveries enable your caregiver to provide the timely education you and your family may need to prepare for Baby's arrival. This was the goal of ultrasound's founding fathers.

1.2 What Is Ultrasound?

Ultrasound is just that...ULTRA sound, or sound waves that operate at a frequency far beyond human hearing in the megahertz (MHz) or millions of Hertz.

For comparison, human hearing ranges from about 20 Hz (Hertz) to 20,000 Hz [2].

Ultrasound probes for obstetric use operate at a frequency range of about 2–15 MHz.

The use of Doppler technology is also ultrasound. Your healthcare provider may use a hand-held Doppler transducer to detect Baby's heartbeat, starting at about Week 10. The frequency of these Dopplers ranges from 2–5 MHz. Special training is required for these Dopplers to distinguish maternal blood flow from fetal heart tones.

You may typically find most Ultrasound departments under the umbrella of Diagnostic Radiology within a hospital, but ultrasound does not emit ionizing radiation like an X-ray. The reason your dentist might shield your abdomen when taking X-rays of your teeth if you are either pregnant or unsure would be to protect you from potentially harmful effects of ionizing radiation emitted by this type of exam.

1.3 Is Ultrasound Safe?

Let's put some truth out there, shall we? The Internet and even a couple of popular pregnancy books on the market today incorrectly fill their pages with baseless and unsupported information about ultrasound. So, without further ado, let's get to the bottom of what is safe and what is not, what is recommended, and what is not encouraged. And most importantly, why.

Let me begin with two statements of critical and essential fact despite what you may have read anywhere else:

Ultrasound is NOT radiation.

This is a well-known and proven scientific fact [3].

When modern commercial equipment is maintained and utilized with recommended settings for power and duration of scanning, ultrasound is considered safe for the fetus [4].

Continued biohazard testing has shown that heat can be created over time and with specific power settings, but no reports of adverse fetal effects have been documented. Nor is it believed that a sustained temperature elevation can be targeted to any particular fetal organ structure [5].

This information is substantiated by three long-standing and highly esteemed associations of educated physicians, scientists, and other medical professionals dedicated to the advancement of care and safe practices for all patients served:

- ACOG or The American College of Obstetricians and Gynecologists [6]

- ACR or The American College of Radiology—its patient information site [7],

- AIUM or The American Institute of Ultrasound in Medicine [8]

These websites provide valuable and accurate information for any interested parent-to-be. You'll see mostly scientific and technical information, but they also offer easily understandable explanations for the general public, as well.

Anyone formally educated to use ultrasound should be trained on the ALARA principle—As Low As Reasonably Achievable—using the lowest equipment power settings and least amount of time to achieve needed results. Without this education, it is possible to scan using much higher power settings than recommended for a fetus, especially using today's most modern ultrasound equipment.

For now, because science has yet to show adverse outcomes for the brief time needed to conduct your diagnostic scan, the medical community believes the benefits far outweigh any potential risk. Again, those benefits include ruling out fetal/maternal abnormalities and closer management, if found, for the safety and health of mother and fetus.

Let's look at an example of how ultrasound makes a difference. The discovery of a severe malformation of the heart by ultrasound would elicit pursuit of a diagnosis with further testing and Maternal Fetal Medicine visits with a perinatologist, or high-risk OB doctor. Baby's well-being would be monitored throughout the pregnancy to determine the best timing and method of delivery. Parents would be counseled and educated on what to expect before and after delivery. A plan for delivery is discussed in advance.

Because not all hospitals are equipped to handle the needs of a newborn with a severe heart abnormality, especially one requiring surgery at birth, preparations for delivery must be made in conjunction with a major hospital that can offer such facilities and staff.

Often, parents must make travel accommodations to a nearby major city or state which can offer such state-of-the-art care—for prenatal care as well as delivery. Without ultrasound, such findings go undetected severely limiting Baby's chances for survival.

Everyone wants a healthy baby. Ultrasound screenings have proven to be a reliable and safe method of diagnosing many conditions which help your physician to better manage your pregnancy and to more effectively care for you and your baby, ultimately leading to healthier maternal and fetal outcomes.

In fact, the United Nations implemented a plan for improvement in maternal health in countries with few resources as Goal 5 of the Millennium Development Goals, 2009–2015. In 2013 alone, an estimated 289,000 maternal deaths occurred globally, 14 times higher than in developed countries. In data gathered from 2003–2009, an estimated 27 percent of deaths were due to hemorrhage. Many of these deaths were preventable if certain conditions had been detected and managed earlier in the pregnancy [9].

Part of this goal for improvement included access to ultrasound and training for healthcare providers in obstetric care to help decrease this rate. The use of ultrasound can detect life-threatening conditions, such as multiple gestations, ectopic pregnancy, and placenta previa [10]. Early detection means early intervention and lives saved!

In short, a diagnostic ultrasound provides far more than just a fun peek at Baby. The keepsake images, gender guesses, and moments of bonding as you watch your Baby kick and yawn in utero are all side perks of this technology.

1.4 Non-Medical Ultrasound Businesses

Okay, maybe a few words! Sure, they offer the movie-theater experience as a special bonding event for you and your family. The desire is understandable! Who doesn't want to see Baby on the Big Screen?

The medical community understands these non-medical facilities fill a void. Parents want to see their babies more often than physicians can provide a valid, medically indicated scan, which is the only time a healthcare provider is justified in ordering an ultrasound exam.

Thus, elective, non-medical, privately owned businesses have cropped up on practically every street corner in major cities all over the United States and beyond. They offer what your doctor's office cannot—a view of Baby any time you are willing to pay for it. They fulfill your desire to see Baby and guess gender, but how safe are they and who is scanning you? The expectant parent, feels "surely, it must be safe, or they wouldn't be open." You would be wrong in that assumption.

Actually, anyone with the money to purchase an ultrasound machine can open one of these businesses—regardless of whether he or she possesses the expertise to operate it. Scary? I think so, too. And here are a few things *you* should know before you decide to go.

Non-Educated Users

These facilities are not required to hire formally educated sonographers to scan you. I have personally received advertisements in the mail regarding the purchase of an ultrasound franchise where "I could learn ultrasound in days." I assure you this is not possible.

Granted, they won't be providing you with a diagnostic examination, but wouldn't you want someone scanning you to *be able* to recognize a problem? And let's go back to the ALARA principle. Do they know anything about safe power settings, and how long are they scanning you?

Some businesses even call themselves "diagnostic imaging" centers. Again, they cannot perform a legitimate diagnostic scan "to make sure everything is okay." Even if they reassure you this is part of your visit, a diagnostic exam can only be performed in a medical facility for which your physician has ordered a scan. A report must be generated, interpreted, and signed by a physician, and a physician must be present on-site before any examinations can begin. These centers cannot legally make any assurances about your baby's well-being.

True story: A reader emailed me once saying she arrived for her elective ultrasound—at someone's private residence. She was unsure at first whether she had the correct address. She did. The setup was very informal with a machine and table configured in this woman's living room. The "sonographer" was quick and abrupt and less-than- friendly/professional. My reader proceeded with the visit though the whole awkward arrangement caused her a bit of unease. She left declaring it was something she'd never do again. Hmm. Formally educated sonographer or graduate of the quickie weekend course? Please don't allow this to happen to you.

No Safety Standards

These businesses are not regulated like medical practices. What's more, they are not required to meet the same standards for patient care and safety as medical practices. Ultrasound equipment is expensive and costly to maintain, with a single probe costing $10,000 or more. Probes crack, old cords fray; these problems can result in an electrical hazard. Are they properly maintaining their equipment? Is equipment inspected on a regular basis to ensure it is safe to use? Are probes disinfected between each customer? This last question is so important, and one can only hope. But, would you know otherwise? Furthermore, would the person scanning you, if not a real sonographer, even know to monitor these things?

True, ultrasound is recognized as a safe and useful diagnostic tool for the management of health of mother and baby. But biohazard testing is on-going and no one can say positively that harmful effects won't be a future discovery. This is the very reason why minimal exposure is recommended, for diagnostic purposes, and only by those formally educated on how to properly use the equipment. No one can *keep* you from visiting these businesses; they can only advise you. So, what's the advice?

- Do your research on the facility.
- Ask your healthcare provider about elective scans and whether he/she takes issue with your having them.
- Ask if your sonographer is formally trained with RDMS (registered) or DMS (registry-eligible) credentials (pertaining to U.S. sonographers).
- Never assume an elective scan at one of these businesses can replace a diagnostic scan ordered by your physician.

And I'll add one more piece of advice here. If during one of these visits, your "sonographer" makes any concerning comments regarding the health of your pregnancy, call your doctor. Know that a physician will not typically be on site in a non-medical facility. Do not assume your physician will be alerted. Only an evaluation by your healthcare professional can assure you that all is okay or confirm a problem exists.

To be sure, I do not maintain that all non-medical businesses offering entertainment ultrasound do not employ formally trained sonographers and utilize safe equipment. I am only here to inform you that some do not. And it isn't something these businesses advertise—because they aren't required to do so.

Parent-to-be, physician, sonographer, physician's assistant, or midwife— even though we may differ in our views of ultrasound, no one will argue that anything is more important than the health and safety of you and Baby. So, do your homework in advance and be informed. Expectant parents certainly have the right to make choices that best suit their family. Just know before you go who's scanning you and whether you're driving up to someone's living room.

1.5 How Does Ultrasound Work?

Everyone is familiar with the visual of the ultrasound probe smearing gel all around a pregnant belly. You may not realize, however, that sound waves act like a "fish-finder" sent from crystals in the transducer (the probe placed in the vagina or rubbed on your belly). These sound waves then penetrate maternal tissues until they reach Baby, bounce back, and create the image you see on the monitor. A 2-dimensional (2D) image is reflected off the structures that lie directly under the probe.

Moving the probe around the belly allows the sonographer to create a 3D mental picture of Baby's position and other parts. Once we learn to identify certain structures, creating the 3D image in our minds becomes easier. It takes time and experience to become good at this, which is why deciphering what you see on the monitor is difficult to the untrained eye.

1.6 What *IS* That Stuff?

People commonly ask about ultrasound gel. It's made up mostly of water and aids in the transmission of sound waves. Sound travels well through liquids but not through air. Without gel, a tiny layer of air exists between the surface of the skin and the probe, producing only black on the monitor. No gel, no image!

Most places are nice enough to keep the goop warmed in a little electric heater made for just that purpose—which, by the way, has been around longer than my career. And since room-temperature gel feels like ice, using warm gel is just plain nice. Most patients greatly appreciate it!

Kids are equally fascinated by the goopy stuff smeared all over mom's belly. I always enjoyed squirting a bit of gel into the hand of a willing and adventurous sibling and watching his or her reaction. They either laugh and play with it, make a disgusted face and look to wipe it off immediately, or simply stare at it. The varied reactions usually prompt a good chuckle from everyone.

Another comical observation is that I could always seem to differentiate veteran moms from the first timers. The patients who have been around the motherhood block, for example, always jumped right off the table after an exam and took a quick swipe at the gel before adjusting her clothes with a, "Oh, who cares, it'll dry in a sec!" Conversely, most new moms were grossed out, using tissues and wet wipes galore to ensure not a trace was left. It's just funny to see how most of us moms really do undergo a dirt-and-grime metamorphosis by the time the stork drops the second child on our doorstep.

1.7 Why Are Some Images So Clear and Others Fuzzy?

Factors such as a patient's size and fetal position can (and do quite often) limit what parts we see and how well we see them. The laws of ultrasound physics dictate that the more tissue sound must travel through before reaching Baby, the weaker the signal by the time it gets back to the monitor. So, the more abdominal fat and tissue that exists between the probe and Baby, the more difficulty in seeing Baby clearly.

Fetal position very frequently presents challenges for visualization. Bones become more calcified over time, absorbing the sound waves and creating a shadow over anything behind it. Figure 1.7-1 is a good example of this limitation.

Can you see here how part of the femur near the top of the image casts a shadow below it? Everything in the shadow is nearly obliterated. Now, can you imagine if Baby was turned just a bit more? The shadow could have obscured male genitalia in this view. What's important to note here is that any shadow from any bone at just the right angle can obstruct the view of any organ we need to document for your diagnostic scan. This is a well-known limitation of the technology, which is one of the reasons why we cannot diagnose 100 percent of structural fetal problems with ultrasound. We cannot diagnose what we technically cannot see.

If Baby is napping or otherwise comfortable, he or she typically stays put, despite belly jiggling or rolling mom to each side. We rejoice when these tricks of the trade actually work.

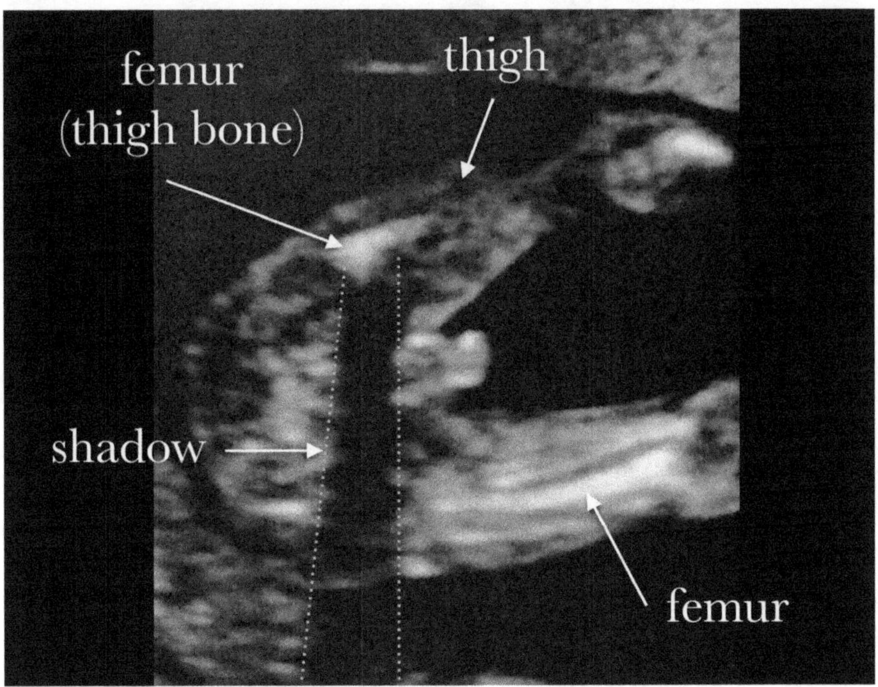

Figure 1.7-1: Femur Shadow in a Week-16 Male Fetus

Another obstacle when scanning is the presence of gas or feces (sorry, there's no better way to say this!) between the probe and desired subject. The more that's there, the more difficult the scan, no matter how thin the patient. Ultrasound does not travel well through air and gas which always create a poor or limited view on the monitor.

Additionally, because sound does travel so well through fluid, decreased amniotic fluid certainly hinders image quality. Even if the level of amniotic fluid is normal, the presence of very little fluid around a fetal area in question limits the ability to see it well. This is a common problem when determining gender if Baby's legs are closed or the cord gets in the way.

All these factors can create a fuzzier image or one of very poor quality. Impeding variables which lie with the patient or Baby stretch beyond any sonographer's control. We cannot change them and can only try to work around them, which is why the sonographer is constantly adjusting buttons with the left hand and always attempting to improve the image with every movement of the probe in the right hand. Many patients have asked over the years if I'm left-handed. I'm not, but I'm doing all the real work with the right.

1.8 Sonographer or Ultrasound Technologist?

Either! Sonographers are not nurses, or X-ray technicians (though some do transition to ultrasound). We have specifically studied a curriculum for ultrasound training or cross-trained in ultrasound from another field in Radiology. Once a sonographer completes and passes the training program, he or she uses the credentials, DMS, or Diagnostic Medical Sonographer. This person needs supervision for a certain period of time along with obtaining work experience before taking certification examinations provided by the national certifying body in ultrasound, the American Registry of Diagnostic Medical Sonographers or ARDMS.

After passing the examinations, a sonographer then earns the credentials of a Registered Diagnostic Medical Sonographer or RDMS and is certified to work as such anywhere within the United States.

Ultrasound has many specialties for which a sonographer can be registered, but it's practical and encouraged that a sonographer becomes certified in whatever specialty he or she practices most.

Sonographers must maintain their credentials with Continuing Medical Education (CME) credits, the same as most other professions in the world of healthcare.

1.9 Ultrasound versus Sonogram

We'll address these two words briefly…ultrasound and sonogram. What is the difference, you ask? Well, if you'd like to get super-technical here, ultrasound refers to the study or practice, as a whole. For example, "the Department of Ultrasound" or "the use of ultrasound in obstetrics" refers to the technology, study, or practice. Sonogram refers to the examination itself, a study using sound waves with a recording of images or other information. The use of these terms may vary depending on regional preferences, but even those of us in this field use them interchangeably. Neither is wrong!

1.10 The Art of Scanning

Learning the art and practice of sonography were the most difficult tasks of my entire life. It was a whole new world and not one for the meek, I must say. The adage "sink or swim" comes to mind. Confidence in my work did not come quickly or easily, and like so many other arts in life, honing the skill takes many months of everyday practice. Becoming an exceptional sonographer in all respects can take years. The goal is to obtain registry status and, in my opinion, to proactively learn something new every week through normal and abnormal examinations and co-sonographer/physician feedback.

So, in the most superficial and basic of terms, yes! I was a "fetal photographer." And in the most complex of descriptions, sonographers have the sometimes-daunting task of finding and diagnosing fetal and maternal abnormalities, reporting them accurately, and providing a level of quality patient care regardless of distractions and time constraints. It was always my desire to deliver the caliber of education and entertainment a patient expected from the visit.

It's the reward of patient care that keeps us going…and keeps us caring about doing a good job. It's a great feeling to receive reassuring feedback from a physician or a heartfelt hug from an appreciative patient. They filled me with a sense of purpose—that I had done something good for a fellow human and made a positive contribution.

I learned so much from so many; the invaluable lessons made me a better sonographer. At the end of the day, I believe it's the desire to help others that drives most of us to the field of healthcare. But it is how others, in turn, affect us —in so many unexpected ways, both big and small—that keeps us there for our entire careers.

References

1. Campbell, S., *A Short History of Sonography in Obstetrics and Gynecology*, Facts Views Vis Obgyn. 2013; 5(3): 213–229. (https://www.ncbi.nlm.nih.gov/pmc/articles/PMC3987368/)

2. Purves, D., Augustine, G.J., Fitzpatrick, D., editors. *The Audible Spectrum, Neuroscience.* 2nd edition. 2001. (https://www.ncbi.nlm.nih.gov/books/NBK10924/)

3. The American College of Radiology and Radiology Society of North America, Radiology Information Resource website. Obstetric Ultrasound. (https://www.radiologyinfo.org/en/info.cfm?pg=obstetricus)

4. The American College of Obstetricians and Gynecologists, Ultrasound Exams, FAQ025, June 2017. Reviewed June 2020. (www.acog.org/Patients/FAQs/Ultrasound-Exams)

5. The American College of Obstetricians and Gynecologists, Committee Opinion No. 723: *Guidelines for Diagnostic Imaging During Pregnancy and Lactation*, October 2017. (https://www.acog.org/clinical/clinical-guidance/committee-opinion/articles/2017/10/guidelines-for-diagnostic-imaging-during-pregnancy-and-lactation?utm_source=redirect&utm_medium=web&utm_campaign=otn)

6. The American College of Obstetricians and Gynecologists (ACOG), About Us, Home Page, Accessed January 2021, (https://www.acog.org/About-ACOG/About-Us)

7. The American College of Radiology (ACR) and Radiology Society of North America, Radiology Information Resource website, Accessed January 2021, (https://www.radiologyinfo.org)

8. The American Institute of Ultrasound in Medicine (AIUM) Information website, Accessed January 2021, (https://www.aium.org/aboutUs/aboutUs.aspx)

9. *The United Nations Millennium Development Goals for 2015*, page 39. (https://www.un.org/millenniumgoals/2015_MDG_Report/pdf/MDG%202015%20rev%20(July%201).pdf)

10. Stanton, K. and Mwanri, L., "Global Maternal and Child Health Outcomes: The Role of Obstetric Ultrasound in Low Resource Settings." *World Journal of Preventive Medicine*, 2013; 1(3): 22–29. (doi: 10.12691/jpm-1-3-3, (https://www.researchgate.net/publication/258281071)

Chapter 2

LMP & How That Egg Thing Works
(aka Your Period and Ovulation)

What is LMP? Initially, how far along you are or your gestational age (GA) is determined by the first day of your last menstrual period, otherwise known as your LMP. These are the calculations used for ultrasound purposes instead of "actual fetal age." And just so you know right up front, this field is partial to acronyms and abbreviations, so I'll do my best to explain them along the way. I promise, there will be no test at the end.

2.1 How to Calculate Gestational Age

Getting back to our monthly friend…you know the one who always makes an appearance on a day you chose to wear white. After working exclusively in Obstetrics and Gynecology (OB/GYN) for so many years, I was surprised by the number of women who didn't fully understand their cycle and what part of it makes them most fertile. I can relate. Maybe they just daydreamed like me or passed notes during that day in seventh-grade Health class. I eventually figured it all out. But we were all taught something a little different about our menstrual cycles, weren't we?

You may recall feeling embarrassed beyond belief during a Middle School Science class, or maybe your parent or mother-figure felt uncomfortable with the subject and simply avoided the topic. Maybe what you learned came from friends with older sisters—and maybe some of it was incorrect. Sometimes, those teaching us didn't necessarily have all the answers themselves. So, for these reasons, this very short chapter is dedicated to this very worthy cause.

Most of us ladies have had to put up with this "thing" for decades, spending nothing short of a college education on tampons, pads, and new white shorts. We might as well get on board with how it all works, right? With that, let's get right to Day 1 of your menstrual cycle.

2.2 Calculating Your Fertility

The first day of your period kicks off your menstrual cycle and is considered Day 1. If you have a day of spotting before your period starts to flow more heavily, that day of spotting is considered Day 1. If you spot for several days prior to what you would call a normal flow, your doctor may want to chime in on what he or she would technically label as the first day of your cycle.

Ovulation, as you may well be aware, is when an ovary releases an egg. Most women with reliable cycles ovulate between Days 10 and 14. If you have a period like clockwork, every 28 days, congratulations! You are very regular and predicting ovulation will be much easier for you. But some women ovulate earlier or later, depending on whether they have short or long cycles. Some women may have 26-day cycles and ovulate earlier. Others may last 33 days, ovulating later.

Others have a much more difficult time predicting ovulation. Some women experience very irregular cycles with a period every other month or even skip them for months on-end. Trying to conceive with periods like this can be challenging. Some need the intervention of a fertility specialist and, as a result, some women have serial endovaginal ultrasound exams (next chapter!) prior to conceiving to help predict ovulation. These scans, in part, count the number and size of follicles on each ovary. So, what are follicles, you may ask?

Follicles are tiny sacs of fluid on the ovary which look like little black circles on ultrasound. Each follicle contains an egg, but the egg itself cannot be seen. And I've already anticipated the next question you might have rolling around up there in your head: How can ultrasound predict ovulation?

2.3 Time for the Egg Toss

Most women do not realize that a cyst on the ovary can represent pending ovulation; it's not always considered pathology or a worrisome finding. Seeing an ovarian cyst can certainly be a very normal and expected finding during this time of your cycle. If you are one of the lucky women with a regular cycle every month and you are nearing mid-cycle (somewhere around Day 14 or two weeks after the first day of your last period), a cyst on one of your ovaries may be a good indication that ovulation is around the corner.

Now, before we get ahead of ourselves, let me just disclose that cysts come in all sizes with many varying characteristics on ultrasound, and some develop due to other factors. Since this book is not a medical reference, I will keep it simple and only discuss the functional ovarian cyst as it pertains to ovulation.

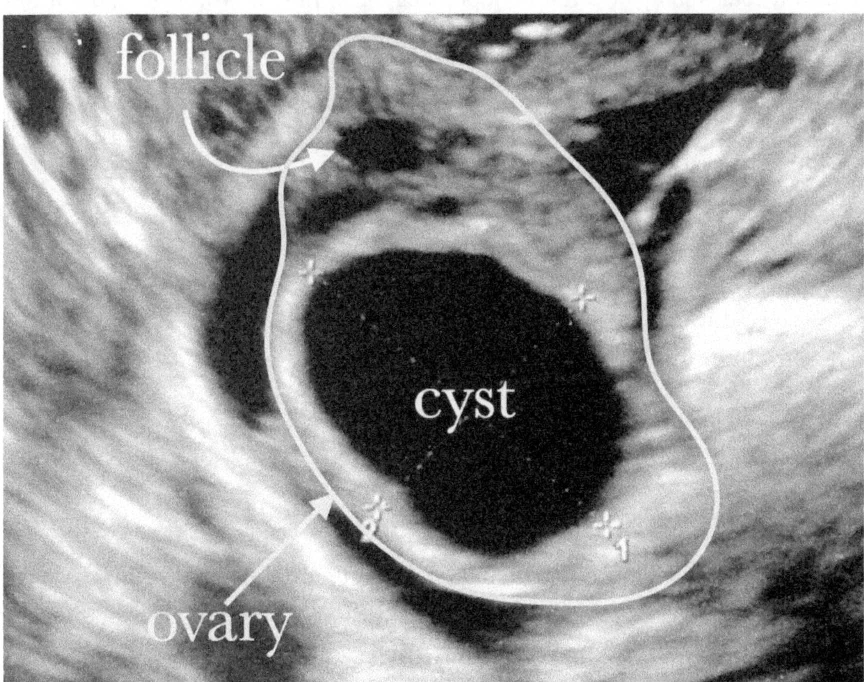

Figure 2.3-1: The Ovulatory Cyst

Hormones tell a follicle to get bigger and become a cyst. These cysts are usually small, filled with fluid only, and contain one egg. If you are desperately trying to conceive, seeing a mid-cycle cyst like this would be welcome news! The cyst will rupture and release the egg somewhere around 3 centimeters (cm), or 1 inch or so. Figure 2.3-1 is an example of what a functional or ovulatory cyst might look like prior to ovulation.

In Figure 2.3-1, the ovary itself is outlined, and the cyst is the black area, representing fluid, inside of the ovary. The white plus signs marked 1 and 2 measure the cyst at 2.7 cm. This means that ovulation can happen any day now, though no one can ever predict the exact moment it actually occurs. If you are desperately trying to conceive a baby and your ovary looks like the one pictured here, put this book down ASAP! Light the candles, pour the wine, and mute your cell phones. You have a very busy evening ahead. (Wink, wink!)

If not, by all means keep reading. You may be interested in the little guy at the white arrow representing a small follicle. "Small" is the operative word here. This tiny follicle may be a future hopeful egg next month or next year, but it has some growing to do to be ready for such an important task.

Within a day or so after ovulation, if you happen to have an ultrasound at that time, we can then see the convoluted walls of the ruptured cyst as it starts to resolve. The black fluid previously seen inside the cyst would be gone. Where does it go? Into the pelvis, typically in the space behind the uterus or around the ovaries until it absorbs back into the body.

Finally, the ruptured cyst takes on an appearance very similar to a deflated balloon. We all know what happens if the egg is fertilized, but what happens when it's not? Not a whole bunch. The egg essentially disintegrates, and you get another period.

Oh, joy…

Everyone is a little different, but most women of child-bearing age have ovaries which demonstrate several small follicles on any given day. Additionally, follicles become fewer and fewer as we get older. Once we reach menopause…no more eggs!

Happy ovulating, everyone. And if you're already expecting as you read this, you are obviously way past this fertilization thing. Hopefully, it was still educational!

Chapter 3
The Dreaded Endovaginal Examination

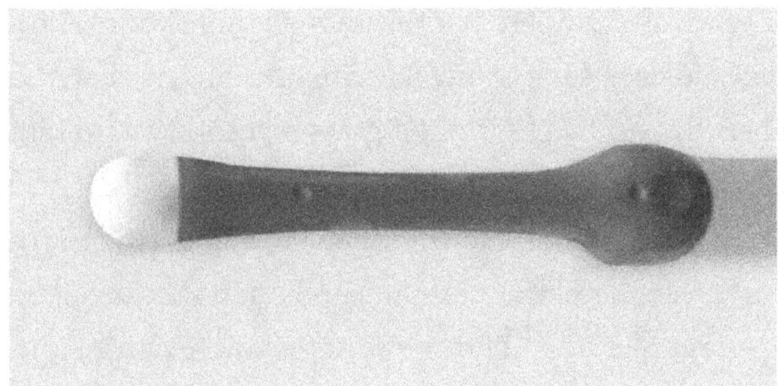

Figure 3.1: The Endovaginal Probe

The transvaginal ultrasound probe...poor thing! It gets such scathing rejection and so little credit. My patient's huge saucer-like eyes always give her fear away when I maneuver it from the machine for an explanation. I surely can't blame her. After all, given its shape, length, and where it goes, vaginal ultrasounds are rarely voluntary. But I can tell you that an expectant mom minds them a whole lot less for the chance to see that little flutter of a heartbeat.

Most patients will undergo this type of exam until about Week 12 of pregnancy. After that, the fetus is a little too big for the image, so an abdominal scan is best. Vaginal ultrasound is (to me anyway!) *the* best invention since ultrasound's inception. In my experience, about 95 percent of the time, I could see everything I needed to see (and saw it better) using the vaginal approach. Scanning this way (as opposed to a belly scan) provides by far the clearest view of Baby in early pregnancy. What's also great about this type of scan is that it requires an empty bladder, unlike the abdominal approach where you may be asked to gulp down an ocean of water.

So, why does vaginal ultrasound help us see so much better? The vaginal probe delivers a higher-frequency sound wave which creates improved resolution. And because your pelvic organs are much closer to the vaginal probe than they are during a belly scan, a clearer and more magnified image of the uterus and ovaries are obtained. Being able to see well is always more satisfying for you *and* your sonographer, whose job it is to choose the best approach for the best visibility.

The probe is covered with a condom or glove. *FYI!* Gloves are made with many different types of materials, but please make sure your sonographer knows if you have a latex allergy. One of my favorite docs always shared a wise thought with her patients: "Down there" is not a great place for you to discover an allergic reaction! I whole-heartedly agree.

The probe is then inserted into the vaginal canal like a tampon. It can only physically go so far as the outside of the cervix and *does not* enter the uterus, a very frequent patient question. The cervix is the lower part of the uterus which holds in the pregnancy and should remain closed until labor. So, while the vaginal probe may sit against the cervix, it cannot pass through it.

Usually, a normal scan with no abnormalities, where Baby is easily seen, takes about 10 to 15 minutes (details in Section 3.1). Once complete, my patients usually commented that the scan wasn't as terrible as expected. Every so often, a patient would tell me about a personal experience or that of a friend where the exam was painful because the sonographer pushed too hard. My first response was that a patient should always tell the technologist if she is using too much pressure! Secondly, we don't need to scan your tonsils. That usually got a laugh, and the end of the exam was always much appreciated.

As a side note, the vaginal probe is disinfected after each patient, and methods vary from one practice to another on how this is achieved. Only a handful of patients in the past inquired about disinfection just prior to an exam. Of course, reassurance was always given. I believe most patients just assume the probe is clean, but it never hurts to ask. It's a valid question!

Many patients may be more familiar with the endovaginal scan today than their mothers, and certainly, their grandmothers. Most every female of childbearing age has either had one or at least forewarned about it by friends or family. Either way, it is still primarily met with a little understandable trepidation.

After all, no one really *enjoys* having her feet firmly planted in stirrups. That said, most patients find it entirely worthwhile to meet her little Sprout for the first time, and I'm betting you will, too.

3.1 The First Trimester Endovaginal Scan

The section describes a little about what sonographers look for in a First Trimester scan. Please note that the following protocol is generalized for many practices within the United States, but it certainly may differ depending on your healthcare provider, insurance, and U.S. region or foreign country in which you live.

If you're seeing a doctor for the first visit to confirm your pregnancy, he or she may perform an endovaginal ultrasound personally. Every physician goes about this a little differently, so some may prefer a sonographer to scan instead. This first scan tells your doctor a few important facts about your pregnancy. Some of the questions your doctor needs answered are:

- Can a pregnancy be seen inside the uterus?
- If so, how far along is the pregnancy?
- Is it a single or multiple pregnancy?
- Is there a normal-appearing yolk sac?
- Is there a heartbeat? How fast is the heart rate?
- Is the pregnancy in its proper place within the uterus?
- Do the uterus and ovaries appear normal?

The more information your examination provides, the better the doctor can manage your pregnancy. From this point, he or she knows just what tests or labs you need next.

How every sonographer narrates a scan for the patient is completely individual and, to a large degree, dictated by sonographer personality as well as the protocol of the department or office in which she works. My protocol was to ensure I saw an embryo with a normal heartbeat first; then I'd immediately point it out to my patient. After all, this is what new parents anticipate most!

Next, I measured the embryo or fetus, then demonstrated for the patient where her baby could be seen on the screen, as well as its size. Moms want to know this stuff! However, in all fairness, all sonographers are limited to some degree as to what they are allowed to show or share with a patient.

3.2 Obtaining Results of the Scan

If a sonographer performs your scan, she'll take the images needed and create a detailed report of what she saw. Any finding documented must be substantiated by images. Then a complete picture of the examination can be presented to your physician. Your doctor examines the information and concludes whether he or she agrees with the sonographer's findings. Your doctor then shares with you, his or her interpretation of the information along with what options are recommended next.

If your ultrasound is performed in a setting where your scan will be interpreted by a radiologist (a physician who reads radiologic exams such as ultrasounds, X-rays, or MRIs), your obstetrician will need that report before discussing the results with you. They may be sent same day if called to your provider, or reports can be as long as about a week depending on their protocol for reporting. This is one of the reasons why many U.S. obstetricians elect to offer in-house ultrasound services. Not only can they order an exam to be performed immediately if they feel it's warranted, they also have immediate access to the images and reports, and they can often provide you with immediate results. Most of all, they can personally observe your scan if a problem is questioned.

One of the most frequently asked patient questions was: "Does everything look okay, healthy, or normal?" Sonographers are not allowed to give you results! We understand patient anxiety, and it is an entirely natural question to ask, but specific medical and legal protocols must be followed. Here's why.

Firstly, sonographers are not physicians. We are trained to perform a diagnostic examination on you and your fetus, and our duty is to share the information we've obtained with your healthcare provider or radiologist interpreting the examination. We do not manage your pregnancy, advise or counsel you, or deliver your baby. This is your obstetrician's specialty who has completed many years of medical training to learn how to manage your care. Other OB healthcare professionals have also under-

gone specialized training. These professionals are the only people truly qualified to answer your multitude of ensuing questions, especially when a problem is suspected.

No matter what news you receive, I do have a bit of advice to offer. Never consult Dr. Google for pregnancy advice! Frantically looking for explanations of a finding from your ultrasound report only creates more anxiety. Letting your fingertips sift through the never-ending abyss of results from an internet search engine provides a whole spectrum of information, ranging from complicated medical studies to another's personal experience.

Because you are unfamiliar with the subject, you end up with more questions than when you began your search. What you read may not even apply to your personal set of circumstances. The Internet is much like ice cream and binge-watching your favorite TV series (one of my personal faves), too much of a good thing really isn't good!

Sometimes, the long-awaited report from your physician is overwhelming, and you have trouble processing all the news. This is understandable. You may be caught off guard with unexpected results, leaving only room for all the Why's and How's. Quite often, patients get home and hardly remember a thing the physician said. It's okay to call your doctor's office to ask his/her nurse for clarification. Create a running list of questions as you think of them and be sure to take that list with you to your next appointment.

It's far better to have accurate information in due time than to have the wrong information right away!

Any distressing issues or worries surrounding you and your pregnancy are best directed to the only person who can calm them…your doctor or medical professional managing your pregnancy. She and her staff are the only people who possess all the medical details of your case and can provide the answers for which you search so desperately. Only your provider and/or staff can answer your questions about your pregnancy and calm your fears or reassure you.

3.3 The Alternative "Full-Bladder" Prep

To drink or not to drink? Some facilities will require you to drink lots of water prior to your ultrasound examination. Being required to fill your bladder depends on a few factors: How far along you are, information needed, and the protocols of your doctor's office, hospital or outpatient center where the ultrasound will be conducted. The protocol for how to conduct your test varies from place to place. Some physicians want to start with a full view of the pelvis, allowing visualization beyond the viewpoint of the transvaginal probe. Others opt for the full bladder only if the transvaginal exam leaves more questions.

At the end of the day, the facility where the exam will be performed will tell you exactly what ultrasound preparation it wants you to follow. And only what they say matters! You may be asked to drink anywhere from 20 to 32 ounces.

The dreaded bladder prep may vary a little from one place to the next, but it goes something like this:

- Empty your bladder 1.5 hours prior to your exam.
- Drink 32 oz of fluid (preferably nothing carbonated) within 30 minutes.
- Have all fluid down 1 hour prior to your exam.
- Do not urinate until your exam is complete!

To clarify, let's say your appointment is 10 a.m. The drinking schedule might look something like this:

- Empty your bladder at 8:30 a.m.
- Begin drinking at 8:30 a.m. and finish drinking all the water by 9 a.m. Most bladders require the full hour to fill completely.

Remember, do not use the restroom before your appointment time! This action, of course, defeats the whole purpose for drinking, but you would be surprised at how many patients overlook this tiny detail.

Will you feel like you need to "tinkle" before this hour is up? For sure (if your bladder filled entirely)! Not many people allow their bladders to fill to this capacity before they feel the urge to urinate. It might very well feel like the LONGEST hour of your life. Don't even look at a toilet or running water from a faucet (if you can help it). A good rule of thumb of patient readiness for us sonographers was when the patient began what we empathetically called the "pee pee dance." If you can't sit still, you're probably ready for your scan!

There is a bit of good news to all this. Once full, the exam should go very quickly, 5 to 10 minutes in most easy-to-see, negative cases. Blame the Laws of

Ultrasound Physics for this one. Figure 3.3-1 is an ultrasound image of a full bladder. Sound waves travel more easily through fluid than tissue. Think of your pelvic anatomy from front to back. First is skin, then fat, then muscle, then intestines or bowel, then your bladder. Your uterus sits behind your bladder. So, if you drink lots of water and fully distend your bladder, it pushes aside intestines containing air and provides a window to the uterus. The effect is cool if you're a sonographer, but not so much if you're the one doing the drinking.

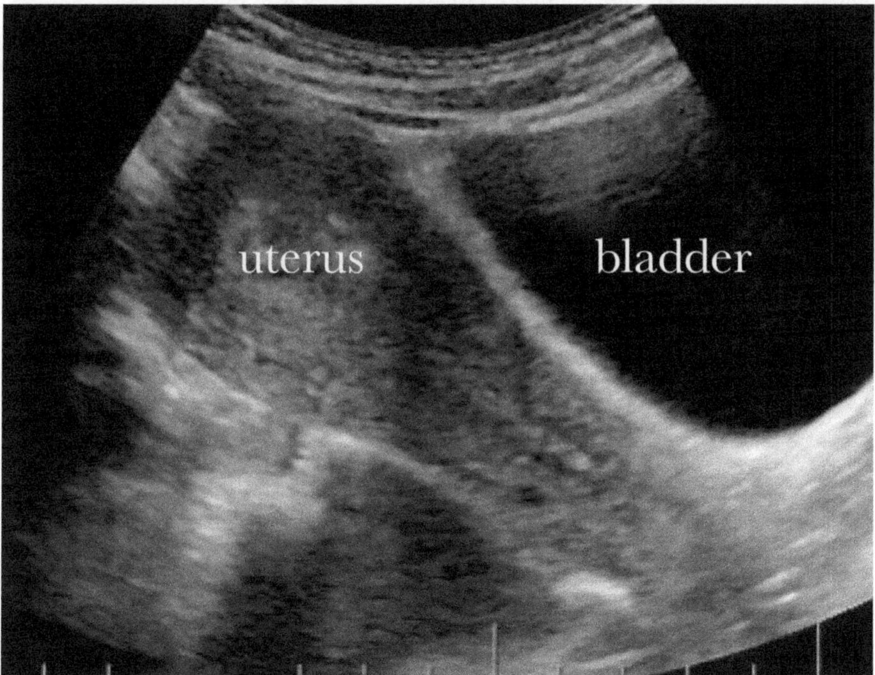

Figure 3.3-1: Pelvic Ultrasound of a Full Bladder

Additionally, the uterus in most women tilts forward (anteverted) or toward the abdomen. Filling the bladder aids in pushing the uterus backward, which allows better visualization. When your uterus tilts slightly back, a better angle is created to see it more clearly.

Occasionally, a uterus decides to go rogue and tilts too far backward instead (retroverted). Sometimes it tilts so far back that it folds over on itself (retroflexed).

These are totally normal variants, though they can be a little more challenging to evaluate.

Everyone's bladder fills a little differently regarding the length of time it takes. If you've been sick or normally drink too little water, you may be dehydrated, which will cause your tissues to absorb much of the fluid instead of sending it to your bladder. If your bladder is not adequately filled at the time of examination, some facilities will ask you to reschedule for another day while others will ask you to continue drinking and be worked back into the schedule.

Hopefully, this chapter gave you some interesting insight into what you might expect when preparing for your First Trimester exam. And if you've already "been there, done that," please share it with another expectant mom who may be anxious about her own First Trimester exam. No one likes to be surprised by our friend, the endovaginal probe.

Part Two ~

First Trimester Growth
Week 4 through Week 13

Week 4

ncredible. Figure 4.1 shows the very beginning of life as we can see it via ultrasound and is our only portal to this new life. But what can we really say, medically, about Figure 4.1?

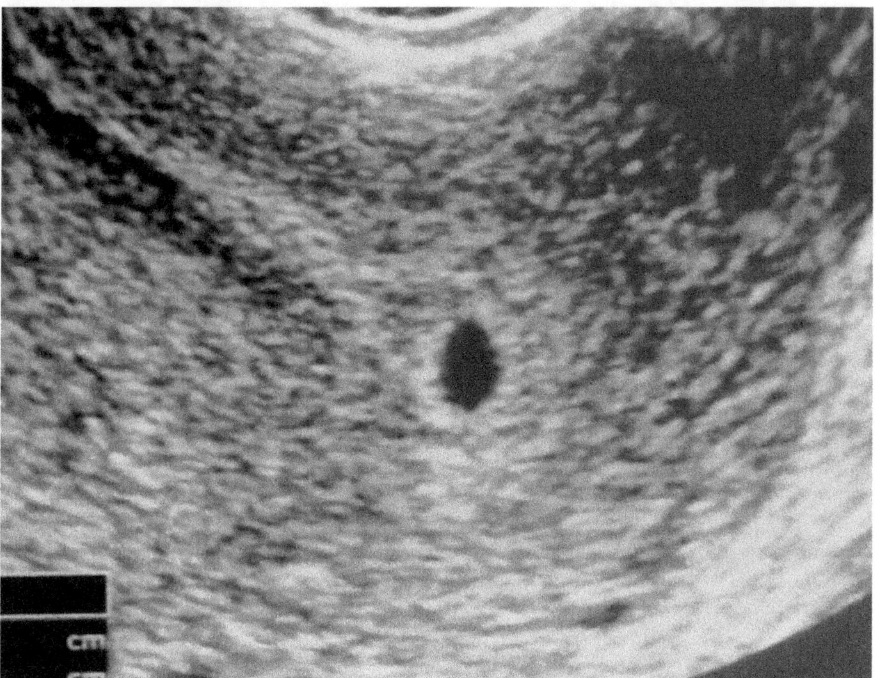

Figure 4.1: Week 4 ~ The Gestational Sac

Unfortunately, not as much as you, the expectant parent, might want to hear —which is why your doctor won't offer to scan you at Week 4. All we can say is:

- This appears to be an early pregnancy.
- It is located in its proper place high within the uterus.

- Measurements estimate gestational age to be somewhere around 4+ Weeks.

This is the extent of conclusions to be made of this ultrasound exam. This waiting may be a real let-down when you call with the exciting news of a new pregnancy. But your doctor needs a bit more time before he or she can provide the reassurance that your pregnancy is off to a good start, usually between Weeks 6 and 8.

Home pregnancy tests advertise that you can know you're pregnant as early as, or even before, the first missed day of a menstrual cycle. Most patients want to see a doctor as soon as the urine pregnancy test reveals that "plus" sign. But for an anxious mom-to-be, the natural next question is, "Can I have an ultrasound to make sure everything is okay?"

We understand the anticipation, but you're likely only 4 Weeks. Remember, pregnancy is calculated in terms of gestational age, not fetal age. So, 4 Weeks would be your gestational age at your first missed period if you had very regular cycles every 28 days. At this point, your doctor can't confirm much more than you already know:

You're Pregnant!

It's also important to mention that in Week 4, no physician can confirm with any real certainty that a pregnancy will progress. What your doctor *cannot* assure you of at this point:

- Whether or not an embryo will develop.
- How many embryos will develop.
- Whether or not a heartbeat will be seen.
- Whether this pregnancy is progressing normally.

Only time can tell. In most circumstances, an embryo is not visible or a heartbeat detectable until the start of Week 6 and best seen with transvaginal imaging. To be sure, some doctors will see you at Week 6. However, if your LMP dates are off, even a few days too early, an embryo with a heartbeat may not be detectable. Your pregnancy needs more time to develop, which may also mean sweating it out for another week or two until you can return for a follow-up scan.

The only thing worse than waiting to see your doctor is leaving without answers. Take my word for it! This can feel like the L O N G E S T and most agonizing weeks of your life.

Also, Baby is *so very small* at this point that cardiac activity can be very difficult to visualize clearly and easily. A *normally developing* embryo and heartbeat are usually much easier to see and measure at Week 7 or 8. So, to avoid unnecessary guesswork or repeat visits, a physician may desire her patients wait the additional 1 to 2 weeks of crucial development.

Trust your doctor's office if you're told it's too early. Typically, office staff ask a few questions about your cycles to determine what you need and when you need it. Moreover, they know what your doctor wants. A longer wait means they're just ensuring that the time of your scan is appropriate to yield the information you *and* your doctor need. Every week a pregnancy progresses successfully, the higher the chances are it will continue, and the more reassurance your doctor can give you—which, by the way, is the goal of your very first visit!

An important clarification here:

You *should* call your obstetrician once you discover a positive home pregnancy test. They'll want to ensure you see your doctor in an appropriate timeframe. The point of this chapter is to inform you as to why your doctor's office may schedule your first visit between Weeks 6 and 8 if you call them at Week 4.

Are there other reasons you should call your doctor before your first visit? Yes! If you have a positive pregnancy test and are also experiencing pain and/or bleeding, your obstetrician will want to know about it. Even though you may be very early in your pregnancy, your doctor (or other provider) may want to examine you for other potentially serious conditions.

Why Start at Week 4?

Week 4 is the very earliest a gestational sac can be seen with ultrasound, though there is not much we can decipher at this age. Most women never get to witness this super early stage of their pregnancies—more reason to share my few and only images of Week 4. Usually, if a patient is scanned this early, it is because of an error in LMP calculation. Now, let's talk about what can and cannot be determined with ultrasound at Week 4 and why your doctor will not order a scan so very early.

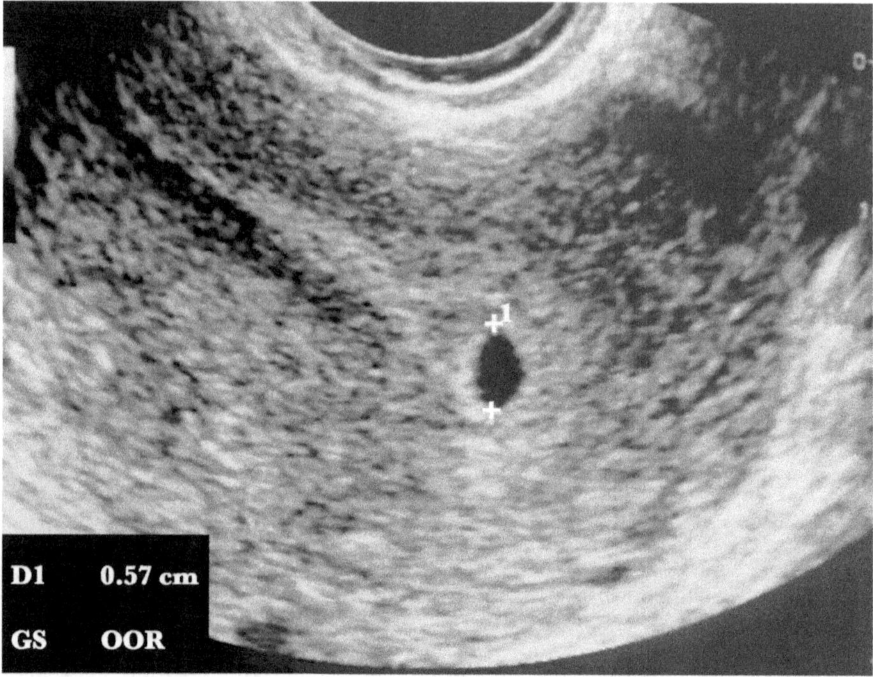

Figure 4.2: Week 4 ~ Gestational Sac

Around Week 4 of pregnancy, a tiny sac of fluid called the gestational sac (GS) can be seen. It first presents as a small black circle or oval. Every day the GS grows slightly. So, how can a sonographer calculate that a sac measures 4 Weeks?

One measurement typically used to calculate gestational age is the sac's longest length, to which 4 is added. Take a look at the image of the sac and measurement in Figure 4.2.

This GS measures 5.7 mm. Now apply the formula:

4 + 0.6 mm = 4.6 Weeks Gestational Age

This rough estimate yields an approximate gestational age of somewhere in the neighborhood of 4w4d. This calculation does not provide as accurate a gestational age as measuring the embryo itself because sacs can vary a bit from person to person. However, this is the only option for dating a pregnancy with ultrasound until the embryo can be seen and measured.

Take a peek at the GS measurement in Figure 4.3.

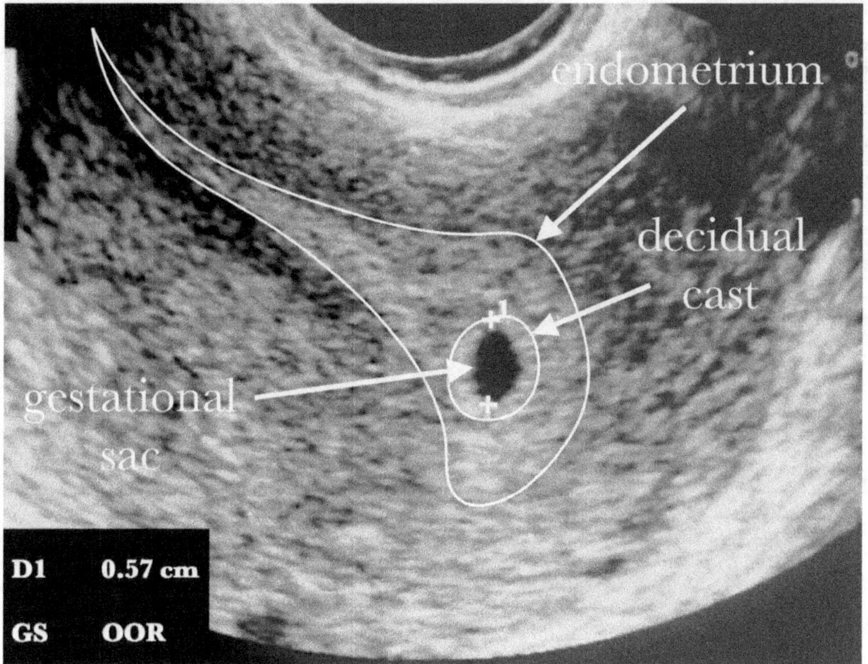

Figure 4.3: Week 4 ~ Gestational Sac, Labeled

Figure 4.3 is labeled the way a sonographer sees it. The GS is represented by a small black circle of fluid. The walls of the GS demonstrate a brighter ring called a decidual cast or ring, circled just outside the GS. The GS should also be located within the endometrium (inner lining of the uterus) and near the top of the uterus. The outer outline demonstrates the endometrium.

The changes observed every week are dramatic and appear essentially the same in every normally progressing pregnancy. Minor differences may be seen from one patient to the next, but what we attempt to document in each one is the same.

Now, how about a test of your mastery of ultrasound knowledge? Here's a hint. Do you see anything particularly special in Figure 4.4?

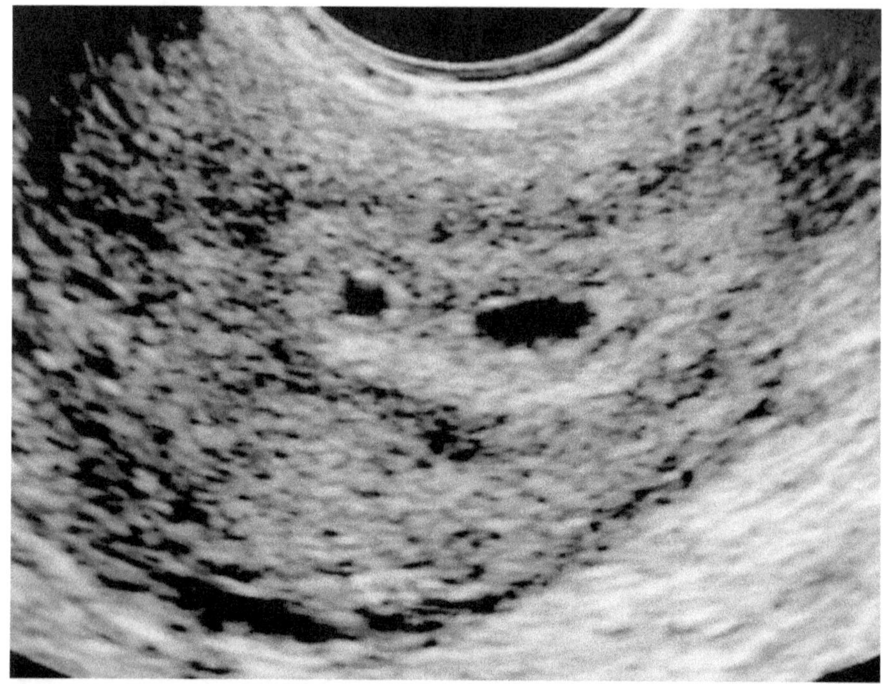

Figure 4.4: Week 4 ~ Twin Gestational Sacs

SURPRISE! If you guessed TWO gestational sacs, or twins, you're absolutely right! I just *love* seeing the shock on a patient's face when I break this news. It's the best! Usually, of course, she is farther along in her pregnancy. The disbelieving, expressionless stares, the near-fainting episodes, the relentless repetitive questioning about how sure I am—and all this is from Dad. Mom and I are usually on the sidelines, laughing hysterically…at Dad. It's some of the most fun I've had at work.

The sacs seen in Figure 4.4 measure just under 8 mm and just under 5 mm. Using the formula, these sacs measure somewhere between 4w4d and 5 Weeks of gestational age. For now, it's only an educated guess!

There is no way to determine at this point, whether one or both sacs will progress. This is precisely the reason a doctor does not want to scan too early. You would want to know if everything looks normal, and she would not be able to firmly reassure you of this. Just too many possibilities exist and there is no reason to speculate. Therefore, there's no justifiable reason to perform an ultrasound at Week 4 unless the patient is symptomatic for other problems.

Some questions you might ask are:

- Will both sacs get bigger?
- Will one or two babies develop?
- Do I have to wait 2 or 3 whole weeks for another scan? (Yes, you likely would.)
- Is it possible that one sac or both sacs may not enlarge?
- Could both sacs be lost to miscarriage?
- Can gestational age be determined on the next scan?
- Will one or more embryos be seen on the next scan?
- Will one or more heartbeats be seen on the next scan?

Can you see how scanning this early would only open Pandora's box of concerns and serve anxiety? There's no reason to put you through this turmoil. You know the adage, "Ignorance is bliss?" The saying certainly applies here.

The only determination to make at this point is that two sacs are suspected within the uterus and they appear to measure between Weeks 4 and 5 of pregnancy. No definitive answers beyond that can be offered with a great degree of certainty. No healthcare provider wants to provide false hope or reason to worry. The only real answer is that time will tell. But, as previously mentioned, a timely wait this early in pregnancy can be agonizing!

And speaking of an agonizing wait, let's meet Dianne, an OB nurse and colleague.

Dianne's Roller Coaster Pregnancy

I had worked with Dianne for many years in an OB/GYN private practice, very knowledgeable and proficient in her expertise. She was always one of my favorite co-workers. She had just gotten married a few months earlier. Exceptionally fun reception!

The practice was fairly large and Ultrasound typically stayed busy. It wasn't unusual for a nurse to pop in and ask when her doc could slide in an urgent scan among our ultrasound schedules.

Dianne dropped into my room one day, stating very matter-of-factly, "I've had a positive pregnancy test." I was thrilled two-fold; not only was there not a patient in distress, but I found myself on the receiving end of super exciting news!

"Oh, my gosh, Dianne! Congratulations! How far along are you?!"

She said her menstrual cycles were very regular—pretty much to the day.

"I'm two days late, so somewhere around 4 Weeks. Can you scan me?"

She knew I could, but she also confirmed my concern and understood. We weren't going to see much of anything at this point except for a possible small gestational sac. I knew she was anxious.

We both worked for the same group of doctors, which was a perk. *Most importantly to note here*, Dianne was also a patient of the same obstetrician for whom she worked, another perk. Doc gave the okay for extra-early scans *only* because she knew Dianne understood early pregnancy as well as anyone in the practice— what and when the first signs of pregnancy could be seen and what to expect this early. (As I mentioned previously, a sonogram this early in pregnancy is not routine!)

So, when both of our schedules allowed for a little free time, she ran into my exam room, quickly undressed, and settled under one of our very fashionable paper drapes. Of course, we began with the transvaginal probe. And, of course, she observed. Now, Dianne couldn't read ultrasound like I could, but she had worked around it enough to be able to recognize a few components of early pregnancy.

The view lying down, however, can be a little compromised due to the angle of the monitor. Any of you reading who've already had this type of examination know what I mean. It can be difficult to see what's on the monitor, especially if the sonographer has it tilted away from you.

I inserted the probe and began my examination, moving the probe from right to left as I scanned through the entire uterus. As previously mentioned, the goal was to identify anything which looked like a sac within the endometrium. As I scanned, I noticed a small black circle, or what I questioned as one very tiny sac. I needed to complete my view of the uterus before I stopped to measure.

I continued moving through the uterus when I inadvertently gasped out loud. I really didn't mean to alarm Dianne, but now she was worried.

"What…?" she asked flatly and nervously as her eyes darted back and forth from my face to the monitor, anxiously studying my face for the problem. She was immediately shaking.

I literally could not keep from grinning ear to ear. I turned the monitor more toward her and froze the image. I turned to Dianne and waited anxiously for her reaction.

Finally, I asked with great excitement, "SO? What do you see?!"

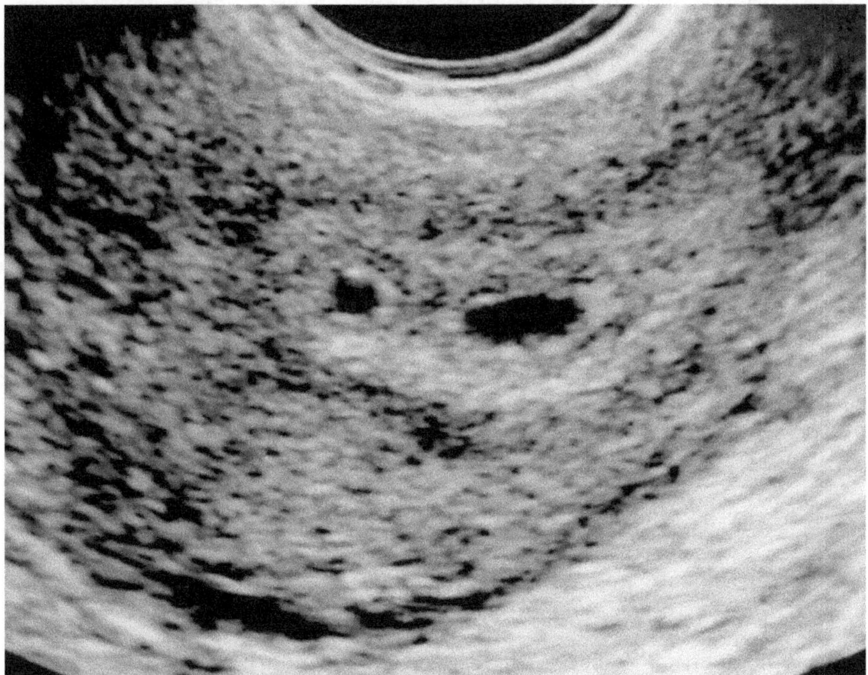

Figure 4.5: Dianne's First Scan ~ 4+ Weeks

Her response was classic! "Oh, shit!" I exploded with a big laugh. With her hand over her mouth in total shock, she sat up on one elbow, staring at the monitor in disbelief! Yes, Figure 4.5 is the very same image as the previous, Figure 4.4 —TWO sacs!

With two small gestational sacs seen side by side, this pregnancy would be labeled as dichorionic. We would later discover that when Dianne ovulated, her ovary released two eggs at essentially the same time, both eggs were fertilized, and both successfully implanted. The most likely result expected would be to see one embryo develop within each sac. This is different from a monochorionic twin pregnancy where one egg is released in ovulation, one gestational sac develops, but the egg splits into two babies which develop in the same gestational sac.

We both laughed at the idea that this pregnancy could very well feel like the gestation period of an elephant. In case you don't know this somewhat-relevant bit of trivia, the gestational period for an elephant is nearly two years. Forty weeks is long enough! I know women often feel like their babies must be the size of newborn elephants by the time they deliver. Thank goodness human babies don't reach 200 pounds.

Like many patients, Dianne never expected multiples and was both nervous and excited at the prospect of possibly carrying two babies at once. What overwhelming news! Two of everything…still, as an OB nurse, she knew quite well how early pregnancies can go, especially ones that begin as twins.

Recalling from the last chapter that we could only estimate the pregnancy was around 4 to 5 Weeks, Dianne knew the likelihood of twins developing was slim. She also knew that multiples meant a high-risk pregnancy, closer attention to care with more antenatal testing, possible premature delivery, and a whole host of other potential issues.

Let's pause here for a minute to talk about how we proceeded going forward and why. We were presented with a unique opportunity and one in which almost no expectant parent is afforded—to witness the on-going weekly development of not only the same pregnancy, but a twin pregnancy at that. We understood that the scans we'd perform on this twin gestation were not typically required for a normal pregnancy. In other words, most women with access to modern healthcare and no complications receive one scan in the First Trimester for a singleton pregnancy (where one embryo or fetus is confirmed). Once a normal-appearing pregnancy is documented, there is no medical indication to scan again unless complications arise, such as bleeding or pain or unless a patient's medical history or prior pregnancies warrant closer follow-up.

As a nursing professional in OB/GYN along with formally educated and registered sonographers in OB/GYN at the helm, she chose to embark on this distinctive journey. We possessed the professional knowledge and access to well-maintained equipment to follow this pregnancy more closely than standard protocols. In light of our awareness and the potential high-risk nature of her pregnancy, she felt that any insight gained was worthy of a few short minutes of scanning. Ultimately, these scans produced no adverse effects on her pregnancy, as continued biohazard testing and the millions of healthy born babies each year have shown thus far.

Who witnesses the weekly growth of the same pregnancy? Of *her own* pregnancy? As a sonographer, I had not even recorded *my* own pregnancy so closely. Perhaps this sort of observation has been pursued by others in healthcare who likewise had the access and knowledge—whether personally or in conjunction with professional trials. We employed the exclusive privilege to observe the very beginning of new lives unfolding before us. And I'm happy to be able to share that with you in this book.

It was an extraordinary once-in-a-lifetime event for each of us and an educational pilgrimage in imaging. I was never before or again presented with such an opportunity in my career. Hopefully, the benefit of Dianne's experience will also provide you with a little knowledge to help you understand your own pregnancy and the growth of your fetus in this First Trimester. For the same miraculous outcome, we'd do it all again...

Moving on!

So, what happened next? We performed another scan a couple of days later, and two minimally larger gestational sacs measuring 8.8 mm and 5.1 mm were noted. See Figure 4.6.

Since an embryo in each sac could not yet be seen, applying the GS calculation equated to an estimated gestational age of about 4w6d and about 4w4d, respectively.

These sacs demonstrated a slight difference in overall size when compared, where we would have expected them to be relatively similar in dimension. While not a hard and fast rule of thumb, it was simply too early to say whether this difference in size reflected a potential problem.

Was the smaller sac progressing normally? Did the larger sac mean she was farther along than she thought? Dianne kept a very practical outlook on the matter and said she was resigned to the idea that only one sac may make it...if she was lucky. A true answer to the questions above would not be made until measurable embryos could be detected. This meant a very long week, or longer, of waiting.

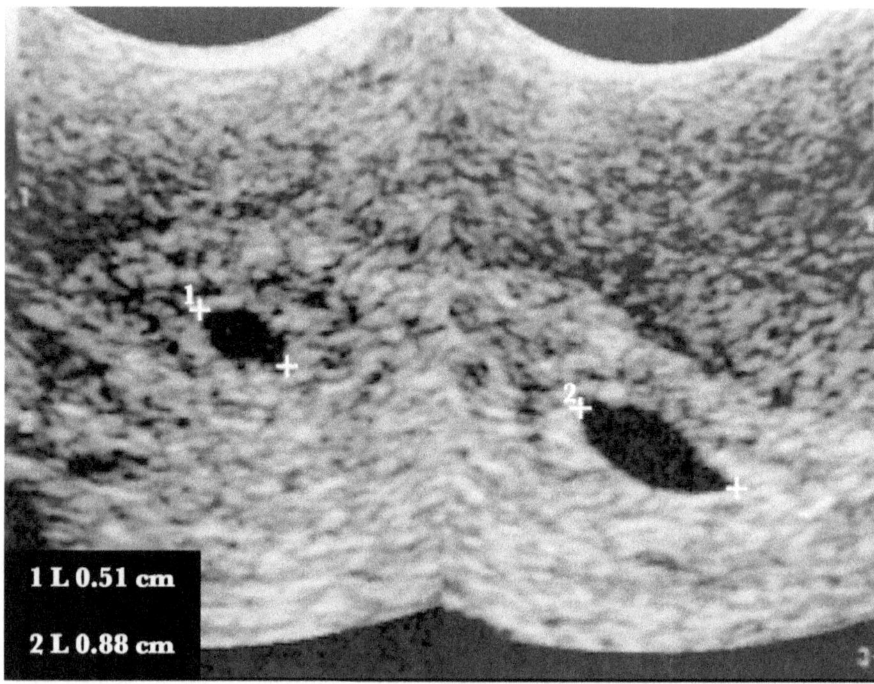

Figure 4.6: 4+ Weeks ~ Dichorionic Pregnancy

What differences can be seen in Week 5? Read on to see what changes await.

Week 5

Your baby is now an embryo and many incredible changes are taking place. However, ultrasound still cannot see the little love bug. So, what can be seen at Week 5?

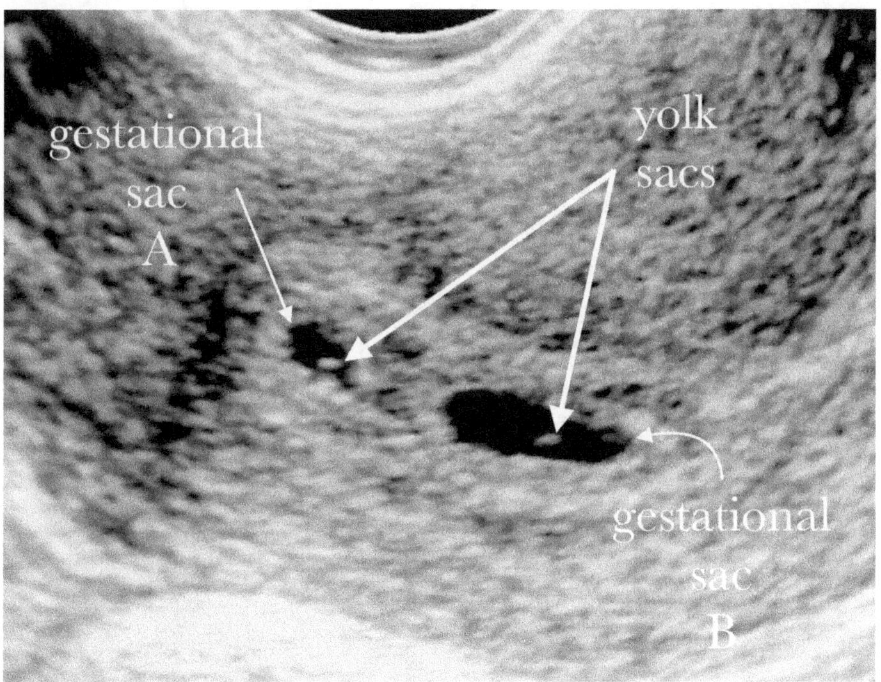

Figure 5.1: Week 5 ~ Questionable Yolk Sacs

The biggest variable here that continued to give Dianne hope was how, in just two days, a very tiny questionable yolk sac (YS) could be appreciated along the bottom wall of each gestational sac (Figure 5.1)! Very plainly put, the YS provides nutrients for the growing embryo until the placenta develops. A yolk sac looks like a tiny white ring and can be very difficult to distinguish so early.

According to Dianne's LMP, she should have still been in Week 4 at this point, so we didn't expect to see yolk sacs for another few days or so. We wondered:

- Did she conceive earlier than she thought?
- If she was already in Week 5, was the GS for Baby A abnormally small?
- Would the GS A for Baby A progress at all?
- Would an embryo develop in both sacs?

Seeing these yolk sacs meant it was *possible* for one embryo to grow in each gestational sac. In other words, we expect to see one YS per embryo in any normally developing pregnancy. We couldn't speculate, and only time would tell.

Ultimately, the size of a gestational sac this early can appear quite variable. But the presence of yolk sacs was a positive finding, and Dianne elected to allow a little more time before scanning again. Otherwise, our patient could drive herself crazy with trying to pick apart these very early observations. So would most moms-to-be. It's only natural.

Your doctor will spare you the agony of these unanswered questions that every patient would inevitably face with a scan at this gestational age, precisely why your first ultrasound will not be performed so early in pregnancy.

The takeaway here is that there was just no way to know whether these findings were negative or positive. Five days passed before taking our next look. What did we see?

Five days later, bigger gestational sacs *and* bigger yolk sacs were noted. Can you appreciate the differences between Figures 5.1 and 5.2?

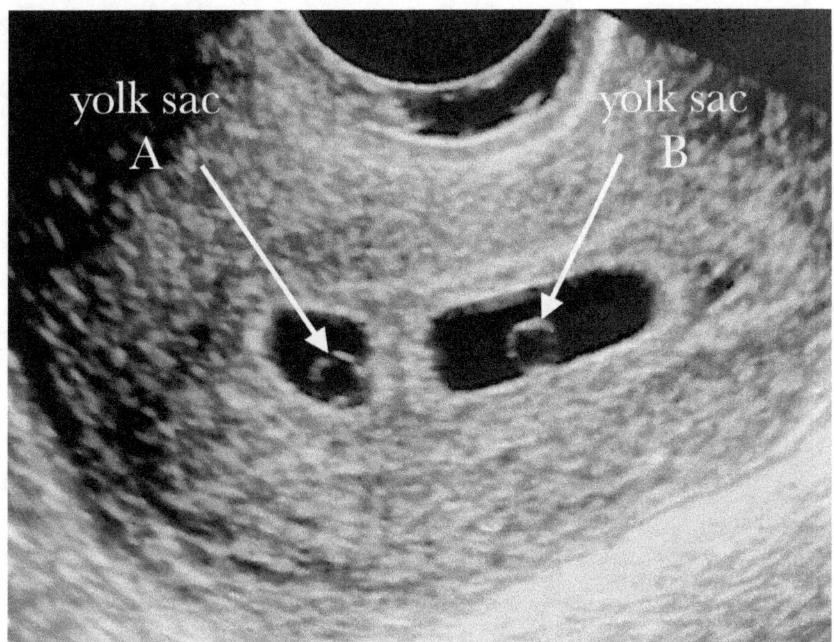

Figure 5.2: Week 5 ~ Yolk Sacs

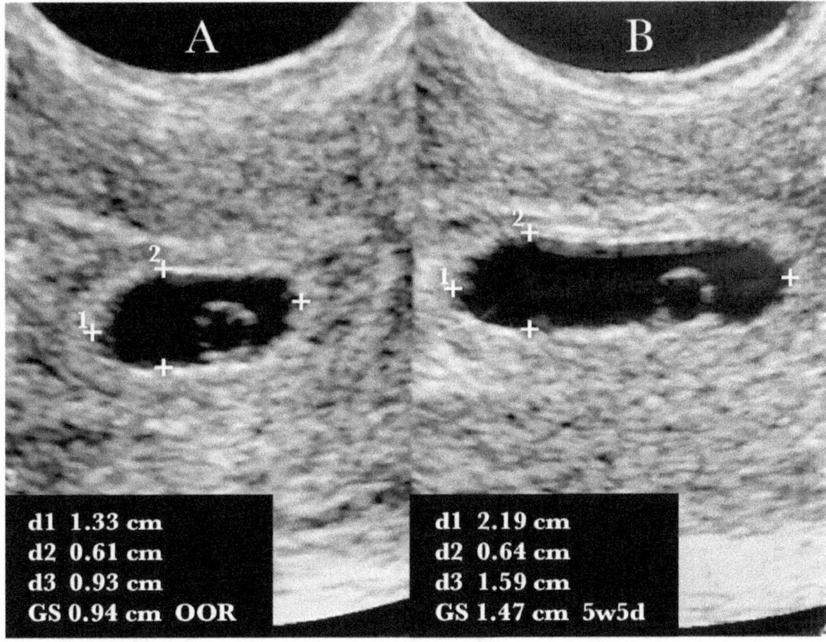

Figure 5.3: Week 5 ~ Gestational and Yolk Sacs

This was a great sign. The yolk sacs were much larger *and* nice and round. Just what we want to see.

Dianne's LMP placed her at 4w6d, but considering the appearance of the yolk sacs, we guessed she was somewhere in the middle of Week 5. Again, this was simply an educated guess until we could accurately date the pregnancy with the more-reliable embryo measurement in Week 6.

So, what did the gestational sacs measure this day? And was there normal interval growth compared to the last scan?

Here, I used a more accurate method for estimating the gestational age of a gestational sac which includes taking a length, height, and width measurement. The three measurements are entered into a software program which then calculates an estimated gestational age of the sac based on those dimensions. The split image of Figure 5.3 displays only the first two measurements for each sac but the overall estimated gestational age for each.

Notice the discrepancy seen between each sac. Sac A's calculation showed OOR, out of range, meaning it was too small to estimate a gestational age with the three-measurement formula. However, utilizing the single-largest-dimension formula discussed in Chapter 4, we could estimate a gestational age of about 5w4d for Sac A.

1.35 mm + 4 = 5.4 (rounded up) or 5w4d

Sac B was estimated at 5w5d. At this point, Sac B's size appeared more consistent with the size of the yolk sacs, and Sac A appeared a bit small. Even though the changes in the yolk sacs were a good sign, the differences in gestational sac size were still a little worrisome. Many unanswered questions remained:

- Was Sac A abnormal?
- Could we expect to see an embryo develop in Sac A?
- Was Sac B representative of true gestational age?
- Would embryos be visible at the same time?
- Would we see two heartbeats?

Figures 5.4 and 5.5 show you another example of a yolk sac and measurements of the GS in three dimensions provided by a reader.

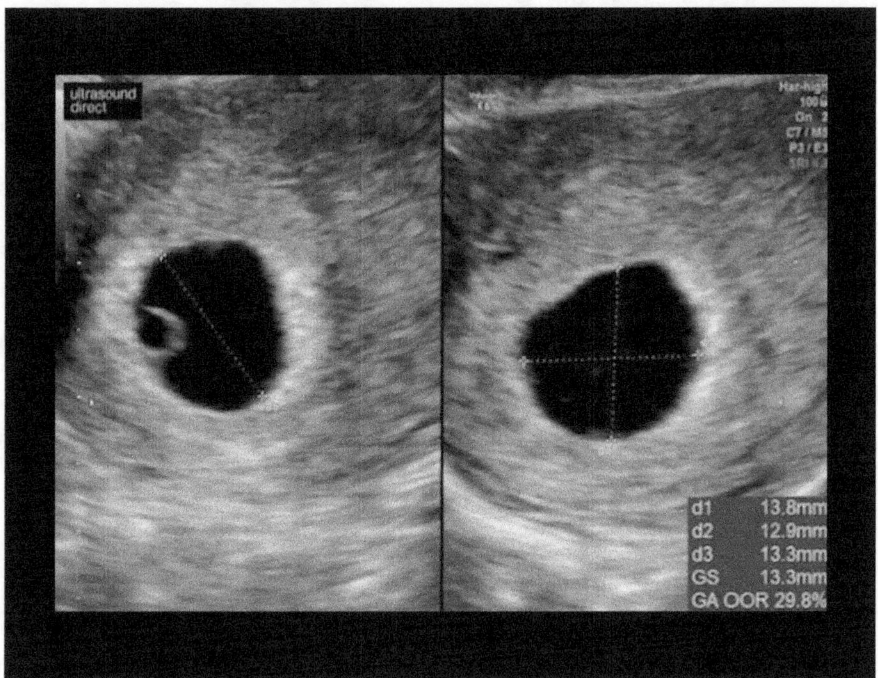

Figure 5.4: Week 5 ~ Gestational Sac Measurement

I would have measured a little differently, but the end calculation would have been similar. Just as we saw for Sac A in Figure 5.3, this sac also yielded an OOR estimation for GA. Again, using the longest-dimension formula, GA could be estimated at 5w4d.

1.4 mm + 4 = 5.4 or 5w4d estimated GA

Again, one of the reasons for sharing this information is to help you understand why ultrasound scans are not routinely ordered this early—because your obstetrician cannot definitively assure you that your pregnancy is on a good path…which is ultimately what most parents want to know after having a first pregnancy scan. Of course, a physician can, at any time, opt for early or additional scans if she or he believes a patient's condition warrants them. The early or additional scans would have to be expected to provide beneficial information to aid in the management of a pregnancy or health of the mother.

Figure 5.5 shows us yet another great representation of a beautiful and well-rounded yolk sac as we'd expect to see in Week 5.

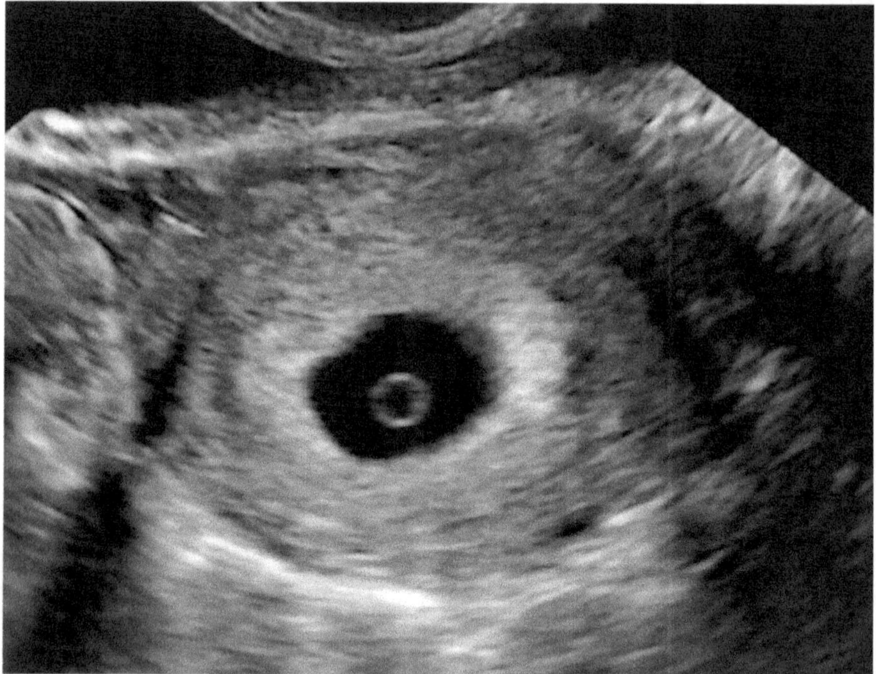

Figure 5.5: Week 5 ~ Yolk Sac

Hopefully, this chapter helped you better understand what we can and cannot see during Week 5. So, as much as patients might beg and plead for an ultrasound, most doctors order a scan at a time when definitive answers and information can be provided to the patient.

Ignorance is bliss! Knowing a little is sometimes worse than not knowing anything at all. No one wants to hear, "Yes, we can see a sac, but we don't know if an embryo will develop." Just ask anyone who has had to wait a week or two for a heartbeat! Not many enjoy the state of limbo, however, Mother Nature needs time to do her thing. And she will not be rushed.

Because we suspected Dianne's gestational age was nearly 6 Weeks, we performed the next scan two days later. Can you guess what was seen?

Bigger gestational sacs only?

One or two embryos?

Heartbeats?

Let's turn the page to see if you're correct…

Week 6

think Dianne must have thought of little else on her way to work that morning. She made a beeline straight to my room and hopped on my table. There are some definite perks to working in an OB practice. I was honestly anxious to see what had developed in the interim, too—even a little nervous for her. Sonographers never enjoy giving bad news, plus she was one of our own. We both held our breath as I started the scan. And I can only imagine how Dianne felt.

(Drumroll, please!)

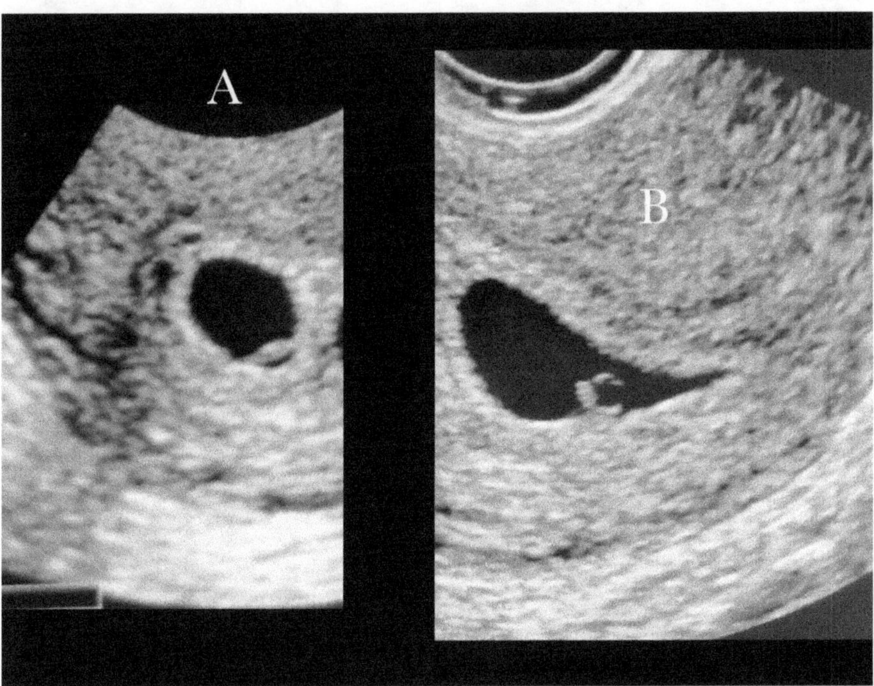

Figure 6.1: Week 6 ~ Dianne's Twins

SUCCESS! Baby on board!

TIMES TWO!

Figure 6.1 shows one embryo in each sac, both measuring right at 6w0d and with two strong and steady heartbeats! "Oh, thank God!" Dianne let out a huge sigh of relief. I did the same. Woohoo! Dianne told me she was feeling cautiously optimistic after the last scan but was afraid to keep too high an expectation. I agreed. After all the surprises brought by the past two weeks, variations of each scan, and the associated roller coaster of emotions, she was hoping and praying for at least one baby.

What a beautiful sight it was to see those flutters! Even though she knew she had far to go to be "out of the woods" of the First Trimester, the chances of miscarriage dramatically drop once a normal heartbeat is seen. Baby steps and a great milestone!

The yolk sacs still appeared normal and the gestational sacs were a little bigger, as we would expect to see in a normally developing pregnancy at Week 6.

Measuring Baby

So, how did I determine that my guess was correct and Dianne's gestational age was consistent with Week 6? For either a single or multiple pregnancy, the Crown-Rump Length (CRL) calculation is used to measure the actual embryo. The CRL early in the First Trimester provides the most accurate estimate of gestational age and due date.

Though a head or body cannot be distinguished at this point, a caliper is placed at each end of the tiny area around the flutter of cardiac activity which represents the embryo, otherwise known as the fetal pole. The software then converts this measurement into gestational age and applies a due date. If measuring an embryo that dates Week 6 or later, the flutter of cardiac activity *should* be visible with the naked eye.

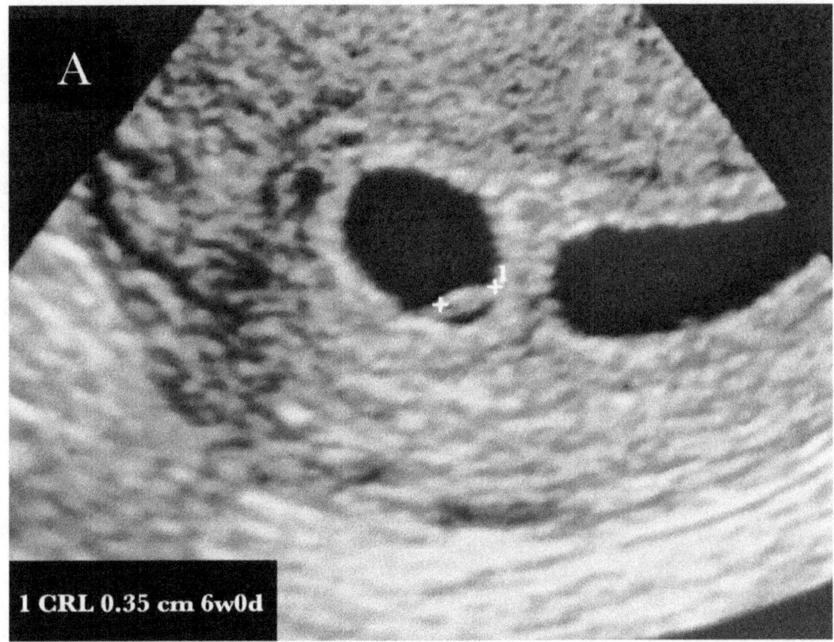

Figure 6.2: Week 6 ~ Baby A

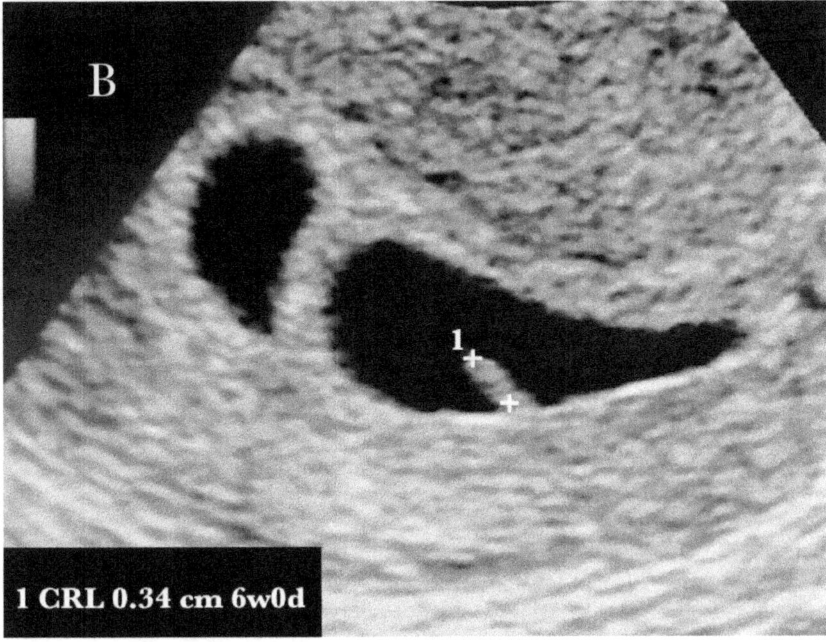

Figure 6.3: Week 6 ~ Baby B

Remember, Figures 6.2 and 6.3 are very magnified images taken with the endovaginal probe, and the actual size of each embryo is shown in the box at the bottom left.

Here, you can see that Baby A was measuring a whopping 0.35 cm (or 3.5 mm), in the smaller sac to the left-hand side of the image. Baby B measured about the same at 0.34 cm (or 3.4 mm), found in the larger sac to the right-hand side of the image.

All ultrasound machines are calibrated to use the Metric System. Dimensions are demonstrated in mm for millimeters or cm for centimeters. As a guideline, 2.54 centimeters equals 1 inch.

Figures 6.4 and 6.5 show the first two measurements taken of Baby A's gestational sac, length and height. Figure 6.5 demonstrates the third measurement, the sac's width, which is obtained by rotating the probe 90 degrees.

As you'll see on the bottom, left-hand side of the image, Baby A's estimated gestational age for the GS according to these calculations was 5 weeks, 3 days (shown as 5w3d)—slightly smaller than the GA of the embryo. Typically, gestational sac measurements are less important once measurable embryos can be seen, unless a gestational sac appears unusually small as it did for Baby A. Could this be a cause for concern? It could, but only time would help us determine if this embryo was a healthy one.

Now, check out the same measurements for Baby B's gestational sac in Figures 6.6 and 6.7 which were taken the same way: longest length and height first, then a width in the next.

Baby B's gestational sac measured 6w2d—right on target! With Baby A's gestational sac measuring 5w3d, these sac comparisons showed almost an entire week's discrepancy. This finding was a bit concerning for Baby A, but both embryos measured the same and demonstrated strong heartbeats. Also, both yolk sacs appeared nice and round. Seeing two strong heartbeats and two babies who measured essentially the same were very reassuring at this time.

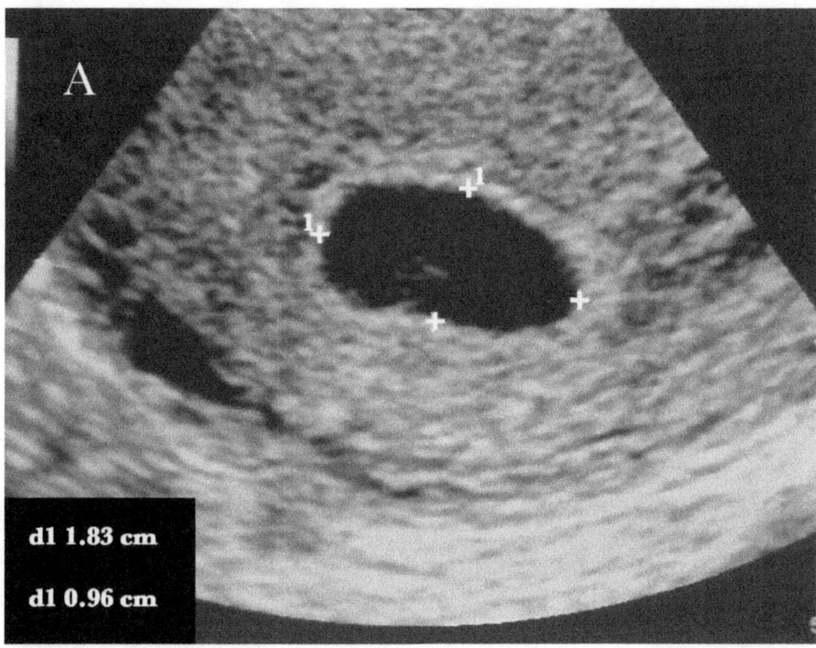

Figure 6.4: Gestational Sac A, Length and Height

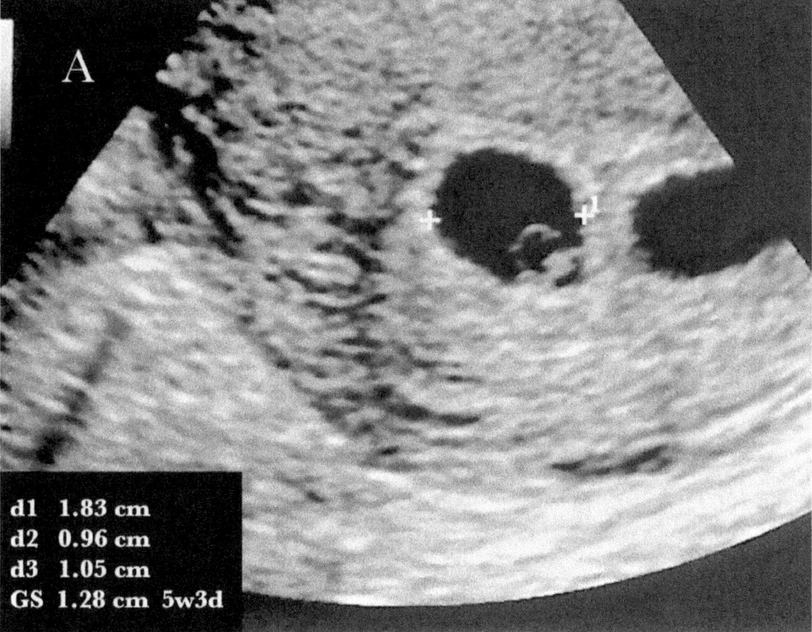

Figure 6.5: Gestational Sac A, Width

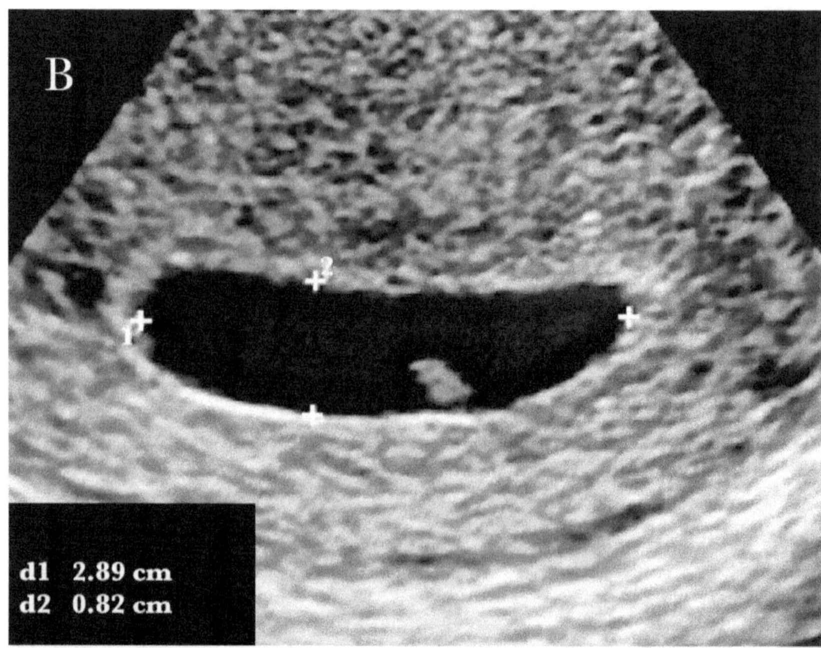

Figure 6.6: Gestational Sac B, Length and Height

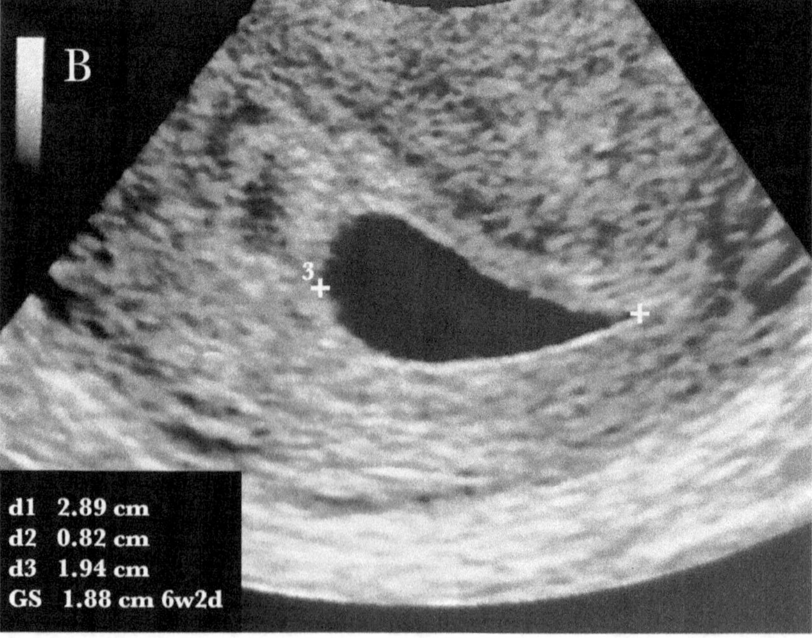

Figure 6.7: Gestational Sac B, Width

Why the labels of "A" and "B"? This is how we keep track of the growth of multiples in ultrasound. The smaller gestational sac was labeled "A" because it was positioned lower in the uterus or closer to the cervix. Thus, "A" would be the first to be born in a vaginal delivery. The larger gestational sac was labeled "B" because of its position closer to the top of the uterus. Later in the pregnancy, the babies are referred to as "Fetus A" and "Fetus B." Labeling allows separate tracking of each baby's individual growth on future scans.

Measuring Baby's Heart Rate

Can you identify what's happening in Figure 6.8? This sonogram image shows a survey of the heart rate for Baby A.

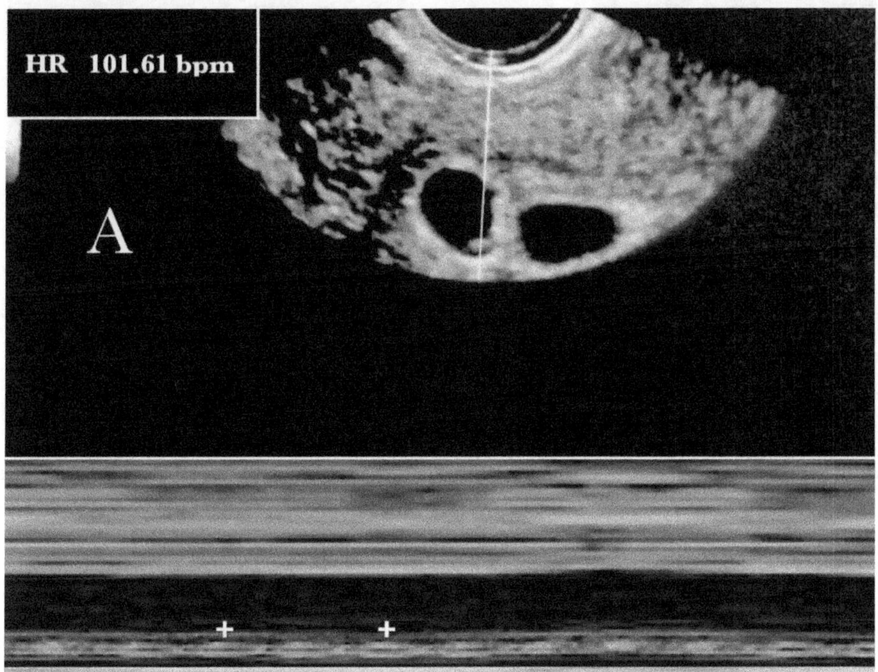

Figure 6.8: Week 6 ~ Baby A, Heart Rate

Note in the upper left-hand corner that the heart rate is calculated at nearly 102 BPM (beats per minute). What a great start!

At this gestational age, any rate around 100 BPM or faster is reassuring. However, your doctor may consider a minimally lower heart rate to be entirely normal. If a *much* slower and/or irregular rate is detected this early in pregnancy, your doctor may order a follow-up scan within a couple of weeks to confirm the embryo is growing properly. It can be a concerning sign for the health of the pregnancy. Figure 6.9 shows that Baby B's heart rate was just a tad faster than Baby A, at 108 BPM.

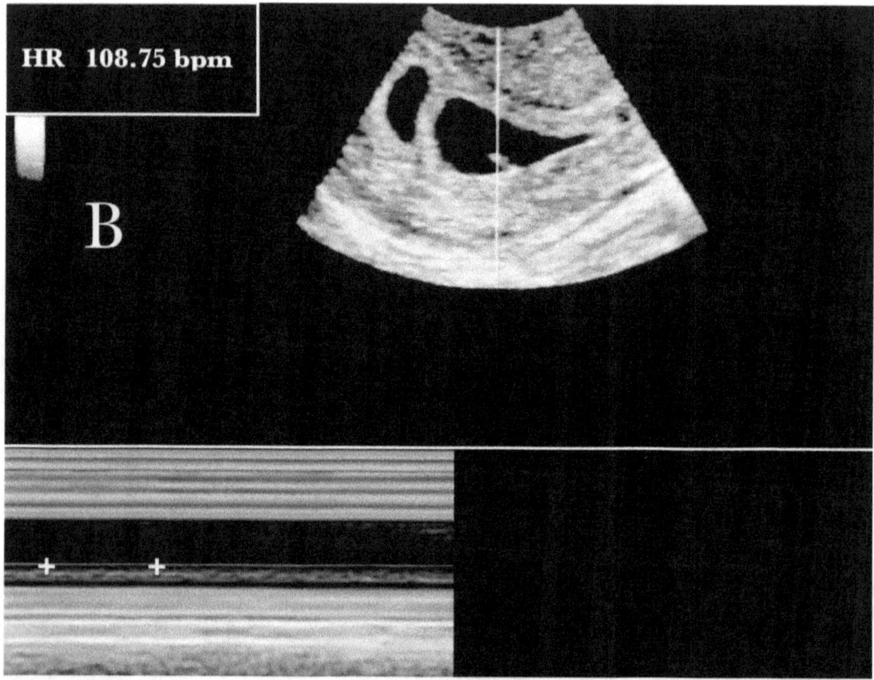

Figure 6.9: Week 6 ~ Baby B, Heart Rate

In my experience with the modern equipment I was using at the time, Week 6 of pregnancy signified the very earliest that an embryo and heartbeat could be discerned. Also, measuring a 3 mm embryo can present quite a challenge as it is so very small. If the embryo is positioned against the wall of the gestational sac or if the uterus tilts backward (a normal difference in some women), visualizing the embryo well and obtaining an accurate measurement can be difficult. To reiterate earlier information from Week 4, an obstetrician or other healthcare provider may avoid such challenges by waiting until Week 7 or 8 of gestational age to perform your first sonogram when the embryo is much larger and easier to evaluate—as you'll see in the chapters to come.

From a sonographer's standpoint, a slightly later gestational age always makes for a much easier scan. Scanning at Week 7or 8 will show the Baby more distinctly, producing an almost effortless means to attain and measure that heart rate. Whatever can be done to limit cause for concern is usually every doctor's preference. Sometimes that means waiting a little longer to get the best imaging.

Figure 6.10 of Baby B is labeled showing what is expected at Week 6, although you may spot your baby in a different position inside the gestational sac.

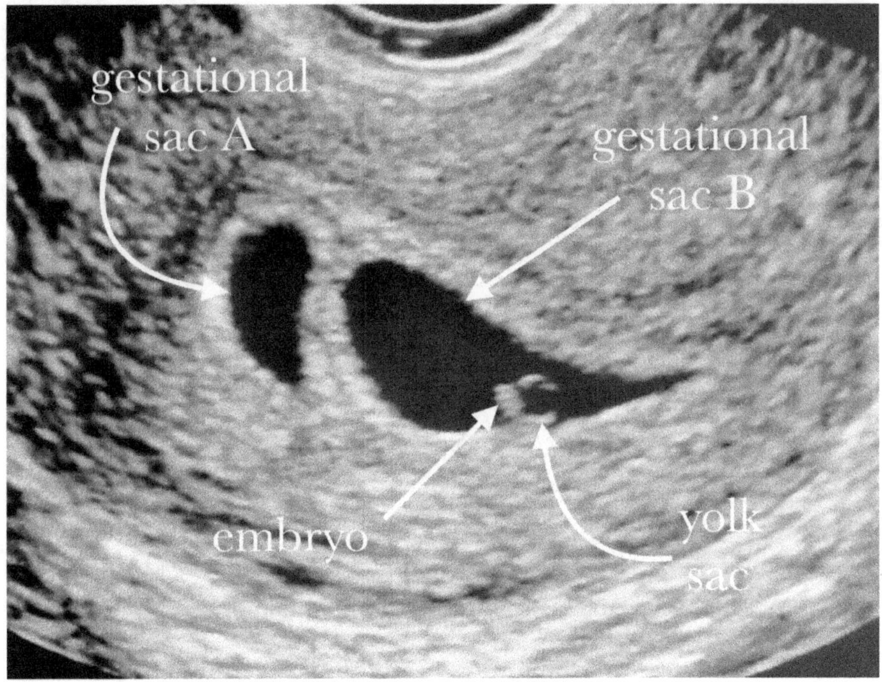

Figure 6.10: Week 6 ~ Baby B, Labeled

The embryo is clearly delineated, lying just adjacent to the yolk sac. Perfect! And, of course, the energetic flutter of Baby's heart in real-time (live scanning) should also be observed.

Know that if you're expecting one baby (a singleton pregnancy) versus multiples, you would subtract the "gestational sac A" component from this photo which represents only part of Baby A's sac. One baby means you'd see only one gestational sac.

Early Miscarriage

It is important to address the unfortunate topic of early miscarriage here in Week 6 because it is a very real and frequent occurrence relative to pregnancy, especially early in the First Trimester. Miscarriage can be quite an emotional, traumatic, and bitter pill to swallow. Still considered taboo to many, women are discussing it more openly today than ever before. There should never be shame associated with a loss. But because the experience is so personal, friends and loved ones struggle with how to provide words of comfort—when few exist.

The yolk sac provides nutrients for the embryo until the placenta develops. If a yolk sac is not seen within a gestational sac at Week 6 (or later), it is not expected that an embryo will develop. This is providing, of course, that your doctor has solid data dating your pregnancy at least to Week 6. A gestational sac that never develops a yolk sac or embryo is called a blighted ovum or an anembryonic pregnancy, making up about half of all miscarriages in the First Trimester [1].

Yes, you are pregnant. But this type of occurrence in pregnancy means that something thwarted development very early, before a baby had a chance to grow. Only a gestational sac developed; an embryo never formed.

Sometimes the suspicion of a blighted ovum will accompany successive scans in order to confirm the diagnosis. The sac may continue to grow because pregnancy hormones may tell it to do so. But not seeing a yolk sac or embryo leads to no other conclusion after serial scans and appropriate time between scans.

For many expectant parents, knowing an embryo never developed can be helpful in the grieving process. Patients have expressed having an easier time coping with such losses knowing that a *baby* didn't die, that a heartbeat didn't stop. Even though it still leaves an emotional scar or the disappointment of an unhealthy pregnancy, the diagnosis of a blighted ovum can feel like less of a loss to some women.

True story: A friend was one of the first to read my book. She came to me in tears after reading this section and confessed she suffered a miscarriage many years prior. It was diagnosed a blighted ovum, but she never knew an embryo never formed. She always grieved the baby she "lost"—for 30 long years! The physiology of a blighted ovum was never explained to her or her husband. It's so unfortunate, and heart-breaking, that she carried around this pain for SO long. She could finally "let go" that she never really lost the son she never had.

A blighted ovum will appear as an empty gestational sac and might look something like the image in Figure 6.11. Please note your physician may wait until Week 7 or 8 before feeling confident in this diagnosis.

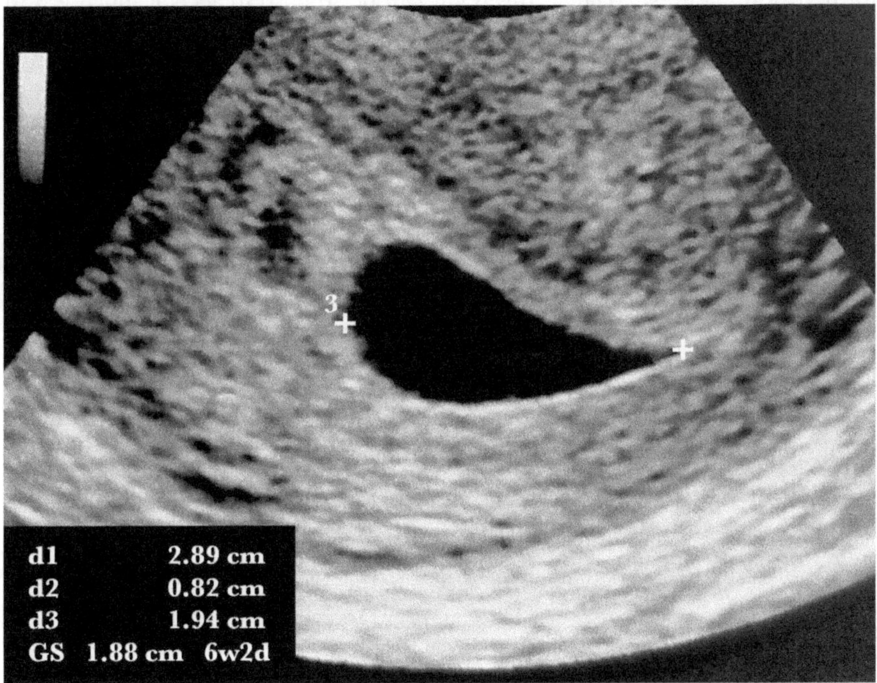

Figure 6.11: Blighted Ovum

Sometimes, a heartbeat is seen one week and not the next. After already documenting the presence of a heartbeat in an earlier scan, this finding can be especially difficult and painful for the patient. Though I cannot claim such a loss myself, I can certainly empathize. There's something about witnessing that flicker for the first time—you see with your own eyes that the pregnancy is real and not just a pink plus sign on a stick.

My personal observation as a sonographer has been such that the farther along a pregnancy progresses before a miscarriage is confirmed, the more traumatic the event and the greater the loss the patient may experience. I'm no clinical psychologist, but I can share what I've experienced with my patients and loved ones who've been through it. And I can imagine what I might have experienced myself.

All are emotions we feel at the outset of a planned or desired pregnancy, the building excitement for the new addition, the announcement of your good news to the world…a miscarriage at this point can be so hard to accept, much less to have to break to others. Obviously, a loss later in pregnancy, becomes tragic for the entire family, including children, for all the obvious reasons.

I have scanned probably one thousand or more early First-Trimester miscarriages. I have held patients' hands, and they have cried on my shoulder more times than I can recall. It's always a sad event and especially heartbreaking for the patient who is so excited for her new addition or who maybe struggled with years of infertility.

Of course, the next attempt at pregnancy is naturally met with much fear and anxiety that history will repeat itself. And for those moms who miscarry after a very normal first pregnancy, the shock is typically surreal. Often, the idea that the next pregnancy would not be a healthy one never occurred to her.

And then there are those who suffer *several* recurring miscarriages. Yes, I've heard doctors say that the hardest part is actually getting pregnant. But this provides no solace to the patient with a poor OB history. If you are one of these women, please know that many have gone on to carry healthy pregnancies and subsequently deliver healthy babies despite the bumpy road to start. I applaud your courage to keep trying!

It can be a frightening and anxious time when couples try again after miscarriage. No matter how early a loss happens, even if it is before a baby or heartbeat is seen; it's still a loss and no less painful.

Patients want to know what happened, why it happened, or what they did to cause the loss. I've heard it explained that a miscarriage early in the First Trimester is very common. It was nothing you did but usually Nature's way of taking care of something that was not developing normally, possibly due to a genetic problem.

Of course, even if you understand the cause from a scientific standpoint, it never truly satisfies a patient's need for *why* it happened. Parents usually look for some sort of spiritual explanation, as well. I like to simply think that maybe Baby wasn't ready for this big old world just yet and possibly needed a little more time! It is my preference to think, however, that the next pregnancy will mean this Baby is finally ready for the journey. Who really knows what happens on the other side, right? We can only wonder.

I would always try to console my patients by saying our babies come to us when *they* are ready, not always when we are! Of course, this philosophy cannot be applied to every scenario, but I feel it provides a little silver lining to an otherwise emotional and traumatic event.

If your pregnancy is one with unforeseen obstacles and an unfamiliar future, your healthcare provider, family, and friends, as well as local support groups can provide the strength some women need to cope. It is sometimes difficult to ask for help. But often others who care for you or who have been through this storm themselves can help guide you through such a challenging time.

If you have had the misfortune of a blighted ovum, I hope this chapter brought you a bit of solace. If you've suffered a prior pregnancy loss, I wish you many blessings for a future uneventful pregnancy and healthy baby.

The Twins at 6w6d

Just look at the changes made over six days from the prior scan! Dianne was now 6w6d by LMP, and Figure 6.12 shows each embryo measured 8 mm, or 6w5d. That means these babies grew 5 mm since the last scan. Does one day's discrepancy change Dianne's due date? Was it a cause for concern? Absolutely not. Because different observers may obtain slightly different measurements, these dimensions are still considered accurate within a few days. This early, your doctor would probably change your due date if a difference of about a week or more is seen between a due date by LMP and that of ultrasound findings.

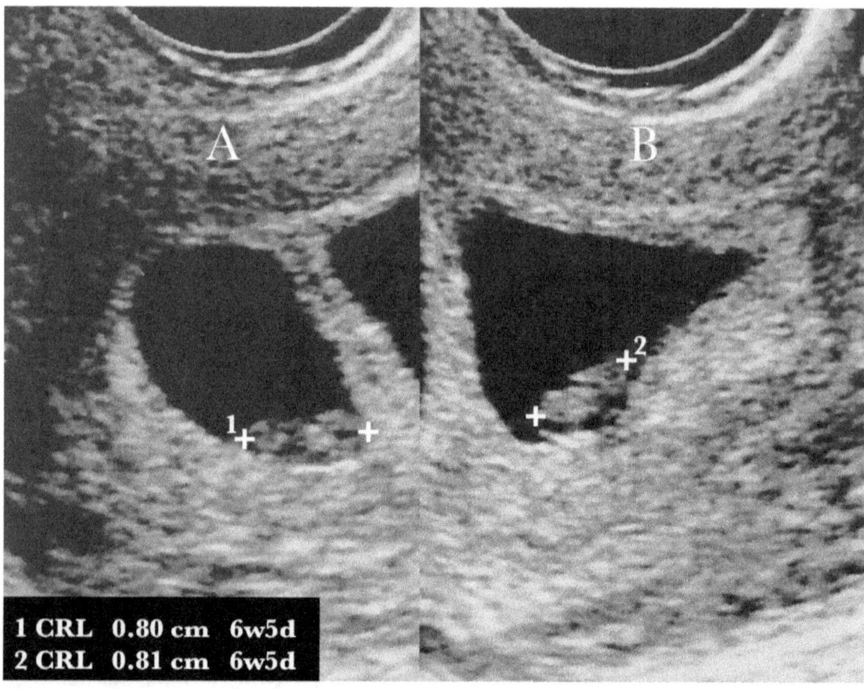

Figure 6.12: Week 6 ~ Twins at 6w6d

Now, let's look at the changes in both gestational sacs. Baby A's sac had always been a bit smaller and caused a little worry for us in the beginning. Figure 6.13 shows the three-dimensional formula for Baby A.

And how did Baby B's sac compare? Check out Figure 6.14 for the correlation. Baby B's sac had been quite a bit larger than A's sac. Here you'll notice that A's sac was average, not quite a full inch and right on target today with gestational age at 6w6d! This was quite reassuring to us both. Baby B's gestational sac now measured just over one inch—one full week ahead of dates and Baby A! Truly, we had no explanation for why B's sac had presented so much larger, but our concern for a miscarriage for Baby A had decreased quite a bit at this point.

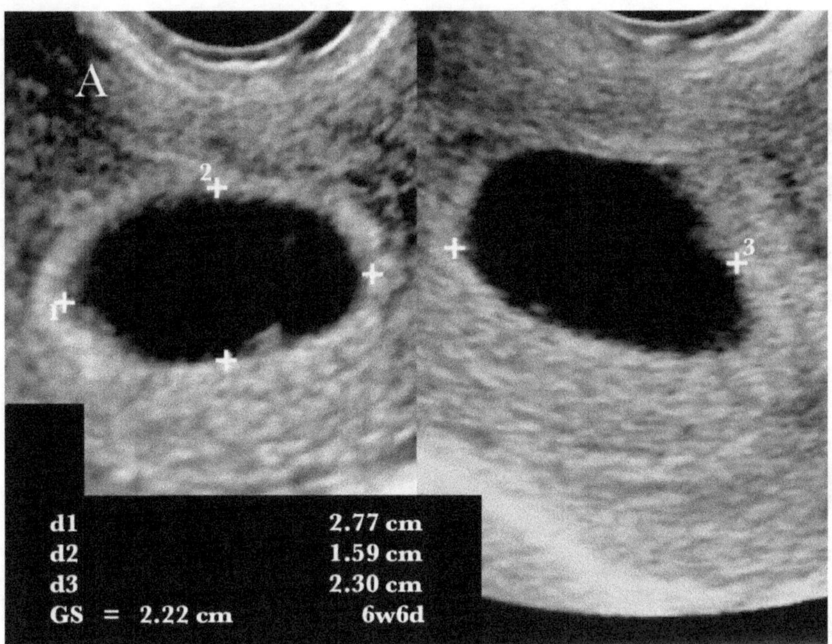

Figure 6.13: 6w6d ~ Gestational Sac A

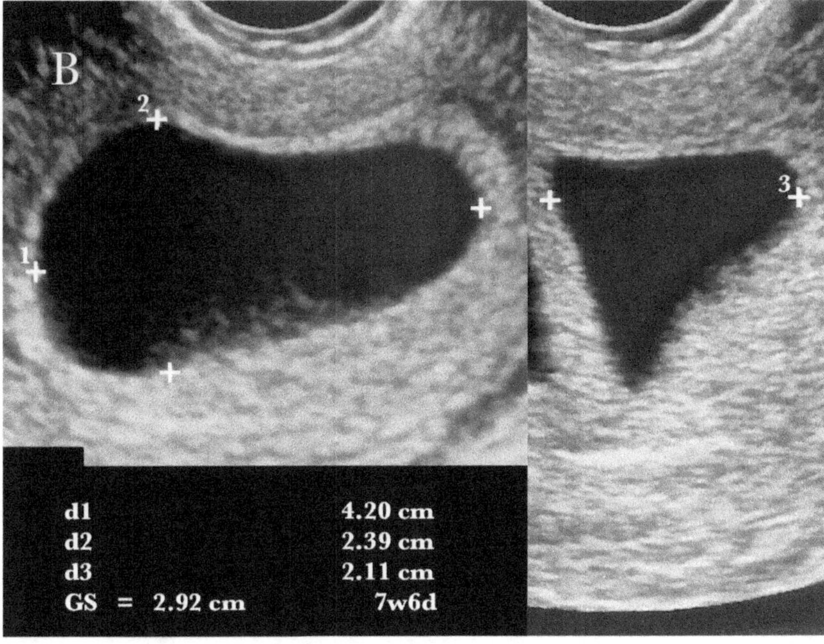

Figure 6.14: 6w6d ~ Gestational Sac B

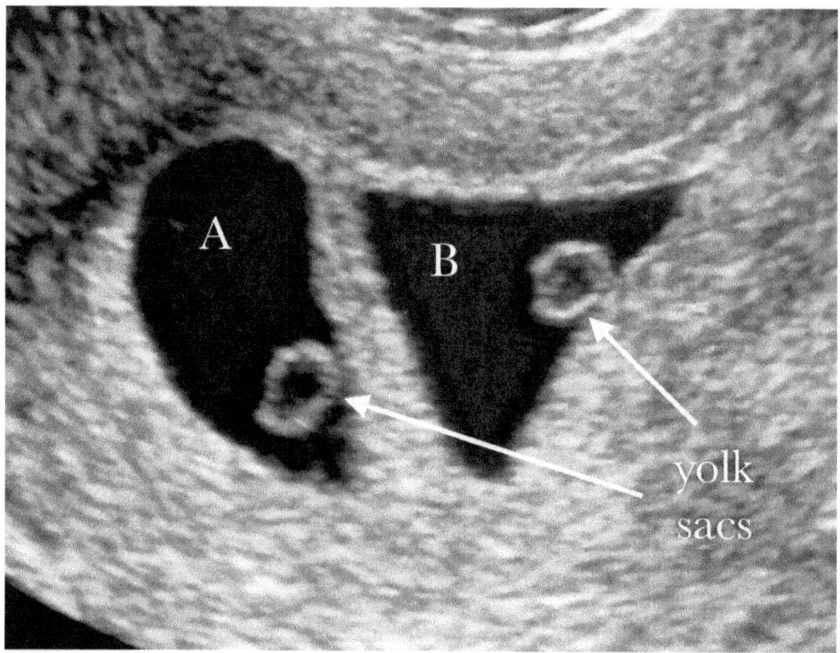

Figure 6.15: 6w6d ~ Yolk Sacs

Finally, Figure 6.15 shows each YS for A and B. They had lost just a bit of their perfectly round shape, and this was entirely normal.

The bottom line as we approached Week 7 was that both embryos had grown appropriately, A's sac now measured consistently with dates, and both heartbeats were steadily pumping with a regular rhythm and normal rate.

Any embryo should continue to demonstrate a normal heart rate with a steady and regular rhythm in a normally developing pregnancy. If a normal heart rate is seen on early scans, it is expected that the embryo should grow normally, too.

Questions to Ask for Your First Trimester Scan

Many patients forget to ask questions after having a sonogram. Maybe this is due to excitement or, possibly, pregnancy brain is already kicking in! Regardless, the following list provides 8 commonly asked questions during a scan at this gestational age. Your doctor or other healthcare provider will have the answers.

1. What is my due date?
2. Is my due date based on my LMP or ultrasound findings?
3. What is my gestational age according to my sonogram?
4. When can I expect to have my next diagnostic sonogram?
5. What would be the purpose for my next sonogram?
6. Can gender be determined (if you want to know!)?
7. Can I record my next sonogram in any way?
8. Where will my next sonogram be performed?
9. When and how will I receive the results?

Considering the positive results of our last scan, our nurse was enjoying a bit of relief. She would wait a full week for the next scan, which we'll address in Week 8. Onward to Week 7!

Reference

1. Chaudhry, K., Tafti, D., Siccardi, M., "Anembryonic Pregnancy," *StatPearls*. 2020. (https://www.ncbi.nlm.nih.gov/books/NBK499938/)

Week 7

As I mentioned in the Week 6, Dianne opted to wait an entire week to scan again so the twins' growth will next be addressed in Week 8. This section will discuss what should be seen in Week 7 of pregnancy and what is meant by "appropriate growth."

In a normally developing pregnancy, we should expect to see more of the same as we saw in Week 6. Gestational sacs should be a little larger, yolk sacs should still be seen even if they are not perfectly circular, and the embryo averages about 1 cm or 0.39 inches [1]. Of course, a strong and steady heartbeat of more than 100 BPM would be expected.

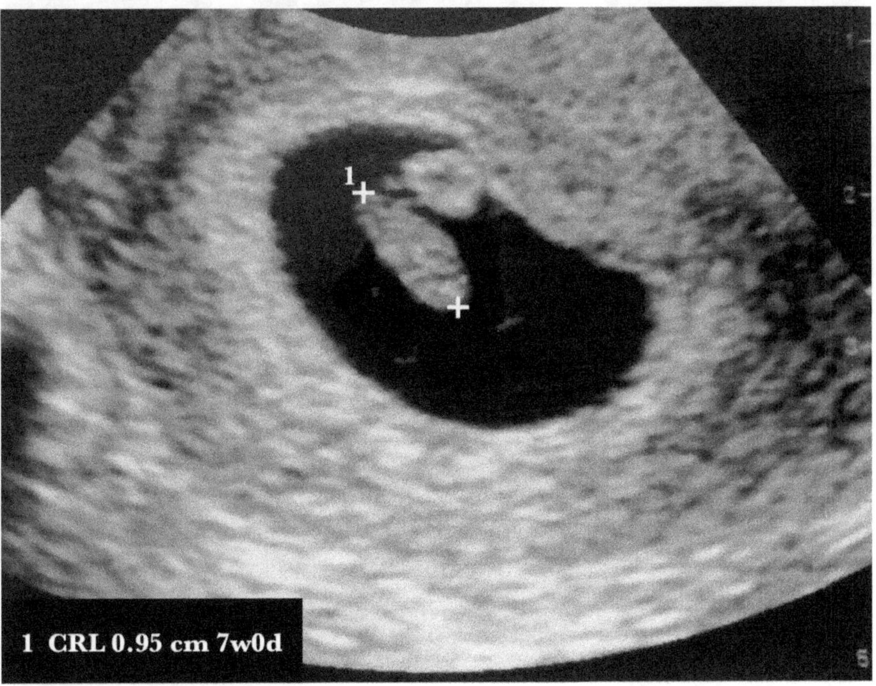

Figure 7.1: Week 7 ~ Embryo & Yolk Sac

Figure 7.1 shows an embryo and yolk sac in Week 7. You can see how it has a slightly collapsed appearance in this view, but only the edge of the YS was visible in this image. Regardless, growth and heartbeat were normal.

Figure 7.2 is another specimen of a yolk sac in Week 7—perfectly circular. You can see how its appearance differs from the YS in Figure 7.1, but both are great examples of how they can look a little different and still be normal.

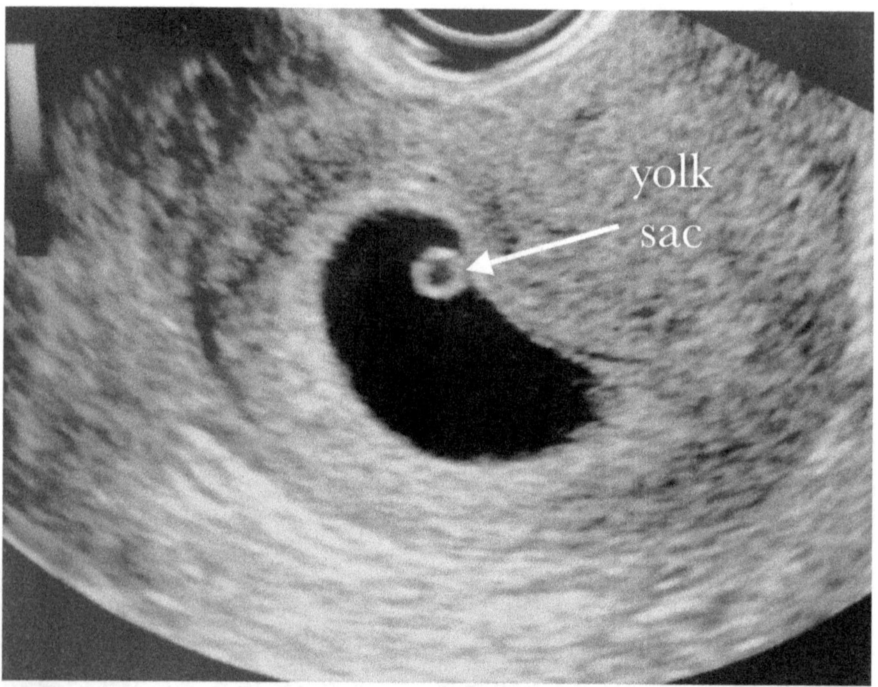

Figure 7.2: Week 7 ~ Yolk Sac

Appropriate Interval Growth

I've mentioned "appropriate or normal interval growth" thus far when discussing growth of the twins from one scan to the next. I'll provide a brief explanation here.

One important feature of serial diagnostic ultrasounds in pregnancy is documenting whether an embryo or fetus is growing as expected. For example, if an embryo measures 6 Weeks and another scan is required (for whatever reason) exactly two weeks later, that embryo should measure right around 8 Weeks, plus or minus a couple of days. This would be formally interpreted as appropriate or normal interval growth. If however, that same embryo only measured 7 Weeks upon return, it would be an alarm bell for the health of the pregnancy. The growth of an embryo or fetus should always show consistency with the established gestational age throughout the pregnancy, plus or minus standard deviation.

What is standard deviation? It's the bit of leeway allowed in Baby's growth via ultrasound measurements which is still considered normal. Baby's measurements should be consistent with gestational age within a couple of days early in the pregnancy, within one week of GA later in the First Trimester, within two weeks in the Second Trimester, and within three weeks in the Third Trimester. This is because as our babies grow, they begin to take on genetic tendencies for big or small which is taken into consideration. These measurements are compared from one scan to the next to reassure of proper growth.

Conversely, this comparison can be very helpful in alerting your physician to a potential problem in cases where growth appears restricted or if Baby is growing too fast, which can be an indicator of gestational diabetes. It's one of the reasons why ultrasound has become a crucial tool for your obstetrician. It allows him or her to better manage your pregnancy when a problem is found.

As for Dianne, she knew she was still quite early in her pregnancy and that there were no guarantees. Her chances of both babies surviving the First Trimester improved greatly with each passing week of normal interval growth and normal heartbeats. So, how were our twins looking in Week 8?

Reference

1. Curran, M., MD, FACOG. *Fetal Development*. 2019. (perinatology.com/Reference/Fetal%20development.htm)

Week 8

It's been a full week, and these babies are growing like weeds! Figure 8.1 shows Baby A at 15 mm now and measuring right on schedule at 8w0d!

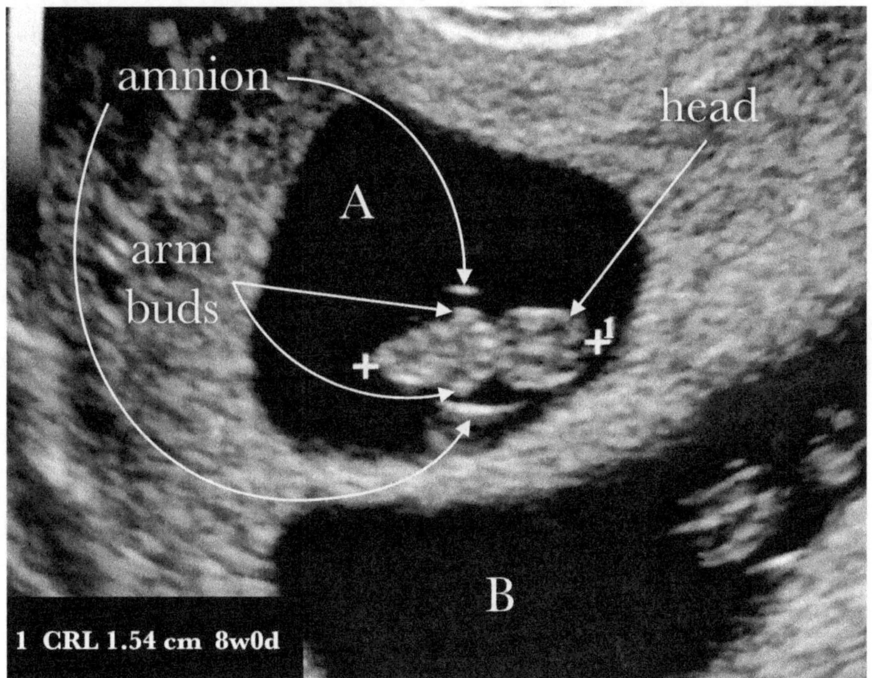

Figure 8.1: Week 8 ~ Baby A

Embryos are also just beginning to sprout little arm and leg buds now which are just slightly visible on your scan. They remind me of a little gummy bear from the front. So cute!

Notice the arrows labeled "arm buds" which point to the tiny white line on each side of Baby's torso. Leg buds are not seen in this image, but they have a similar appearance. Baby's head is to the right, and the thicker arrows point to the amnion.

What is the amnion? It's the membrane or protective sac directly around Baby which contains amniotic fluid, or you may know it as the amniotic sac. A couple of generations ago, your grandmother may have referred to it as the "bag of water." Because the amnion is still so small and thin, only a tiny segment of the top and bottom membrane can be seen well by ultrasound at this GA. The amnion will be more easily seen in the coming weeks as Baby grows all things inside get bigger.

Figure 8.2 shows Baby B who is a gigantic 16 mm and also measures 8w0d! Figure 8.3 is a side view of Baby B with a second CRL taken showing just a bit larger at 8w2d.

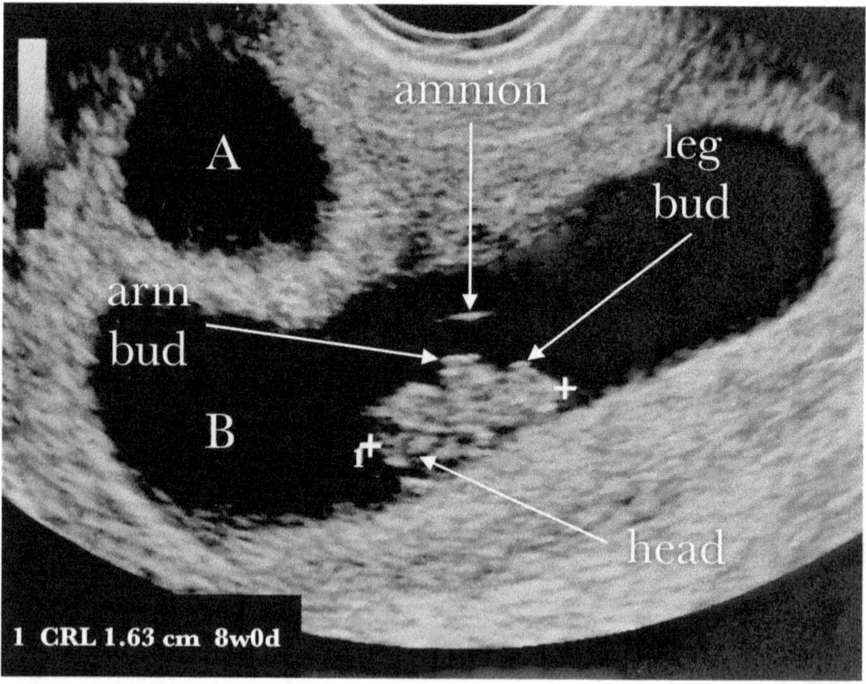

Figure 8.2: Week 8 ~ Baby B, Coronal View

This subtle difference of two days between Babies A and B is considered normal or concordant growth. Concordant growth means the twins are growing at a similar rate to one another, what we hope to document for the duration of the pregnancy. The operative word here is "similar." A small discrepancy can exist and still be considered normal growth. Your physician can tell you whether discrepancies in size and growth exist or are concerning. In other words, do not dismay over the numbers you see on the monitor!

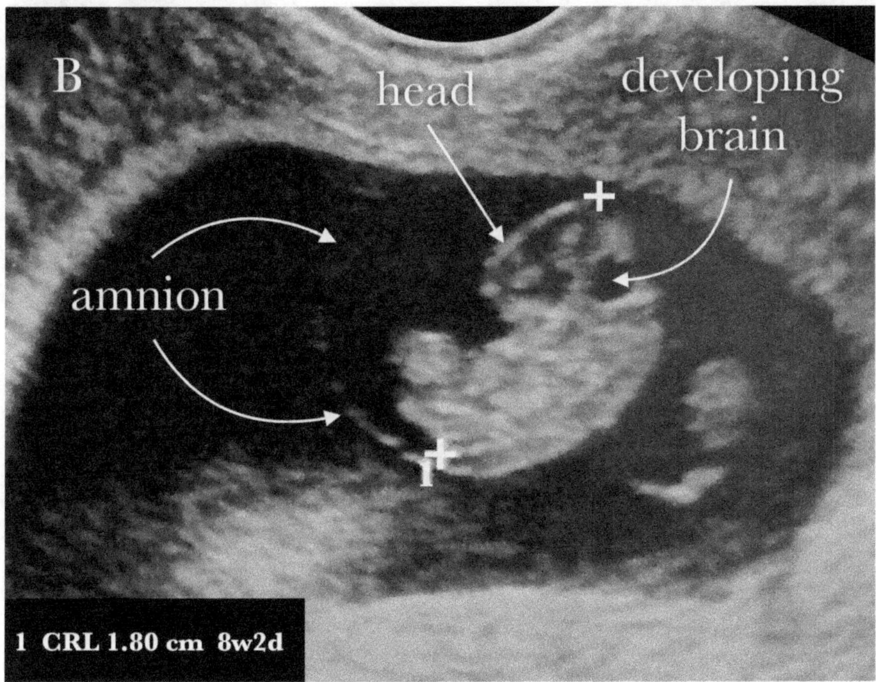

Figure 8.3: Week 8 ~ Baby B at 8w2d, Side View

An ultrasound in Week 8 shows the most miniature of movements with the endovaginal probe! This very sporadic squirm is barely visible, so don't be alarmed if it is not detected during *your* Week 8 scan. Just a great heartbeat and appropriate growth are needed to make this scan a success. A lot more movement can be seen at Week 9, which is discussed in the next chapter.

If you are pregnant with twins or a greater variation of multiples, you may have more detailed questions related to sac development or identical versus fraternal. Because multiples can be a little complicated, I recommend asking your doctor who can provide answers more specific to your pregnancy.

Figure 8.4 is an image of both babies together, each in their own gestational sac. This is one of my favorite shots. A twin pregnancy such as Dianne's is called

Dichorionic/Diamniotic, meaning each baby has its own gestational sac and its own amniotic sac. Having a placenta all to yourself is also a great thing and an important bit of documentation in a twin scan.

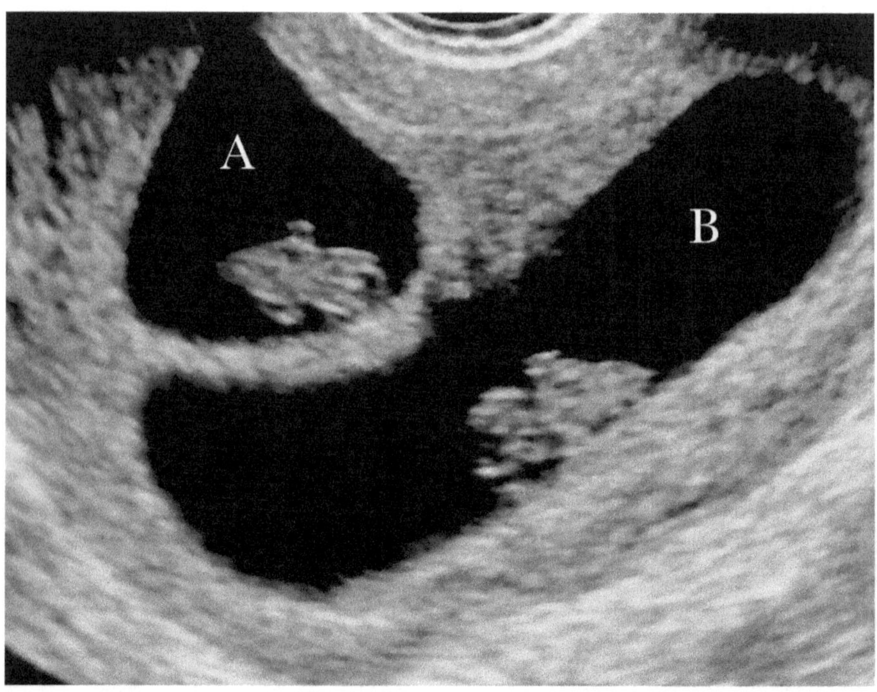

Figure 8.4: Week 8 ~ Dichorionic/Diamniotic Twins

Wanna compare the leaps and bounds our babies make in just two short weeks of early pregnancy? Figures 8.5 and 8.6 show the difference in size of Baby B at Week 6 compared to that of Week 8.

The transformation in two short weeks is incredible. A growth of about 13 mm or right about a half inch is seen, and more than 5 times larger. You may now be able to appreciate how scanning and measuring your baby at Week 8 is so much easier than Week 6.

With another weekly milestone achieved, Dianne became officially a little less anxious with the risk of miscarriage now dramatically decreased. I was a bit relieved myself! We were, however, cautiously optimistic knowing she was not yet out of the woods of the First Trimester. She even allowed herself to feel a little excitement. Let's see what's movin' and shakin' in Week 9!

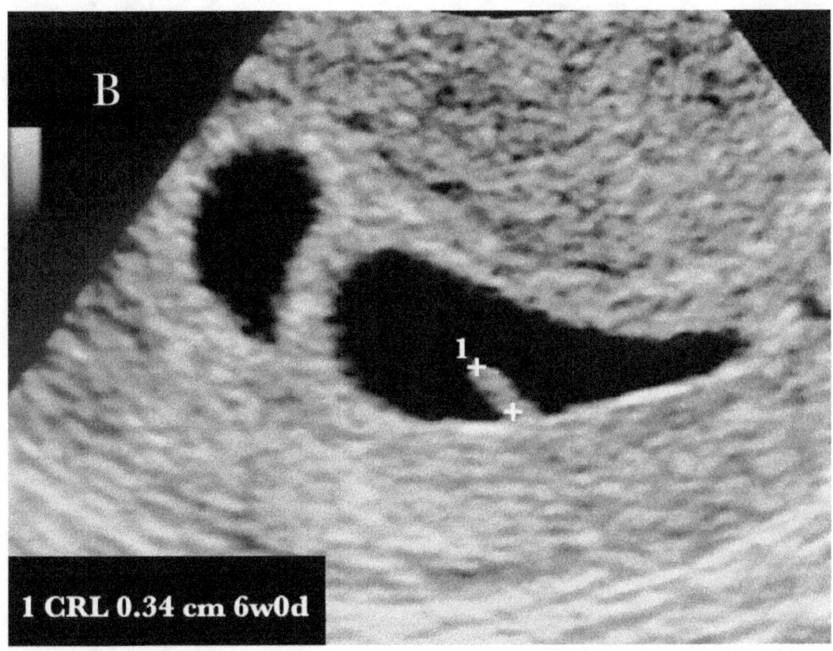

Figure 8.5: Week 6 ~ Baby B

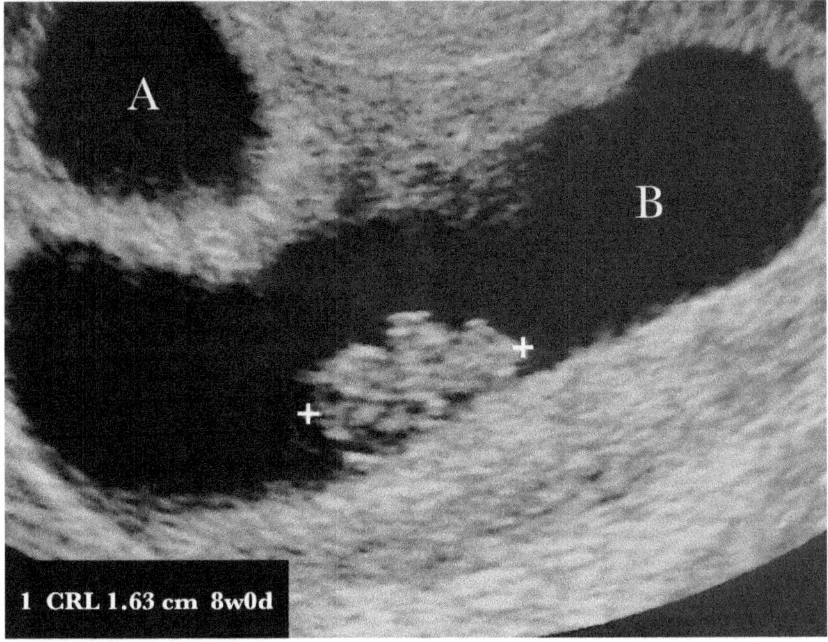

Figure 8.6: Week 8 ~ Baby B

Week 9

Figure 9.1 shows Baby A measuring almost an entire inch at 2.3 cm (2.54 cm = 1 inch) and normal interval growth at 9w0d. Baby A in Figure 9.1 is upside-down with the head toward the bottom of the image.

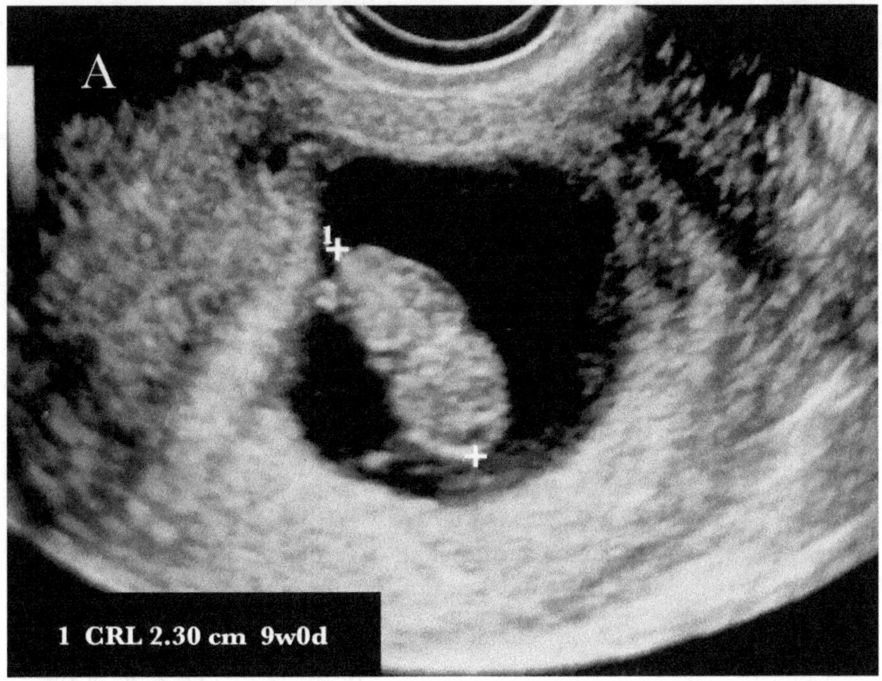

Figure 9.1: Week 9 ~ Baby A

Figure 9.2 shows the concordant growth of Twin B, measuring just about the same at 1.5 mm larger and 9w1d.

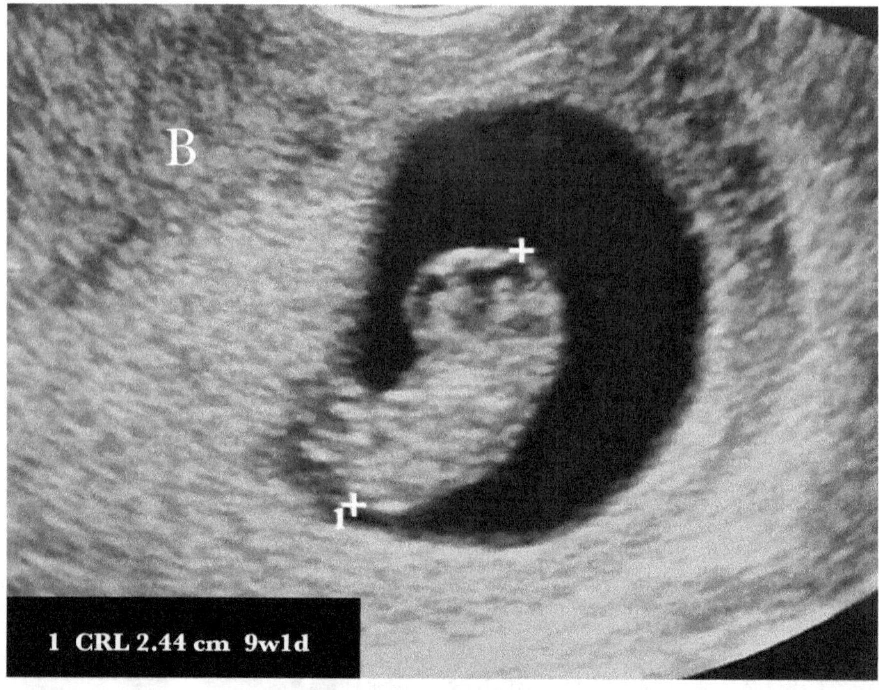

Figure 9.2: Week 9 ~ Baby B, Side View

Dianne was feeling very positive about her pregnancy now with another week of great growth. It is greatly reassuring to see normal growth in a singleton pregnancy, but these findings are especially favorable for multiples.

Their heart rates were also excellent at 178 BPM for Baby A and 176 BPM for Baby B. It is not unusual to see this sort of increase in heart rate at this gestational age. Often, the beginning heart rate starts off much more slowly at around 100 BPM in Week 6 and settles down in the Second and Third Trimesters to a variable 120–160 BPM for the remainder of the pregnancy.

Don't become alarmed if you see the recorded heart rate a bit below or above these numbers. You may notice on your scans later in pregnancy that Baby's heart rate changes based on level of activity, increasing in rate as he or she practices gymnastics and slowing down during nap time. Your doctor may consider slight variations quite normal.

All Baby's parts are labeled for easier understanding in Figure 9.3. The arm and leg buds are a little more prominent now and the dark spot inside Baby's head represents the developing brain.

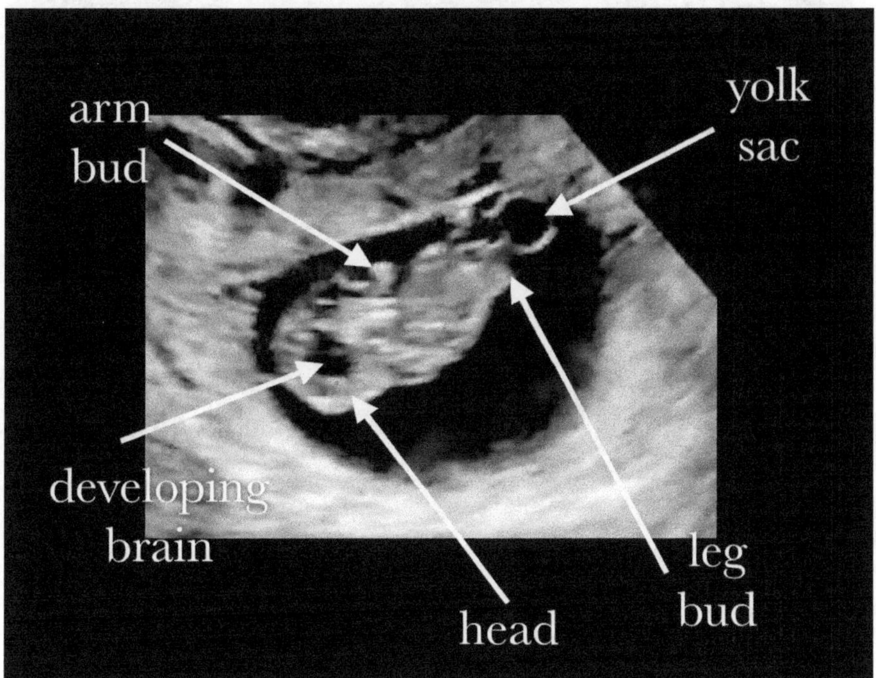

Figure 9.3: Week 9 ~ Embryo, Labeled

Figure 9.4 shows a better view of the amnion, now that Baby's development is a little farther along. The yolk sac is not seen in Figure 9.4 because the focus was to illustrate the amnion. The arrows point to the amniotic membrane or sac immediately around the embryo.

Can you identify Baby's parts in Figure 9.4? Try to guess first, then check them against Figure 9.5 which spells it out for you with labels.

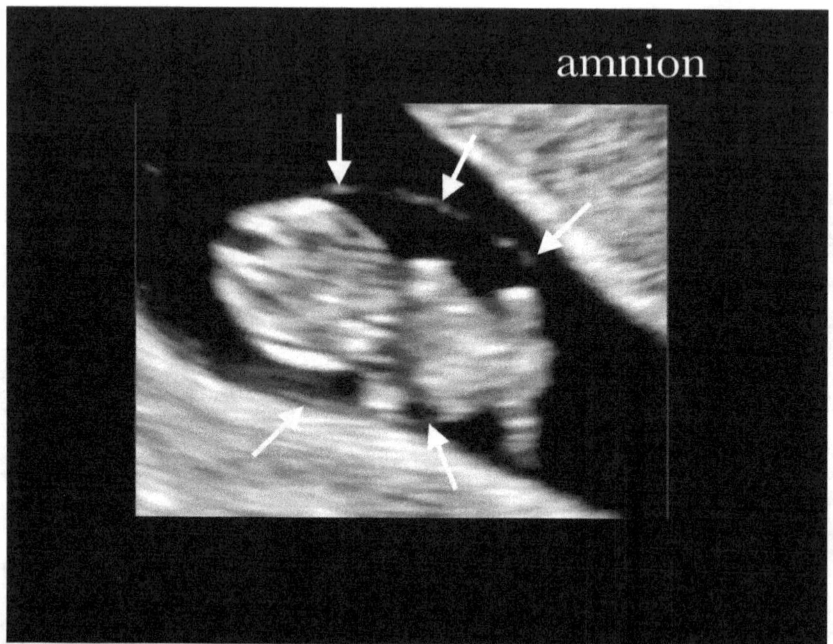

Figure 9.4: Week 9 ~ Amnion

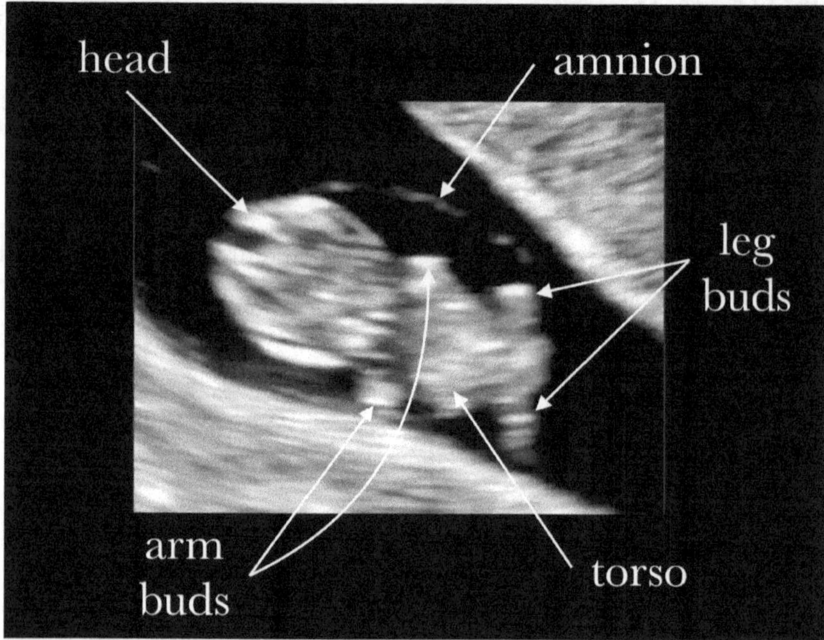

Figure 9.5: Week 9 ~ Amnion & Embryo, Labeled

Week 9 Movement

Have you ever seen a baby move in Week 9 of pregnancy? If not, you are in for some real amusement! As discussed in Week 8, Baby begins to demonstrate barely detectable movements. Seeing the smallest of squirms may require focusing on the screen intently for a couple of minutes. Just one week later, the wiggles really appear quite pronounced.

A reader of my blog, UltrasoundUnwrapped.com, was concerned about her very early ultrasound and emailed a few questions. Two weeks later, she sent me a video to show how well she was doing! You can go to the following link on my site to see this little fella tap dance.

https://ultrasoundunwrapped.com/week-9-wiggles/

Isn't the degree of movement amazing? Of course, none of it is well thought-out choreography but instead the nervous system very hard at work.

Week 10

Congratulations! At gestational age Week 10, your baby has graduated from an embryo to a fetus! This is a huge accomplishment and certainly worthy of celebration.

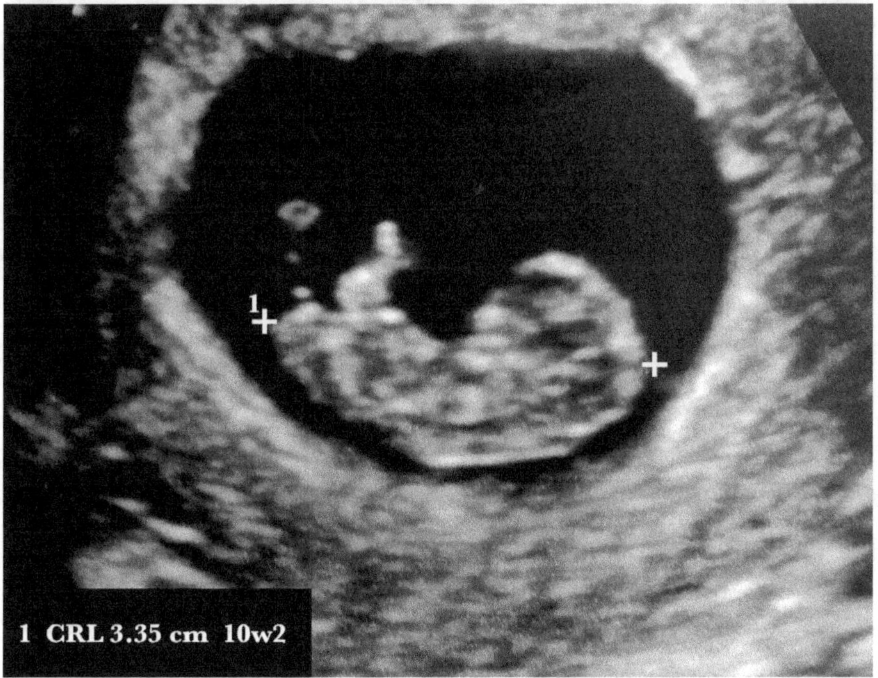

Figure 10.1: 10w2d Fetus

Figure 10.1 represents a side view and a CRL of this fetus at 10w2d. Fetal size that you could expect to see during a scan in Week 10 measures about 3.2 cm or 1.2 inches long [1].

Transvaginal scanning still provides the best views in most women at this point. And because this approach requires an *empty* bladder, hopefully, you won't need to drink a sea of liquids in order to see Baby. However, as I mentioned in Chapter 3, it's worth noting again here that every facility employs different policies regarding how they perform an ultrasound at this gestational age. So, depending on where the study is performed, you may be asked to fill your bladder. Be sure to ask at the time your ultrasound is scheduled if specific preparation is required.

We have just a few quick images of our twins in Week 10, 10w6d to be exact. Their growth will be addressed next in Week 11. Figure 10.2 is a split image of both Baby A and B.

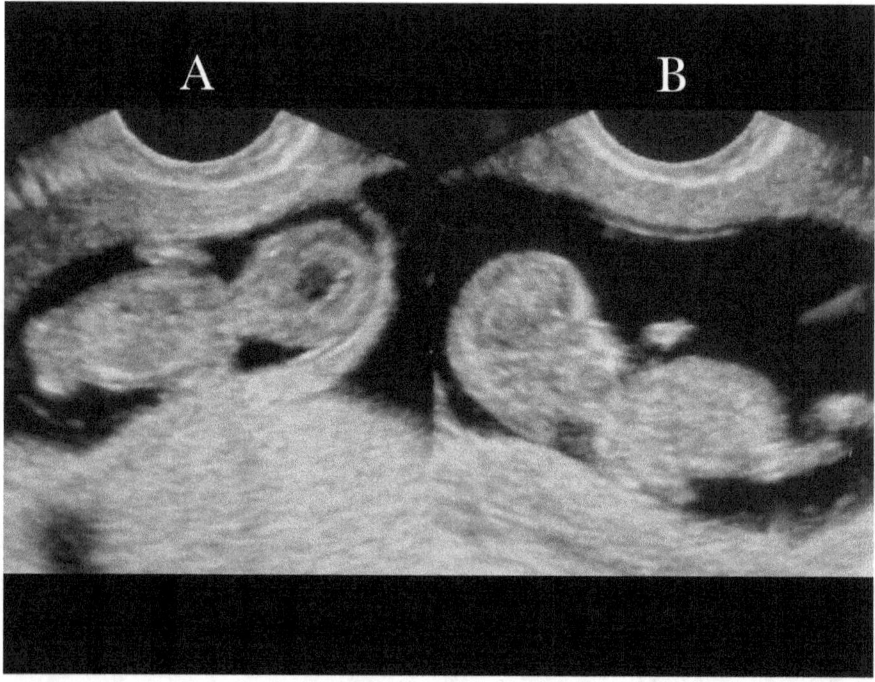

Figure 10.2: Twins at 10w6d

Figure 10.2 shows a split-screen image with Baby A on the left and Baby B on the right. As twins become bigger and more active, it then becomes much more difficult to obtain a great image of them both at the same time. Limited belly space and limited angles make this a challenge.

In Figure 10.3, Baby A shows off his/her bottom half. The leg is so clear here because it lies perpendicular to the sound beam, which always yields a clearer image.

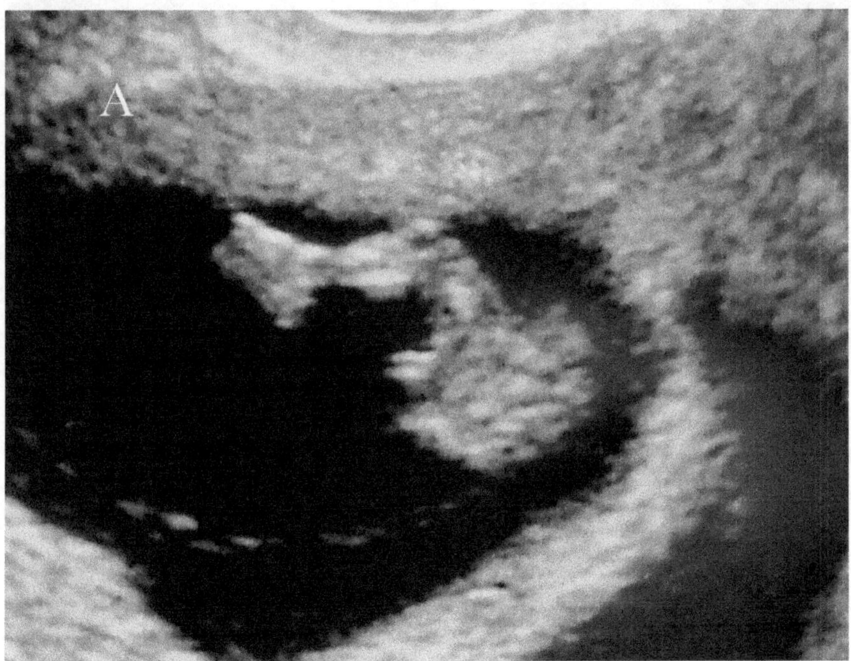

Figure 10.3: Week 10 ~ Baby A, Leg and Feet

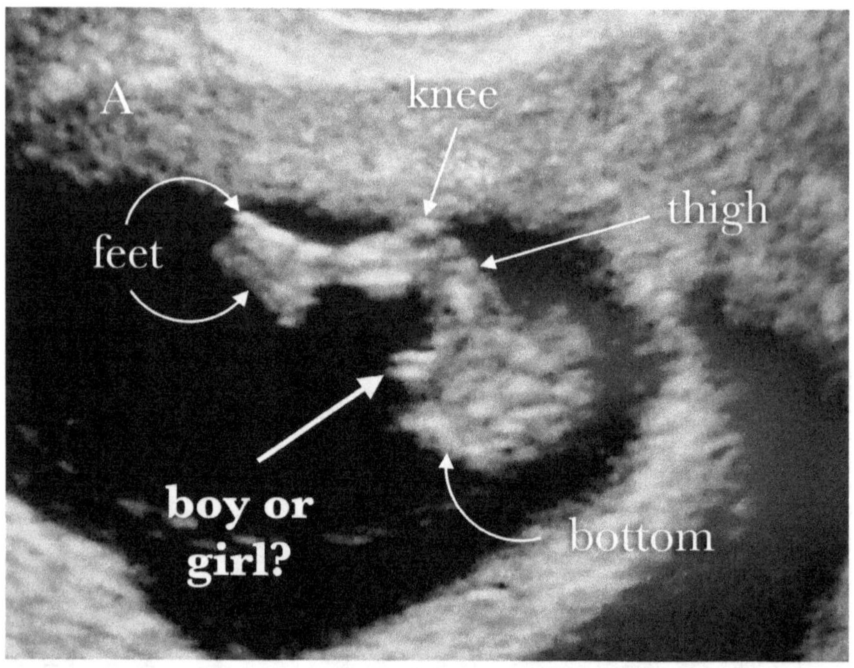

Figure 10.4: Week 10 ~ Baby A, Leg and Feet, Labeled

Figure 10.4 is the same as Figure 10.3 but with labels. Can you see these parts more clearly now?

Notice the question of boy or girl and arrow in bold pointing to external genitalia. We need several more weeks before a confident guess can be ventured about the sex of Dianne's twins! This area could represent either gender. Though they are only a day shy of Week 11, a guarantee at Week 12 is just too early. But more on that in Week 14 in Part Three.

Of course, as the sonographer here, *I* already know whether this baby belongs to Team Pink or Blue. But our twins' genders will just have to remain a mystery for the time being. I can't give away *all* my secrets too soon now, can I?

Reference

1. Curran, M., MD, FACOG. *Fetal Development*. 2019. (perinatology.com/Reference/Fetal%20development.htm)

Week 11

At Week 11 your baby is now just shy of two whole inches or about 4 cm in length from head to bottom. The fetus at Week 11 is looking more and more like a baby instead of a tiny alien and, in real-time imaging, watching Baby flop around like a little fish out of water always creates a chuckle for spectators, including me.

Endovaginal ultrasound remains the (usually) preferred method of scanning because it still gives the best image, and Baby is not yet too big for a magnified view. Sometimes, a sonographer may choose to scan your belly instead at this point, but this is a subjective decision. And, hopefully, you will not need to fill your bladder!

Arms and legs are almost fully developed and can be seen flailing about during periods of extreme activity. Additionally, Baby's head still looks bigger than his or her body, much to the concern of most parents. However, do not be alarmed! A lot of brain is still growing in there.

Some babies are more active than others. Some stay curled up in a little ball and move very little while others perform gymnastic feats. Activity can make it difficult to get consistent and accurate measurements.

Avoid espresso shots and loads of sugar before a scan to limit the hyperactive fetus. Your doctor would *probably* say caffeine and sugar are better off excluded from your everyday diet anyway. That said, it can hinder a successful ultrasound if Baby just won't slow that roll.

Figure 11.1 shows a CRL measuring Baby A from head to rear. A 4.3 cm dimension puts this fetus at 11w1d, as you can see demonstrated in the lower left corner of the image.

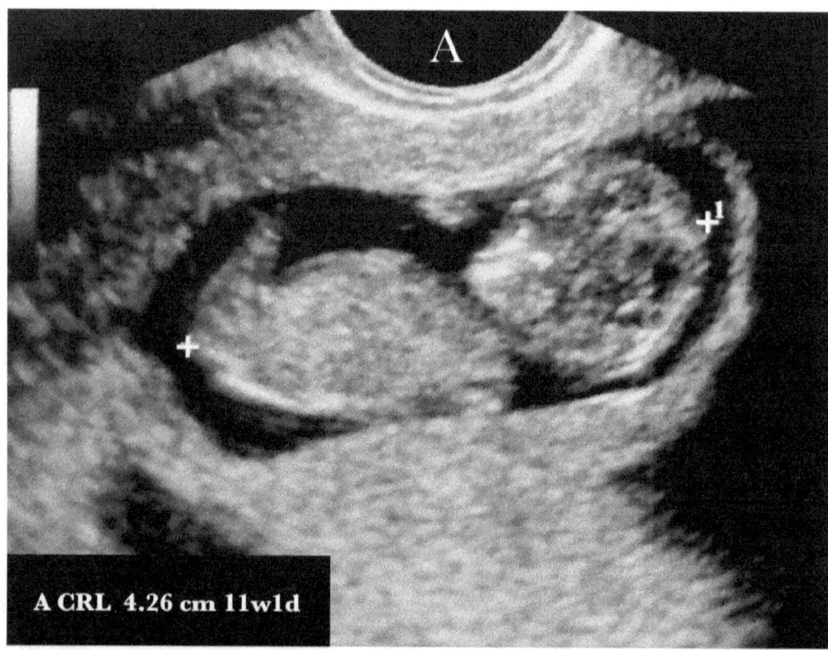

Figure 11.1: Week 11 ~ Fetus A, CRL

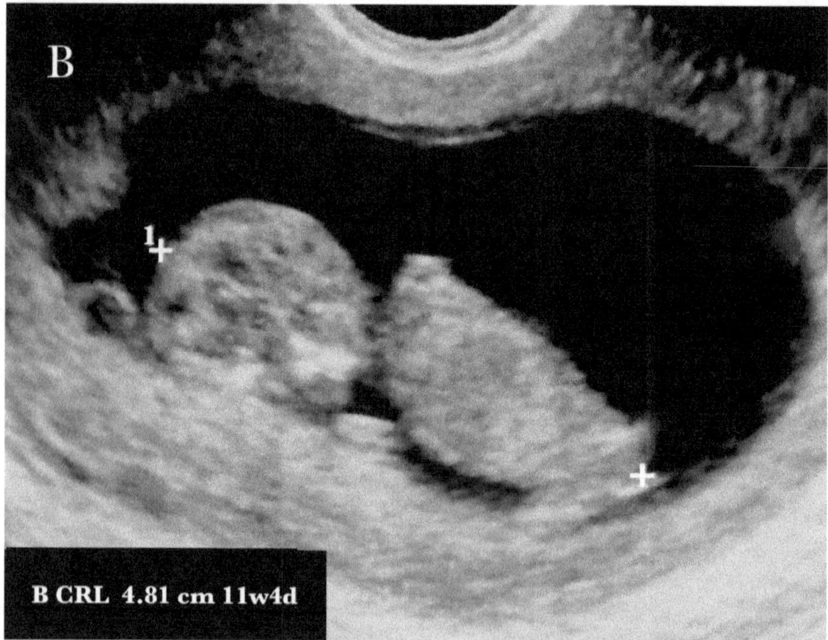

Figure 11.2: Week 11 ~ Fetus B, CRL

Now, note Baby B's CRL in Figure 11.2. His (or her!) measurement is slightly larger at 4.8 cm or 11w4d—that's 5 mm larger than Baby A and 3 days ahead. This is a minor discrepancy and is still considered "within normal limits" or concordant growth.

Remember, the most important factor when measuring twins (or any pregnancy including multiples) is to show that all babies in the pregnancy are growing at about the same rate. A few days discrepancy between babies is no cause for concern, if the gap of growth does not dramatically widen with every subsequent growth assessment performed. Another pertinent factor to note about Baby A's growth—though Baby B was a little bigger, Baby A was *not* small and was measuring right on track.

Even though Baby is not yet two inches from head to bottom, he or she is very active! So, while the CRL on Baby B wasn't the prettiest textbook representation, it was an accurate one. Sonographers want to take this measurement while the fetus is more stretched out as opposed to curled in a little ball. Obviously, a balled-up fetus will produce a shorter measurement than one in which the fetus is outstretched.

Is Figure 11.3 a face only a mother could love?

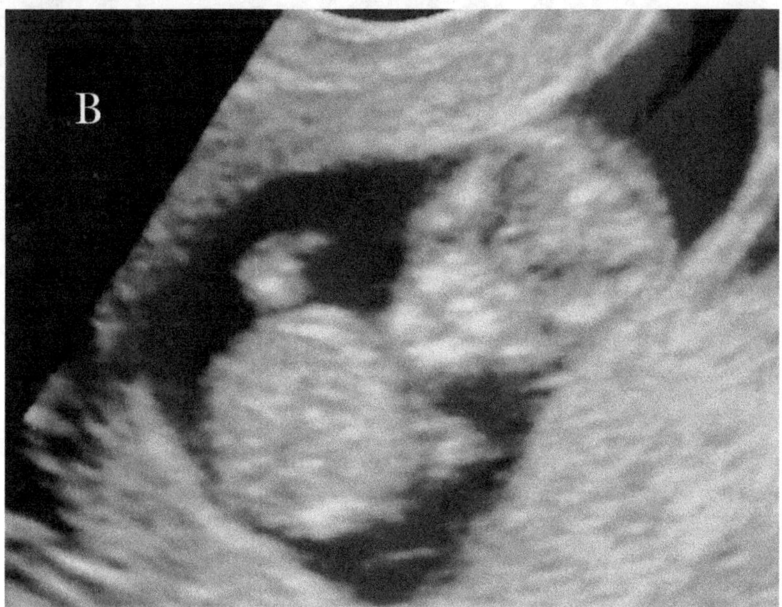

Figure 11.3: Week 11 ~ Baby B, Frontal Face

Well, it depends on which mother you ask. In this case, Dianne thought it was hilarious and asked for me to snap it. She thought "the alien shot" made a great addition to Baby B's collection.

In Figure 11.3, the frontal face image tends to scare most parents and understandably so. The "alien" look, as most patients call it, highlights facial bony features, making it appear more skeletal. I agree that it's not the cutest view. If Baby's position allows, a twist of the sonographer's wrist may provide the cute profile which lets you appreciate the soft tissue features of the nose and lips. They certainly look more like a baby from the side. Week 12 provides more examples of great profiles.

We did have lots of fun scanning Dianne's twins. Baby B's small but very distinct pair of legs and feet are pictured in Figure 11.4. So cute.

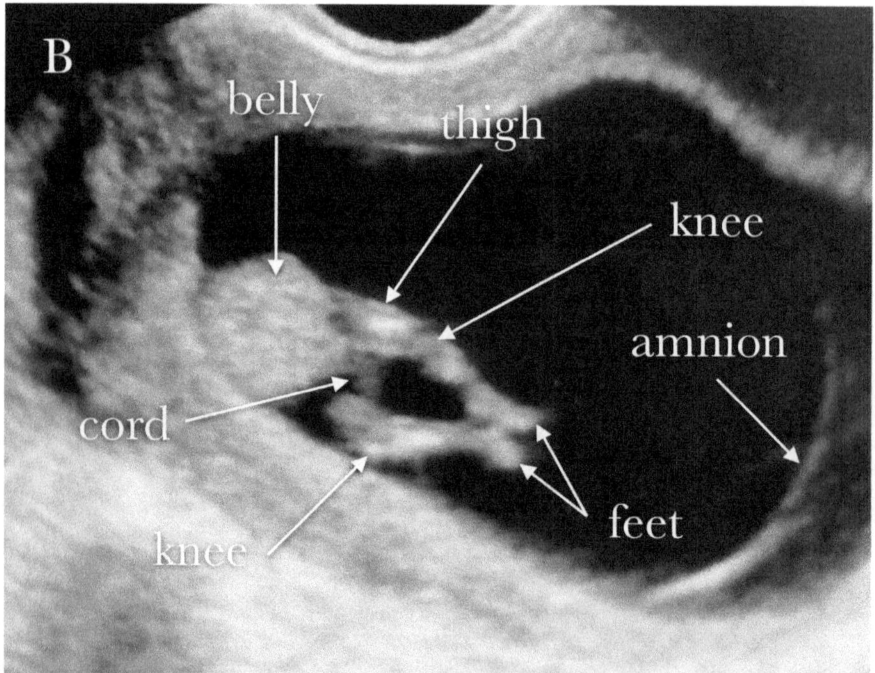

Figure 11.4: Week 11 ~ Baby B, Legs and Feet

Part of my goal when scanning at this gestational age was to obtain an image like Figure 11.4. Hands, feet, and a profile of the fetal face or body are the images that best make for cute keepsake photos, if they are obtainable!

One additional note here—multiples typically warrant more ultrasound examinations than a singleton pregnancy because of the higher risk brought by two babies growing together in the same home. Serial scans ensure how well your babies are growing comparatively, provide a means for your physician to monitor your pregnancy more closely in the event a problem is discovered, and allow intervention for early delivery, if necessary. Your healthcare provider will determine how often scans on your multiples need to be performed.

Week 12

Dianne was so relieved to reach Week 12 with no problems. The twins were growing concordantly, and her pregnancy otherwise was healthy.

Figures 12.1 and 12.2 show that Baby A measured just a few days smaller than Baby B—12w2d and 12w5d, respectively—still considered "within normal limits" for growth.

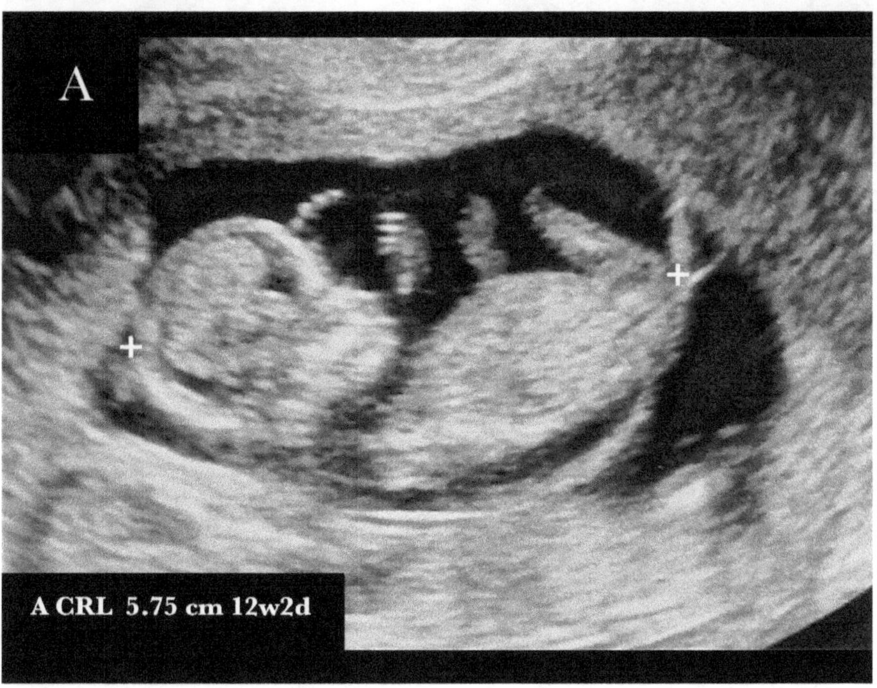

Figure 12.1: Week 12 ~ Fetus A, CRL

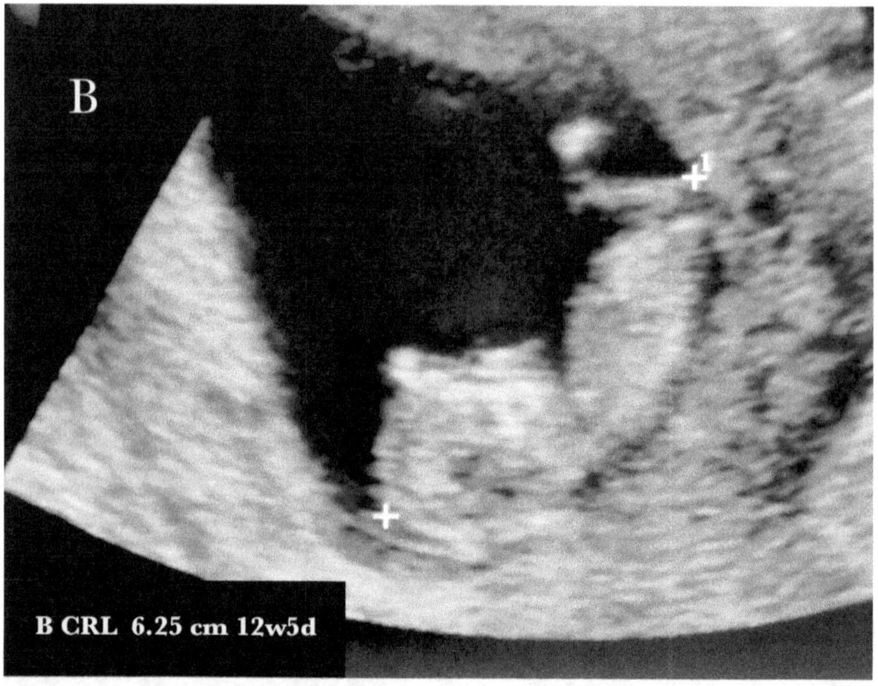

Figure 12.2: Week 12 ~ Fetus B, CRL

Now you may notice quite a difference in how well each fetus can be seen here. Does Baby A appear clearer to you than B? Fetal position can make a great impact on the ultrasound image. Baby B was tilted at a slightly greater angle and performing somewhat of a head stand, creating an image that looks "fuzzier" than Baby A, who was resting peacefully on his/her back.

Figure 12.3 is a labeled image of Figure 12.1. Only tips of the fingers and part of one upper leg are seen here. And because this is not a perfect profile shot, only part of the nose and lips are seen.

Note that only small segments of the umbilical cord are pictured. Most of the time and because of its length, the entire cord cannot be seen from placental insertion to insertion into Baby's abdomen. This is especially true as a fetus grows, taking up more and more room in the uterus. This early in gestation, the cord can appear as tiny white lines, as you see in Figure 12.3.

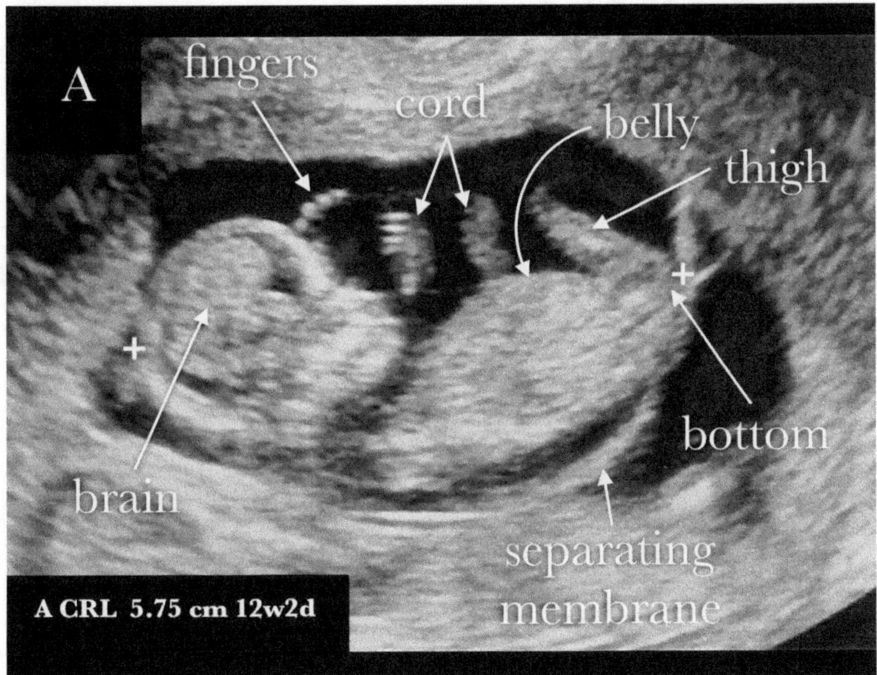

Figure 12.3: Week 12 ~ Fetus A, Labeled

Later in pregnancy when the cord is larger, most parents mistake it for bubbles, especially when it appears in front of Baby's face. Remember, however, that bubbles are not possible—no air in there!

In Figure 12.4, you'll see a great example of this—a beautiful profile shot of Baby A at 32 Weeks with a segment of cord near the lips. The white horizontal lines represent the walls of the three blood vessels of the cord.

A cross-section of the cord gives it the appearance of a tiny cluster of circles, as shown in Figure 12.5. A normal umbilical cord contains three vessels—one vein and two arteries. The vein is larger and the two arteries are usually about the same size. Here, it certainly does resemble bubbles.

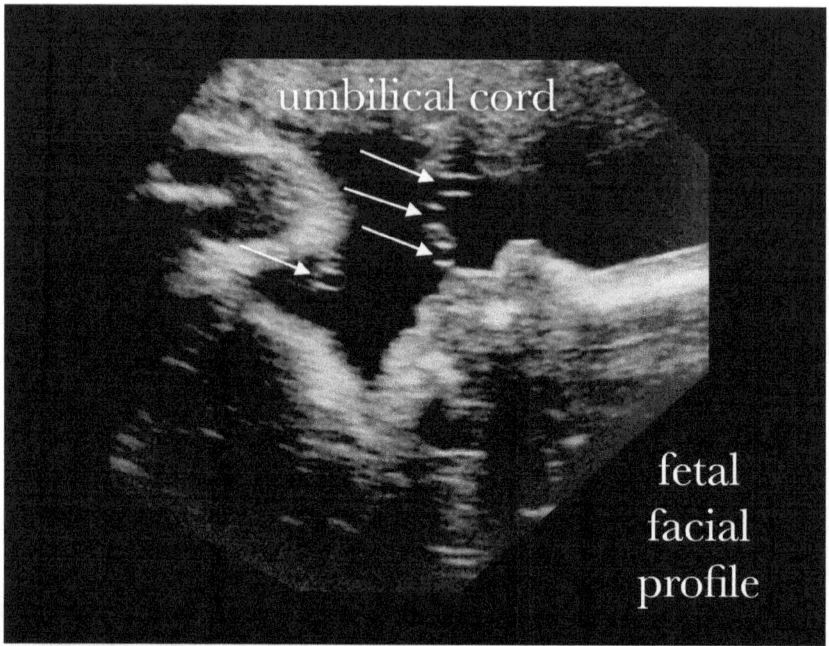

Figure 12.4: Mistaking the Cord for Bubbles

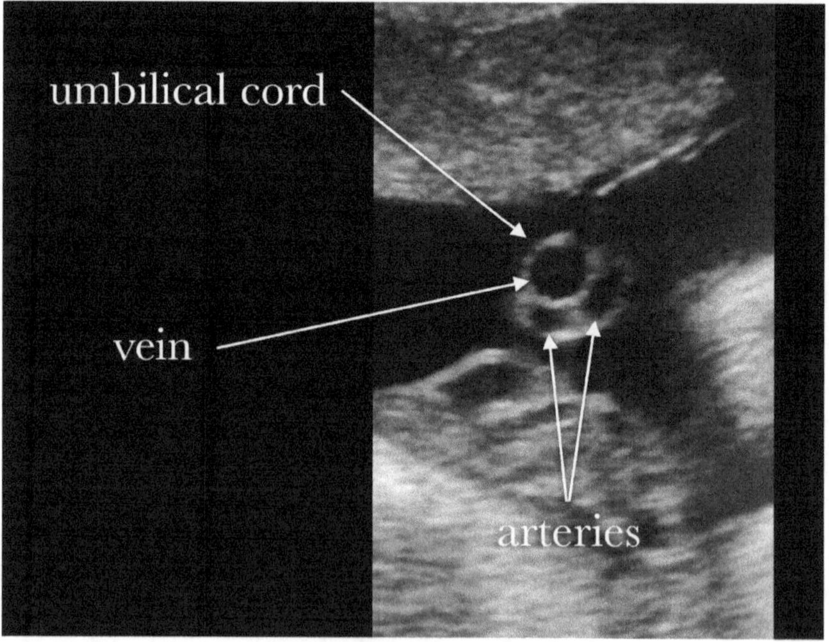

Figure 12.5: Cross-section of Umbilical Cord

Can you decipher what body parts the twins are showing off in Figure 12.6? If you guessed legs and feet, you're absolutely correct. Yes, the legs are indeed connected. They only appear to show gaps due to the curvature of the legs and the angle obtained between the probe and position of these babies.

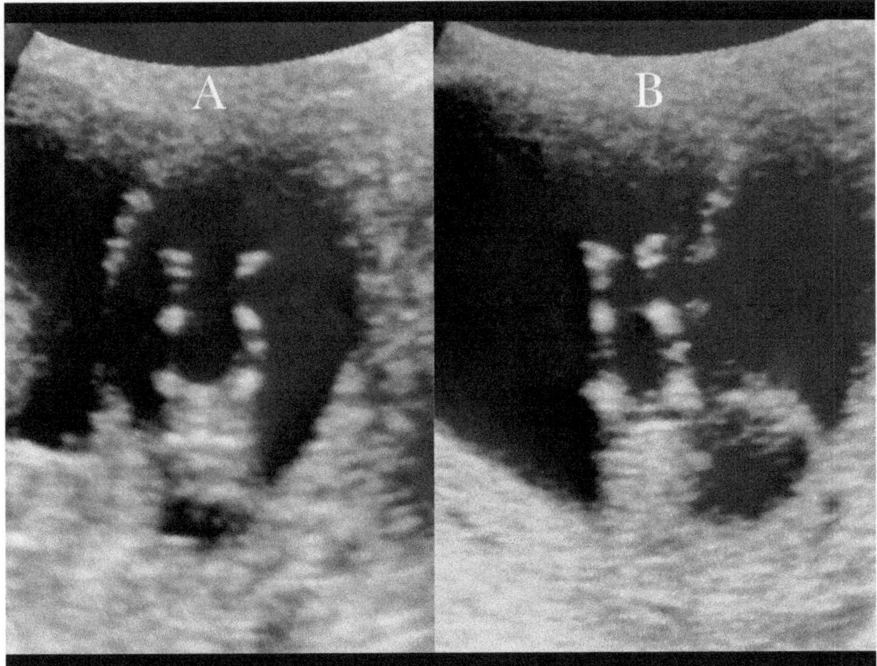

Figure 12.6: Week 12 ~ Twins' Legs and Feet

A Short Word on Genetic Testing

Because I am not a physician or geneticist, I will not discuss chromosomal testing in detail. It's an extraordinarily complex topic. Therefore, I will only provide you with some introductory information on the subject as it pertains to ultrasound.

An expectant parent may have an ultrasound examination around this gestational age if she chooses genetic testing to screen for chromosomal abnormalities, either due to maternal age or a family history of genetic abnormalities. These optional tests may or may not include ultrasound depending on the type of genetic testing performed. Counseling is typically required regarding your options for testing, how the tests are performed, what abnormalities each test is capable of detecting, the risks and limitations. That said, back to my area of expertise!

The scan which may be part of a genetic screening protocol is the Nuchal Translucency (NT) test. This test is an extraordinarily technical examination, requiring very precise magnification, positioning, and measuring. It also requires special training and certification for sonographers to perform the test. The examination involves measuring a fold of skin at the back of Baby's neck, documenting other structures, and submitting the information to a lab along with blood work from mom.

Often, a patient may be referred to Maternal Fetal Medicine to see a perinatologist (a high-risk obstetrician) who would perform the testing and provide you and your general obstetrician with the results. Their specialty lies in maternal and fetal abnormalities, counseling, and education for expectant parents for a myriad of pregnancy-related complications.

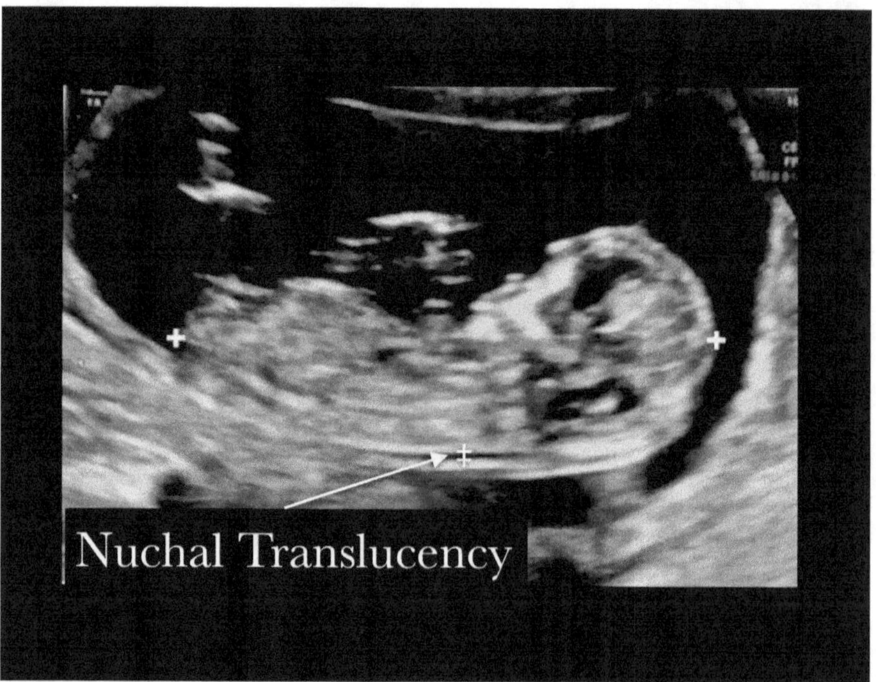

Figure 12.7: Nuchal Translucency

An NT measurement may look something like what you see here in Figure 12.7. A thickened NT can be an indicator of certain structural or genetic malformations. Of course, your perinatologist or obstetrician would discuss with you the results and any findings which may warrant further testing. Fetal position must be perfect or the test cannot be performed—a common limitation of the test. Discuss this path at length with your obstetrician or healthcare provider. It's not a decision to make lightly due to the important consequences of testing.

More and More Week-12 Photos

Everyone has just worked so hard to get to this point! Babies are fully formed now, and tiny hands and feet are distinctly recognizable. What a great shot of Baby B's foot in Figure 12.8!

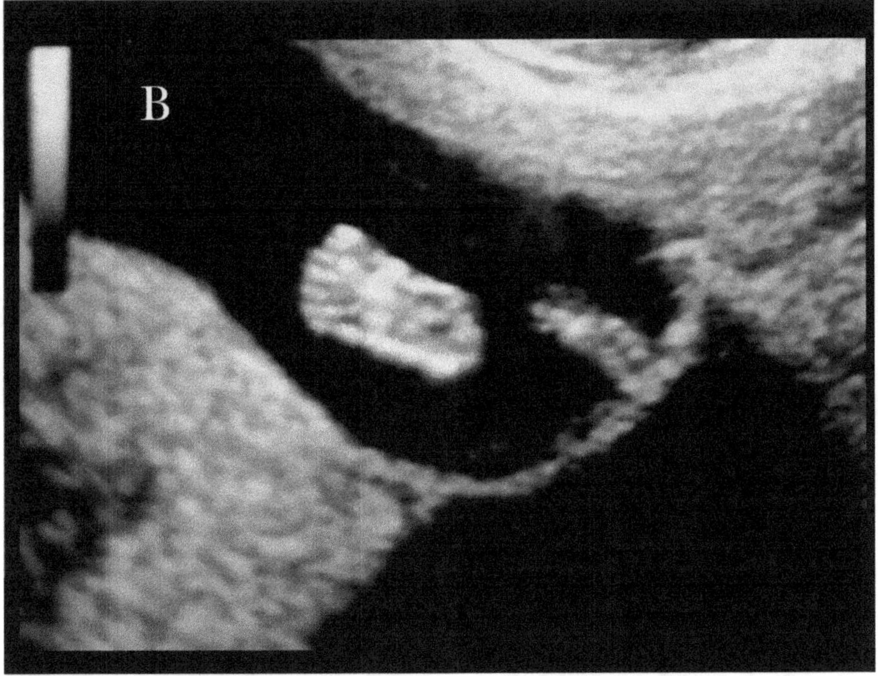

Figure 12.8: Week 12 ~ Baby B's Foot

It's not every day we can see them this well, but it's a favorite when we can. Figure 12.9 shows a little foot currently measuring about 1 cm (or less than 1/2 inch)! You can see five very distinct toes. Some parents become a little concerned and ask if they are seeing six! But they aren't because the outer-most layer is skin.

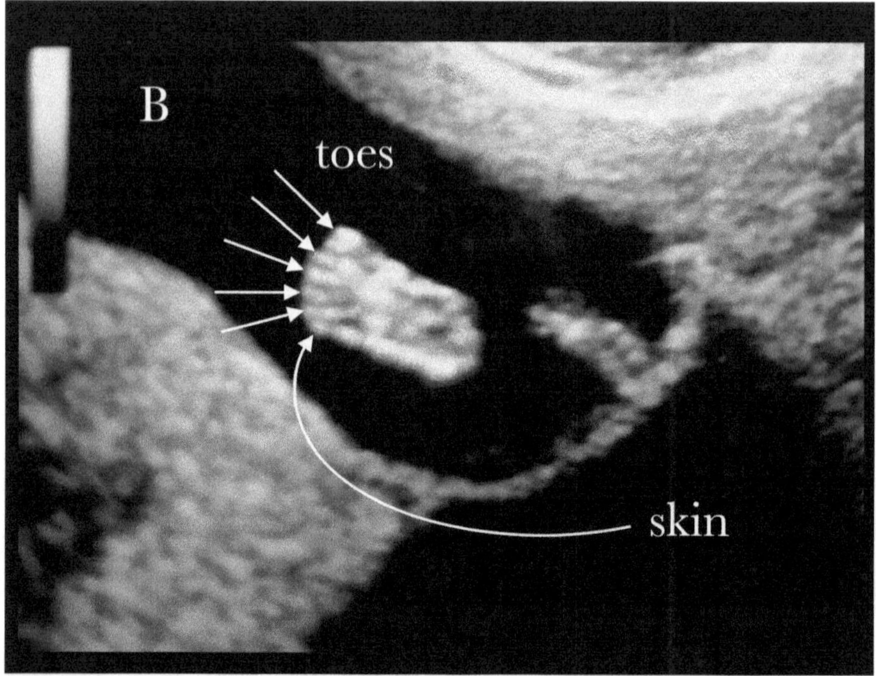

Figure 12.9: Week 12 ~ Baby B's Toes

Figure 12.10 was submitted by a blog reader. Her baby measured 12w2d here with a CRL of 5.7 cm. More than two whole inches from head to bottom. What a great side view for this gestational age. Notice the clearly recognizable nose and lips. This is what we see when Baby is looking up at mom's belly, versus her back like in Figure 12.11. This is a prone position with no chance of seeing that face unless Baby flips over!

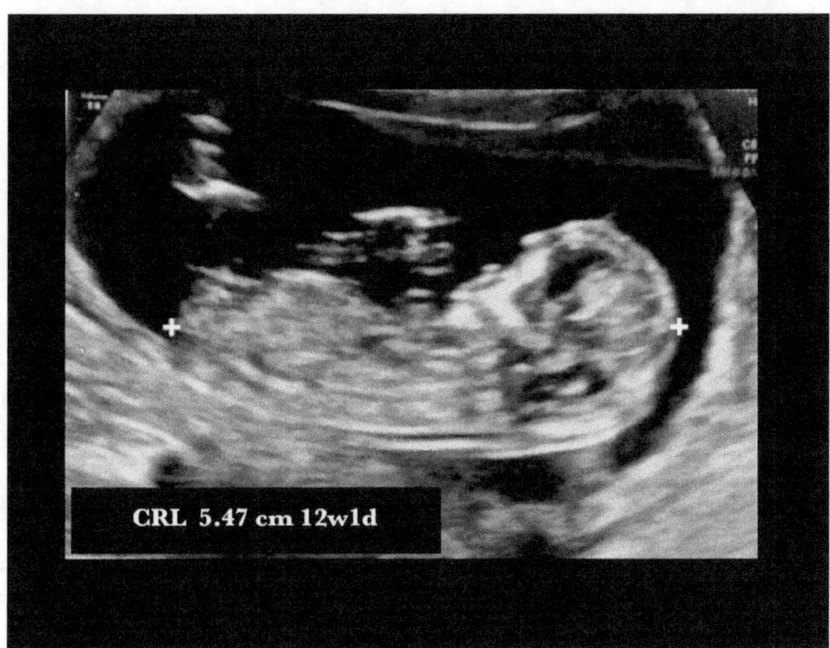

Figure 12.10: Week 12 ~ Fetal Profile

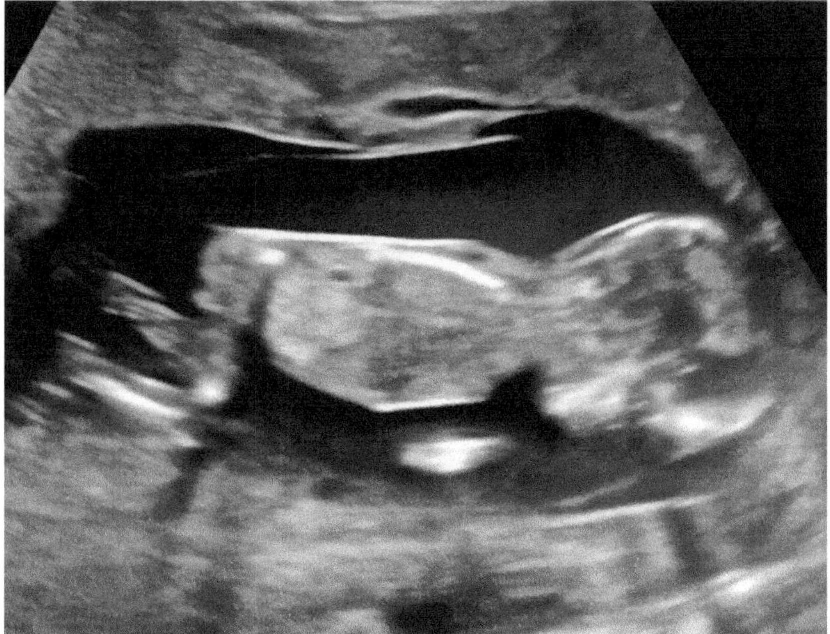

Figure 12.11: Week 12 ~ Fetal Prone Position

A few organs can typically be demonstrated on a scan in Week 12. The stomach appears black because it is filled with amniotic fluid swallowed by the fetus. The urinary bladder is also identifiable as a small black circle in the pelvis as it becomes more distended due to functioning kidneys. A fetus urinates, too! Most parents don't realize that the amniotic fluid is made up mostly of your baby's urine. The kidneys, however, are too small to see very well at this gestational age.

The brain can be seen but will continue to develop and change its appearance with gestational age. The heart is a beating machine but is still too small to see much detail. These and other organs will grow larger and be easier to evaluate mid-pregnancy, per your doctor's orders. The anatomic survey performed mostly between 18 and 20 Weeks is called the Anatomy Screen or "The One Where We Find Out the Sex," according to many parents-to-be. The purpose of this examination is to confirm Baby's growth, to document development and functioning organs, and to rule out structural malformations. Determining fetal sex is *only* a bonus provided *if* Baby cooperates, if protocols of the medical facility allow for this guess, and if all the stars align just so!

To bring Week 12 to a close and leap into the last week of the First Trimester, Baby A sends you off with a first wave, shown in Figure 12.12. This is positively one of my most favorite images! And if you're a fan of my website or Instagram page, @ultrasound_unwrapped, you have seen quite a bit of Baby A there, too.

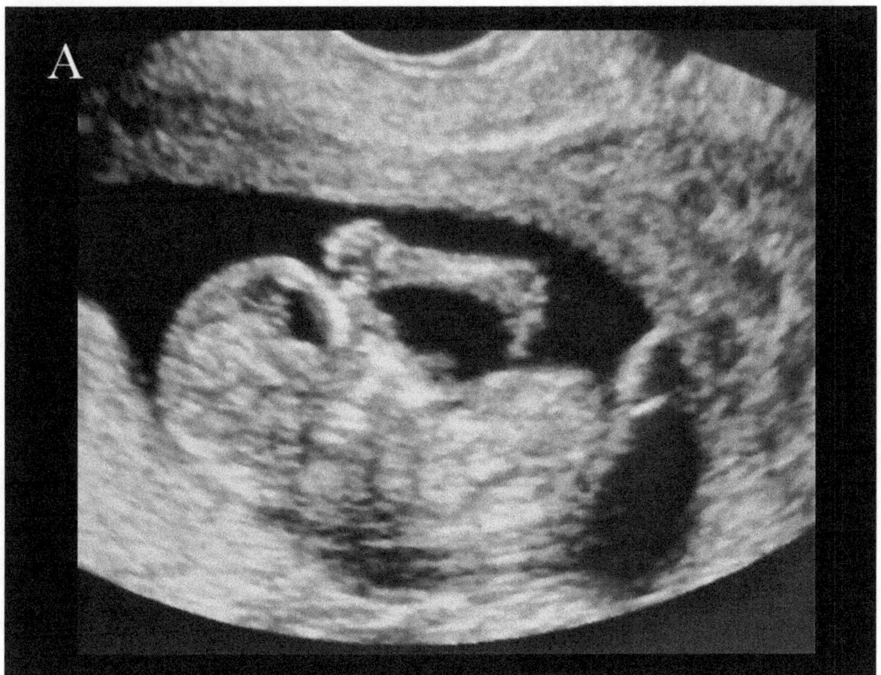

Figure 12.12: Week 12 ~ Baby A's First Wave

Week 13

Congratulations! You are almost out of the woods of the First Trimester which ends at 13w6d. The First Trimester, considered the most crucial time for growth and development, is nearing its end for our nurse. Yay!

The Last Week of the First Trimester

In Figure 13.1, Baby A now measures 7.2 cm from head to bottom at 13w3d. In Figure 13.2, Baby B measures 7.9 cm and 13w6d. Still all good in the neighborhood! This is precisely the kind of growth that we like to see between multiples.

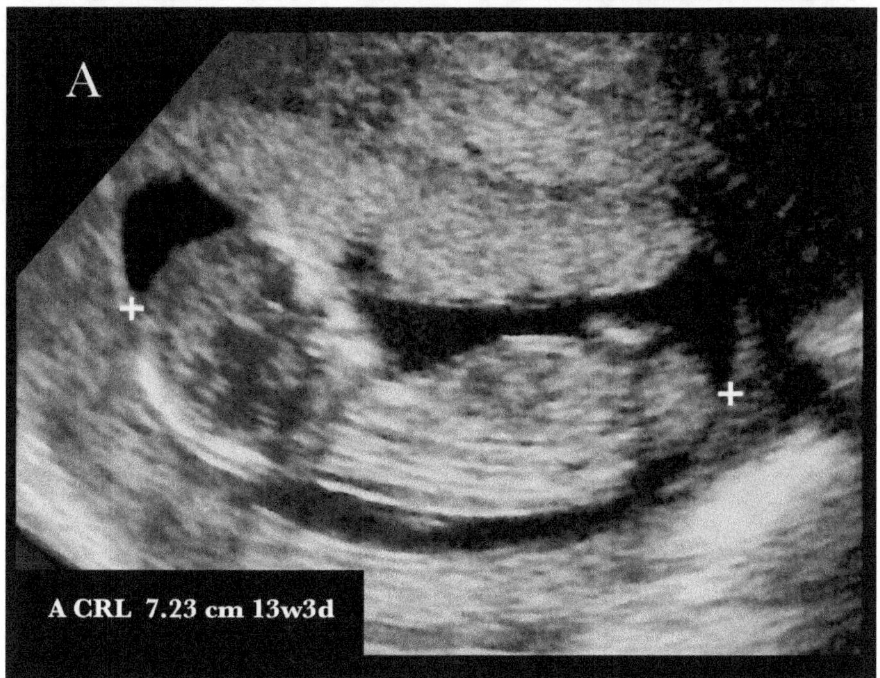

Figure 13.1: Week 13 ~ Baby A

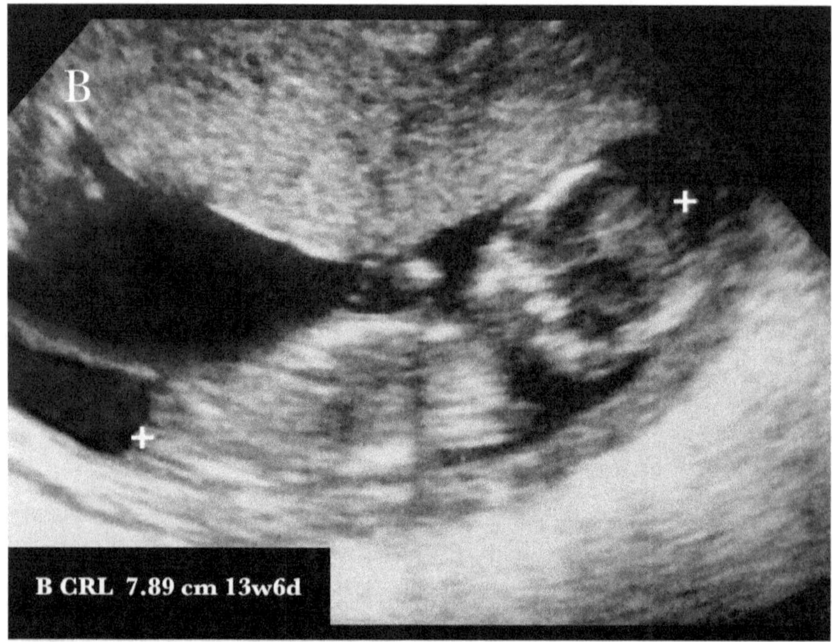

Figure 13.2: Week 13 ~ Baby B

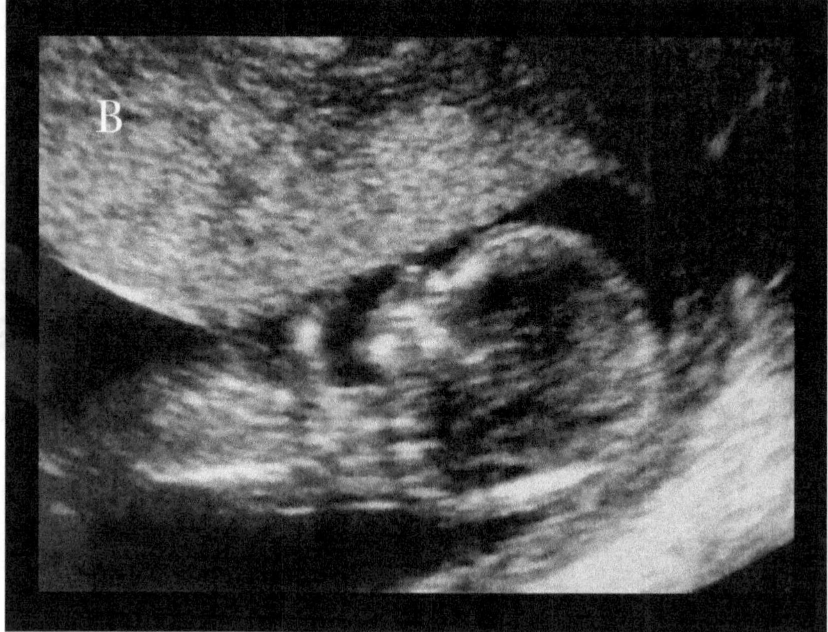

Figure 13.3: Week 13 ~ Baby B Profile

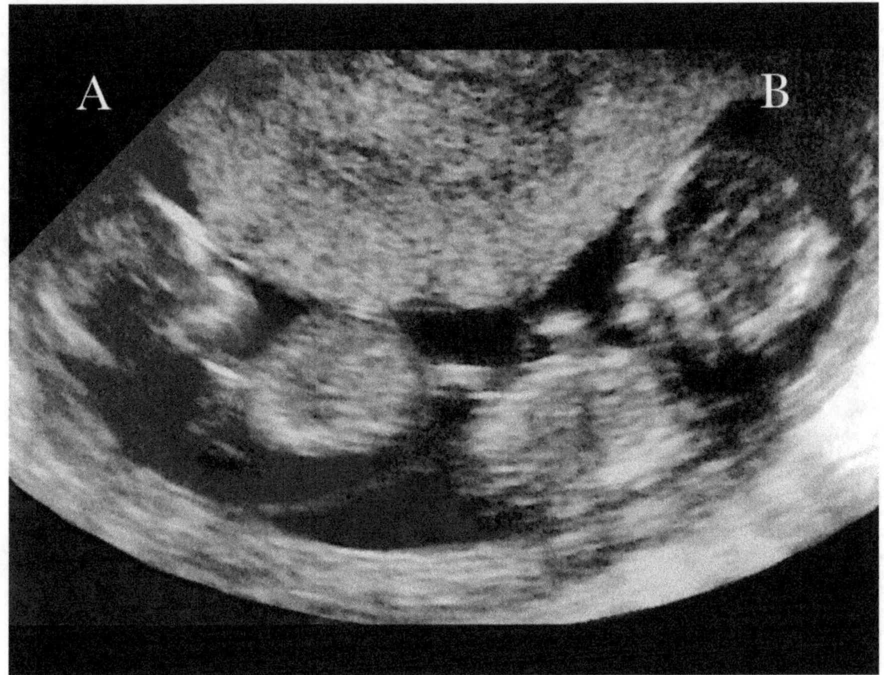

Figure 13.4: Week 13 ~ Dianne's Twins

Figure 13.3 shows a clear view of Baby B's profile. Figure 13.4 shows how difficult it can be to obtain a great shot of both babies in the same image. The chances are slim that they'll both agree to pose exactly in the same way at the very same moment.

If a pregnancy was confirmed very early, this First Trimester has probably felt like a long, emotional roller coaster ride. If you have other children at home or toddlers pulling at your skirt, these weeks have either flown by because you are *so* busy or have crept by because you are simply exhausted. A mother's work is never done! With any luck, the queasy morning (or all day) sickness is subsiding, and maybe your favorite foods are smelling good again.

One of the very best images comes from a reader of my blog and her 13 Weeker seen in Figure 13.5. Baby is kicked back in the perfect position for a great profile, looking up toward mom's belly.

This is as near a perfect fetal image at this gestational age as one could hope to obtain. Baby's face is very well delineated, and its hand is seen just in front of the face. Baby stretches out completely, perfect for obtaining a great measurement.

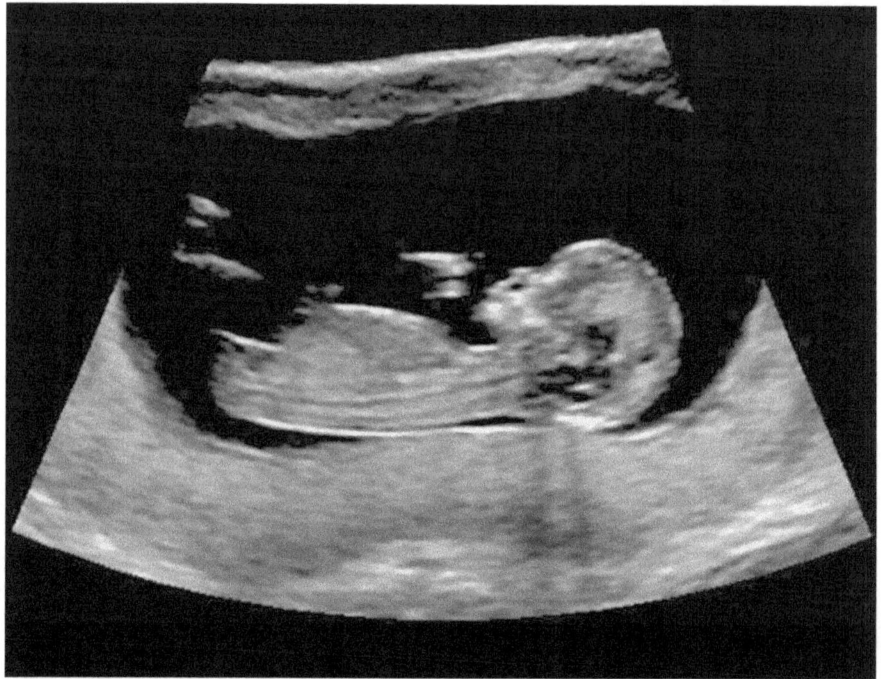

Figure 13.5: Week 13 ~ Fetal Profile-1

The CRL at this GA can be difficult to acquire if Baby curls up too tightly. They rarely stay in the position shown in Figure 13.5 for very long, and by very long, I mean even one full second. They can demonstrate a crazy degree of activity at this point, bending and flexing and performing acrobatic feats. The femur, or thigh bone, may also be measured at this gestational age. The attempt can be quite a challenging one due to Baby's small size *and* the aforementioned acrobatics.

Figures 13.6 and 13.7 are two more Week 13 images submitted by my blog readers. Aren't they cute? Not all of Baby's torso can be seen in Figure 13.6—bottom and legs are not included. In Figure 13.7, you can see Baby's feet and legs hiked up on the left-hand side of the image, as if she's kicked back in a hammock.

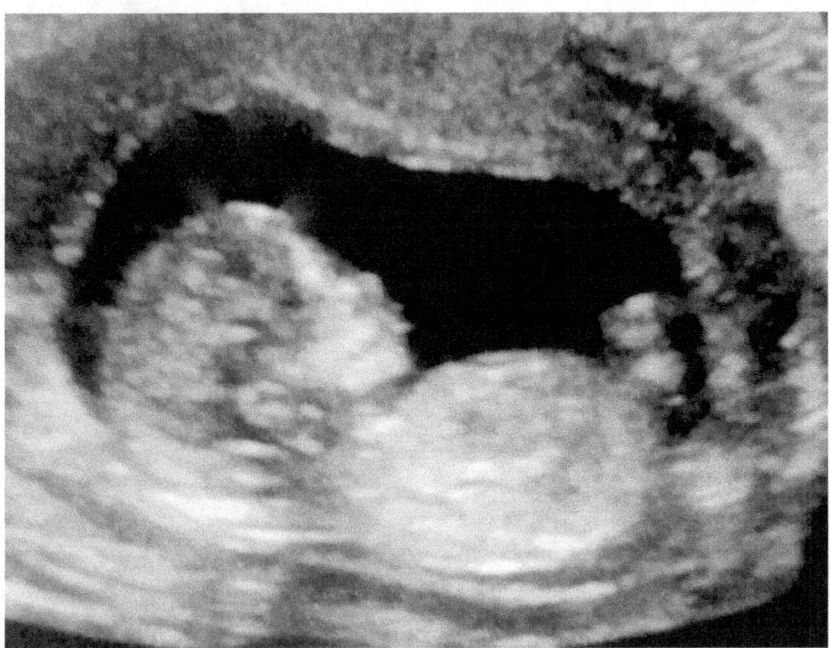

Figure 13.6: Week 13 ~ Fetal Profile-2

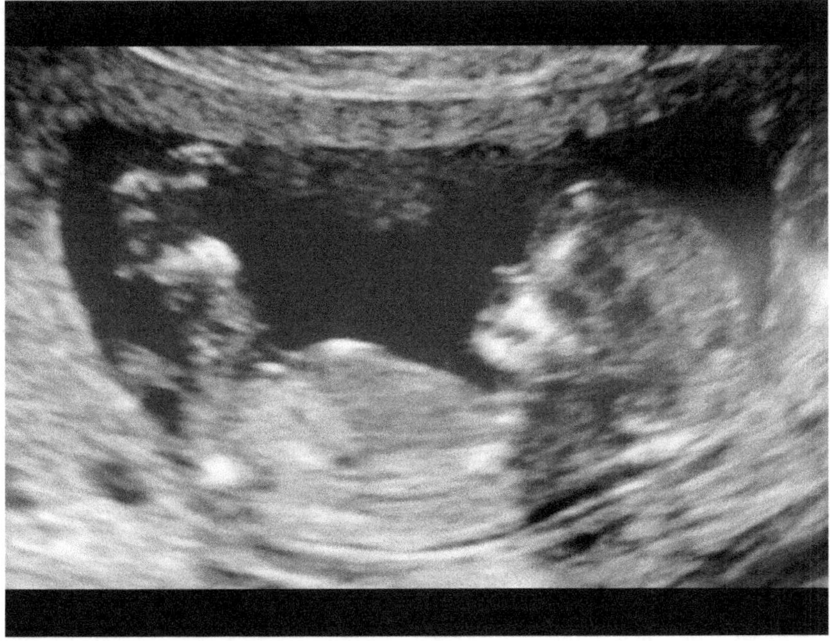

Figure 13.7: Week 13 ~ Fetal Profile-3

As for the subjects of this chronical: all three patients were progressing beautifully at this point in pregnancy. Both Dianne and I felt so very relieved that her twins had come this far with no real issues or complications. Dianne, like so many parents surprised with twins, never expected that a first pregnancy would result in two babies. Even though she could have never prepared herself for this gift times-two, she expressed extraordinary gratitude for two seemingly healthy babies.

Our next scan at Week 14 begins the Second Trimester and Part Three of this book. Here, also begins exploration of the difficulties and differences in appearance of fetal sex.

Concluding the First Trimester

How exciting that you've made it to this point in your pregnancy! Getting through the First Trimester is a great accomplishment. You'll soon begin this all-important but no-less-exciting second phase of your pregnancy with so many firsts to experience. You'll feel Baby kick for the first time, and you will have your anatomy screen or "big ultrasound," as many patients call it, around the Week-18 to Week-20 timeframe.

And if you are itching to paint that nursery, you may have your sights set on gender determination. This trimester brings preparation and celebration: opening gifts, shopping for Baby, decorating his or her new room, and washing all those precious miniature outfits that seem impossibly tiny for any human. That's the fun part, right? For me, it was decades ago! But I still remember it so well.

Next up? Of course, Dianne (as well as the rest of the staff) simply could not wait to find out the sex of Baby A and Baby B! Only time would tell. Team Pink? Team Blue? Or BOTH?!

Part Three ~

Gender Identification

Week 14 through Week 38

Early Gender Determination

Most ultra-curious parents never wait until mid-pregnancy to ask about fetal sex. This inquiry usually surfaces during their first visit with the doc, but oftentimes comes in the form of a screened phone call by a staff of nurses before a patient ever even steps foot in the office. It usually goes something like this:

"Hi. I just found out I am pregnant with five positive home pregnancy tests. I need to make an appointment to see my doctor and, by the way, when can I know what I'm having?"

First things first, ladies! Obviously, not everyone approaches a newly discovered pregnancy with eagerness to this extreme. Some moms-to-be want to begin preparing as soon as that little stick flashes the plus sign. The excitement is completely understandable. After all, there are names to fight over with your spouse and "gender reveal" parties to plan. By the way (as a word of warning), those celebrations should *never* be scheduled the same day as your sonogram because your baby may not cooperate for a guess. This happens a lot!

First, let's begin with a theory for guessing a baby's sex in the First Trimester, which has taken on some popularity in the past few years. I have some personal experience to contribute here and have received many blog emails on this subject, so it warrants some discussion.

The Nub Theory

In case you are not familiar, The Nub Theory entails seeing a "nub" pointing up or out, to determine fetal sex very early in pregnancy, around Week 11 or 12. This nub represents external genitalia which is just beginning to develop. Now, a diagnostic scan is not routinely performed at this gestational age unless:

- You are seeing your doctor for the first time at this point in pregnancy,
- You are experiencing medical complications, or

- You have elected early genetic testing.

Depending on what type of genetic testing your physician offers, the Nuchal Translucency test may be part of that protocol as we discussed Week 12. During this scanning process, the "nub" in question may be seen if Baby is in a good position, and your sonographer may be willing to offer up a guess for gender.

As previously advised many times on my blog, both boys and girls possess tissue which protrudes at this gestational age and both nubs can appear very similar. The school of thought on predicting sex surrounds the "angle of the dangle" as some have referred to it. Check out Figure P3.1 and imagine a fetus lying on his or her back.

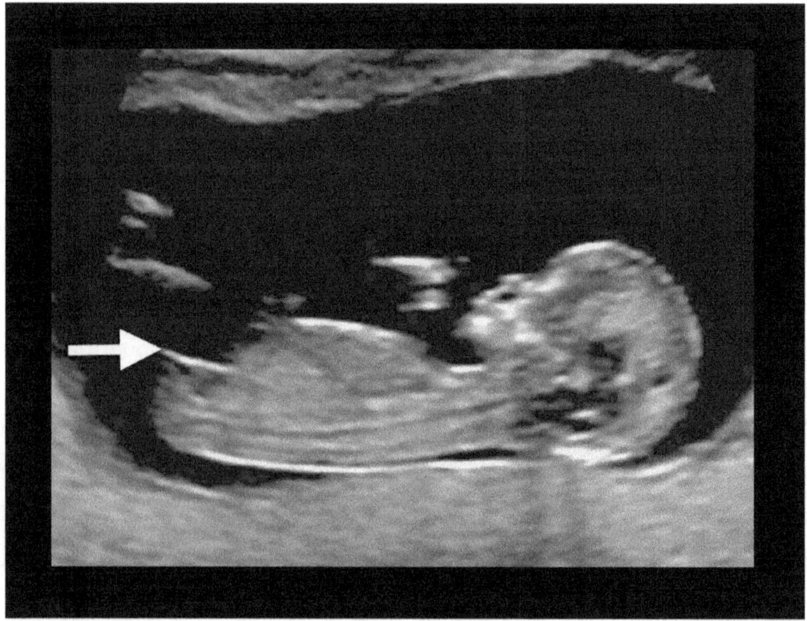

Figure P3.1: Week 13 ~ Female Fetal Nub

Put on your 3D-thinking cap to mentally understand this image. This is a side view of Baby, right down the middle from the head to the bottom. The angle obtained essentially divides the fetus into right and left halves. Legs are not in the image; we would have to angle out to each side to see them, right?

The arrow in Figure P3.1 is pointing to the nub in question. If the tissue appears to stick straight out, as in parallel with Baby's body as we see here, the thought is Baby Girl.

Figure P3.2 is an edited image to depict a male nub based on this theory. If this tissue instead points straight up, or toward the top of the image, the thought is Baby Boy. If the nub fell somewhere between up and out, we'd have to declare too equivocal for a guess—or at least, this is what I was taught way back when!

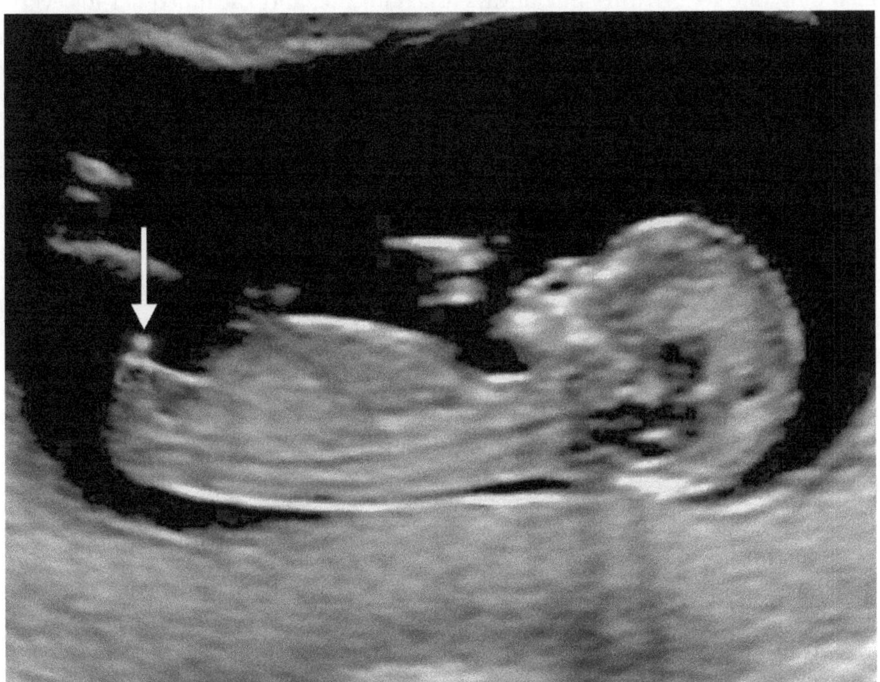

Figure P3.2: Week 13 ~ Male Fetal Nub

Now, the sonographer who trained me boasted that the accuracy rate was somewhere around 78 percent and she seemed to be excited about that number. In my mind, it still left a whopping 20+ percent of moms who are dreaming of ballet recitals only to discover later in pregnancy (and long after social media announcements to the world) that she might be attending baseball games instead. My personal feeling is it's just too large a margin of error to guess, unless a patient says she can remain entirely unbiased. And some certainly can. Here's a little story about one of my patients who (thankfully) did!

For the most part, this up or out thing was right on the money…but not always! Personal experience shows that this little experiment was incorrect at least twice in the two-plus years I performed the NT exams.

So, I guess if this theory is going to be wrong on someone, it's better for that someone to be my patient for whom I had scanned all *five* of her pregnancies, including one set of twins. She always asked for me, and I scanned her for every ultrasound our schedules would allow. Sonographers often develop special relationships with patients we see so often—one of the aspects of my career I loved most.

She opted for genetic testing for her last pregnancy, so we performed an NT at Week 12. She wanted me to take a crack at gender. I gave expectant parents the usual talk about accuracy, but this scan was for fun since they really didn't care about Baby's sex. Her scan was easy, and Baby's nub pointed straight out, *just* as shown in Figure P3.1. It was *textbook* for a baby girl.

Needless to say, we both were quite surprised at her Week 20 anatomy screen. SURPRISE! Boy, oh, boy! And I mean "boy."

Even though I knew the statistics and the angle showed a classic appearance for a girl at Week 12, the Week 19 scan showed his legs wide open with a scrotal sac and penis—easily detected and no guesswork needed. Figure P3.3 is a clear example of male genitalia at almost Week 20, and her image looked a lot like this one.

We laughed hysterically. My patient had three boys and a girl, so the couple was thrilled either way. I was thrilled they weren't upset! They had kept a completely open mind and still had all the gender-specific clothes from other children. That experience made me cautiously hesitant about guessing so early thereafter. From that point forward, I shared this story with every patient who wanted a guess at Week 12.

The patient strongly desiring one sex over the other always received a bit a caution from me. Pregnancy itself causes an increase in emotions as it is, and it's certainly okay to have a gender preference. However, most moms do become emotionally attached to this "guess" from the very first inkling—even if the sonographer isn't sure. If the guess is later determined to be incorrect, those patients tend to feel sadness for the baby boy or girl they "lost" and guilt knowing satisfaction should win out for healthy. The emotional adjustment is real and leaves these parents often regretful and angry if electing and paying out of pocket for an early scan. Many patients and my blog emailers alike expressed both sentiments.

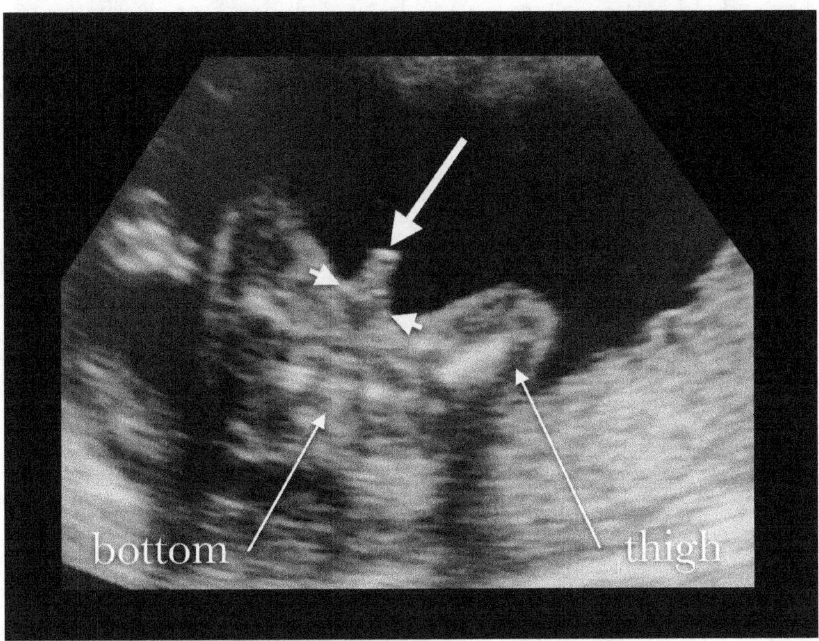

Figure P3.3: Week 19 ~ Male Fetal Gender

So, there is some truth to The Nub Theory. But will you be part of the 70-percent right? Or will you be part of the 30-percent wrong? You might be the gambling sort, and you may even say those odds are pretty good. But I caution anyone who cannot remain impartial or wait until later in fetal development. I've written it many times in blog posts and it's worth reiterating here: I do not recommend paying for fetal sex prediction before Week 16. And now you know why!

The Best Time to Guess

"When is the best time to determine gender?" This a loaded question, but it is the one asked most often. To spare you from reading the entire chapter before answering your most burning question, the short answer is Week 18 and up until the early Third Trimester, around Week 30.

This timeframe is simply my personal preference based on years of experience, but my co-workers also agree. It's a time where external genitalia are developed enough, and Baby is large enough to distinguish between *normally developing* boy and girl parts, if all other variables work in our favor allowing us to see well enough otherwise.

There's so much more to determining sex with ultrasound than just moving down to Baby's bottom and looking between the legs. Ultrasound works in two dimensions, and so many other factors can interfere with determining gender.

In other words, a later GA does not mean a sonographer will definitively be able to identify Baby's gender. The same may be true at Week 20 or Week 36. Determining a Baby's sex accurately using ultrasound depends on a few important variables such as:

1. Appropriate Gestational Age,
2. Good Fetal Position,
3. Good Visualization, and
4. Observer Experience.

Have I ever guessed gender for a patient at Week 14 through Week 17? Of course! Guessing correctly at those ages is not impossible, but the circumstances for correct guesses included a perfect view despite the slightly early age, allowing me to see well enough to provide a confident guess. Additionally, I possessed the skill to be able to offer up an educated guess—or not, if I felt the imaging wasn't optimal enough. At the end of the day, a guess is entirely subjective and hangs solely on the observer's confidence. And sometimes, a sonographer or other healthcare provider confidently guesses wrong!

The chances of accuracy decrease if all other variables are limited. *Anyone* can provide a guess at Week 12 or Week 14; however, a greater chance of an inaccurate guess exists at these ages because Baby is so small and external genitalia is less developed. Conversely, trying to confirm gender later in the Third Trimester presents its own challenges…you've got a bigger baby and bigger parts to work with, but often Baby takes up more room and fluid may be a bit diminished (normally) which limits how well we can see. Far enough along, a great fetal position and observer experience provides the greatest chance that a sonographer will correctly guess fetal sex.

The gender-specific images which you'll see in the following chapters represent some of the best textbook images for male and female of the Second and Third Trimesters, and some need a little help with explanation. I label parts for each and every one.

Back to Dianne and her journey through ultrasound. Dive with us into the Second and Third Trimesters, discover the gender of her babies, and learn about how to differentiate male from female.

Week 14
Beginning the Second Trimester

Twinkle, Twinkle Little Star, How I Wonder What You Are?

start here because, in *perfect circumstances*, Week 14 provides the earliest point to see real changes between the normal development of male versus female. Please know, however, I really cannot (in good faith) recommend anyone pay for a gender scan at Week 14 for all the reasons I've already laid out in previous chapters. Though this seems to be a popular trend, Baby is still very small, and seeing these parts well can be very difficult. Sure, you may know many whose guess was correct at Week 14. I'm simply reiterating that there's more of a chance to get it wrong this early.

First Peeks at 14 Weeks

Though we touched previously on the most common variables that can lend to an incorrect fetal sex determination, it won't hurt to mention them here again:

- Early gestational age: The earlier you are, the smaller the parts and the harder it can be to see well.
- A layperson as your "scanner:" An employee of a non-medical ultrasound business may possess no formal ultrasound education or credentials—a weekend course taught by an ill-informed instructor does not make a skilled sonographer.
- A limited fetal position or uncooperative fetus: Closed legs, breech position and umbilical cord between the legs all limit (or prevent entirely!) a confident guess.
- Obesity: More maternal tissue hampers a sonographer's view.

- Limited amniotic fluid: A late-gestation scan or an earlier scan with little or no amniotic fluid around parts is limiting visually.
- Antiquated ultrasound equipment: The older the equipment, the poorer the resolution or clarity of the image, even in the best of circumstances.

I might also mention here that we all had to learn the art of scanning, and it takes times. A formally educated sonographer who is new to the field or one whose specialty does not lie in obstetrics may find some difficulty in determining gender, especially early in pregnancy.

Remember, a "guarantee" of gender only means that the "peek-a-boo" business you visited will refund your money if they are wrong. A refund only pads your wallet; it can't take away the feelings of disappointment and guilt many women feel if the opposite sex is later discovered as discussed in Part Three, The Nub Theory (page 119).

Here is a rule of thumb I enjoyed passing along to patients:

The earliest time I can recommend a fetal sex guess is Week 16 with the best time for most being Week 18 through the early Third Trimester at about Week 30. In the best of circumstances with the best views, IF Baby cooperates and IF your sonographer is formally trained with skill and experience in obstetrics, the chances her guess is correct are quite high. A bit later usually yields the best chances at an accurate guess, when Baby and his/her parts are bigger and easier to visualize.

And that, my friends, is about the best anyone can predict the reliability of any fetal sex guess by ultrasound. Ultrasound will *always* be subjective. A guess will *always* be left to the opinion of the observer. And whatever you do, *do not* plan a gender reveal party for the day of your ultrasound! Quite often, limited views yield only an appointment to go back another time, often another day altogether. If getting it right is very important to you, wait a little longer and shoot for the educated guess.

Dianne's Twins at Week 14

With that, let's look at a few bottom-side images of Dianne's twins. I've labeled all the discernible parts in Figures 14.1 to 14.4 for the ultrasound challenged.

You're welcome! Please note in these early weeks, I offered these gender guesses posed with tinges of hopefulness. The real vote of confidence comes much later.

What could we see in these images? Dianne did not expect me to commit to gender so early. Thank goodness. But I could offer up some "maybes" with a few appreciative differences between Babies A and B.

Annotations I've made on the images differentiating male and female are:

- *For Male Images:*

    A single bold white arrow points to a questionable or definitive penis with one or two small arrows to delineate the scrotal sac.

- *For Female Images:*

    Three thin white arrows point to a questionable female—the three lines or dots represent a female fetus, the outside arrows point to suspected labia and clitoris in the middle. Later in pregnancy, you may see two arrows labeled labia.

In each chapter after sharing gender images of Dianne's twins, I'll also share gender images from other babies for comparison. Readers will be surprised at how varied they can appear—not just from one week to the next but also from image to image of the same sex. Again, the variables here are (and always will be) the differences from one patient to another, different angles, varied skill set from sonographer to sonographer, equipment differences, and fetal position.

Figure 14.1 reveals Dianne's twins, side-by-side. What do you see? Can you appreciate a difference between A and B? Figure 14.2 is another view of Baby A. Figure 14.3 is another view of Baby B.

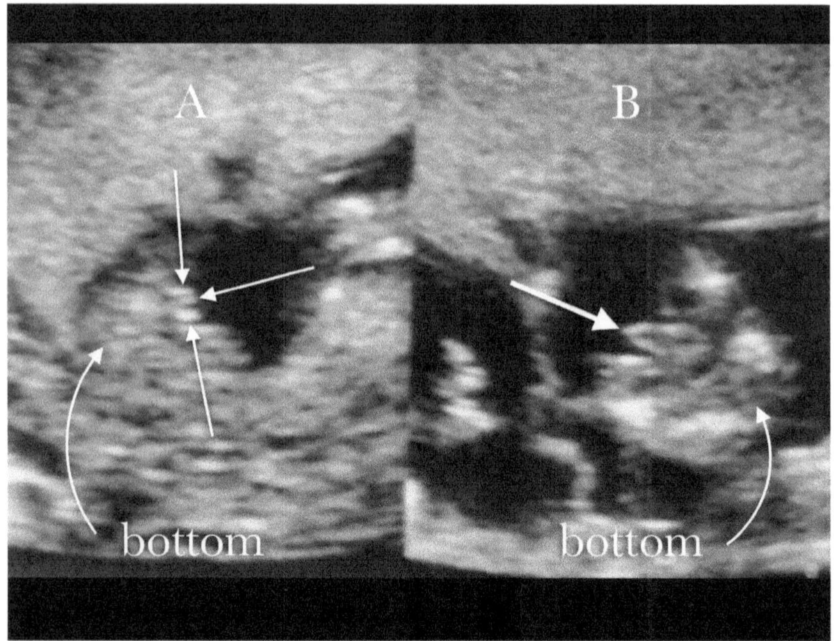

Figure 14.1: Week 14 ~ Babies A & B

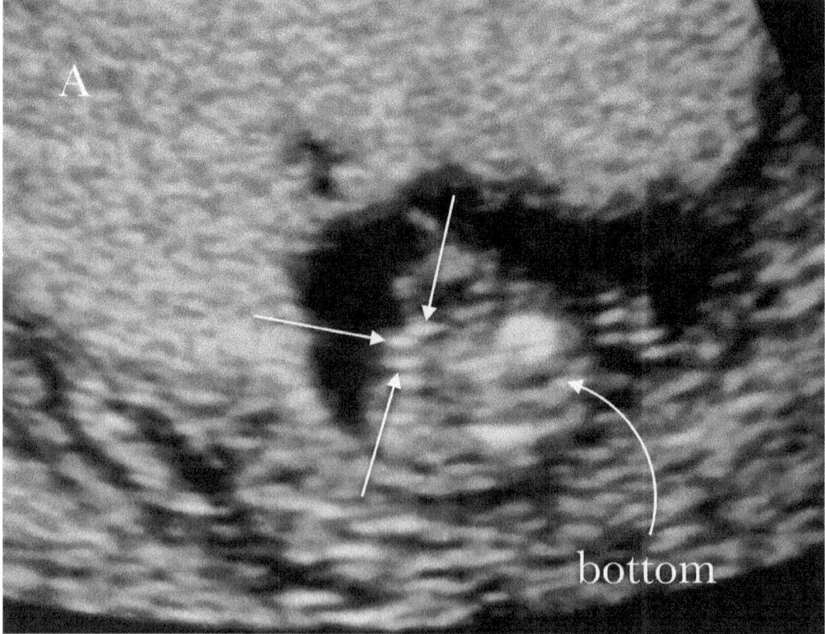

Figure 14.2: Week 14 ~ Baby A

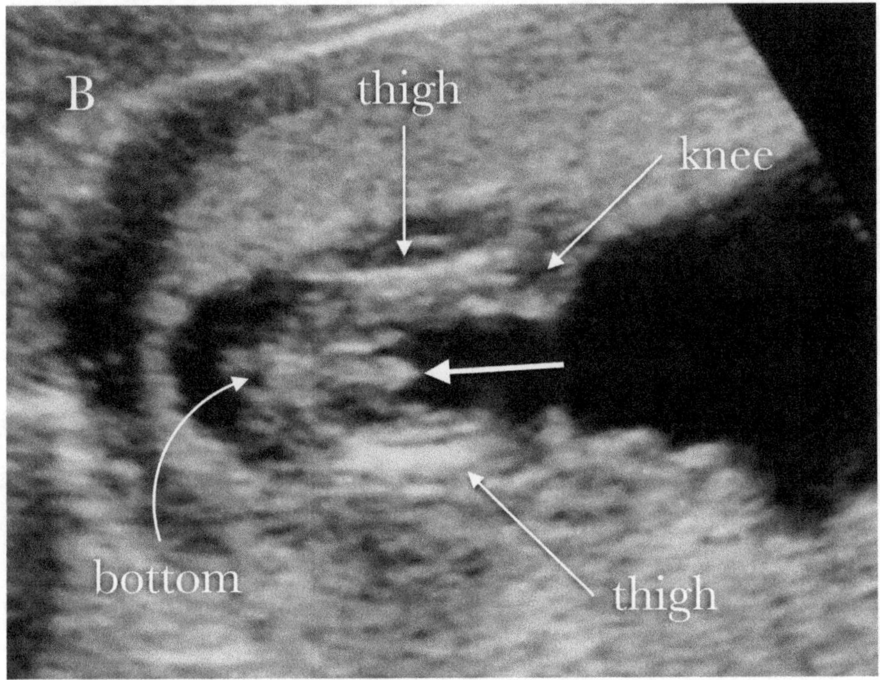

Figure 14.3: Week 14 ~ Baby B

We were cautiously optimistic that Baby A could be a girl and Baby B, a boy. These photos show how both their parts appear different at different angles, one of the reasons why no two ultrasound images look exactly alike. I think it's important to reiterate here that these are great images for 14 Weeks, and not everyone can see gender this well at this age. Dianne was thin, the twins were both lying in optimal positions, there was plenty of amniotic fluid (black) around each baby's parts, I had modern equipment to work with, and I had the skill needed to optimize these views. All these variables play a large role in how well your baby can be visualized at this age.

Baby A was head down, so we couldn't capture a great profile for her. However, Baby B was breech (bottom down and head up), located higher in the uterus, and looking up toward Mom's belly. All those factors allowed for this beautiful shot of B! Adorable.

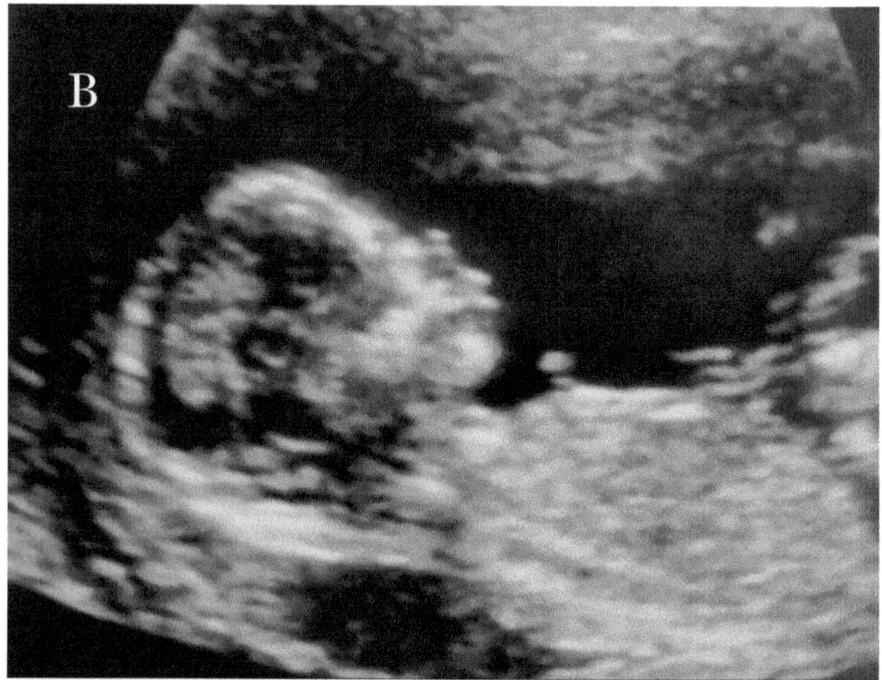

Figure 14.4: Week 14 ~ Baby B Profile

After seeing Dianne's images at Week 14, are you convinced of the twins' genders? We chose not to get too excited just yet but were cautiously optimistic.

Again, I feel Week 14 is too early for most people to receive an accurate gender guess. However, non-medical businesses are happy to take your money for a stab at it. More than a thinly veiled warning should be offered in advance of these scans beyond simply signing a waiver. However, if you choose to go, keep an open mind and don't paint your nursery just yet.

After all, gender lies in the eye of the beholder…the skill and experience of a seasoned sonographer. Ultimately, I can never stress enough that gender can never be guaranteed 100 percent by ultrasound anytime, even if you're told that it is.

Week 15

I t's amazing what one week can show in the world of ultrasound. Did Baby A sprout something unseen the week before? Did Baby B's extra little something shrink? Figure 15.1 is an image of the twins at Week 15. What do you think?

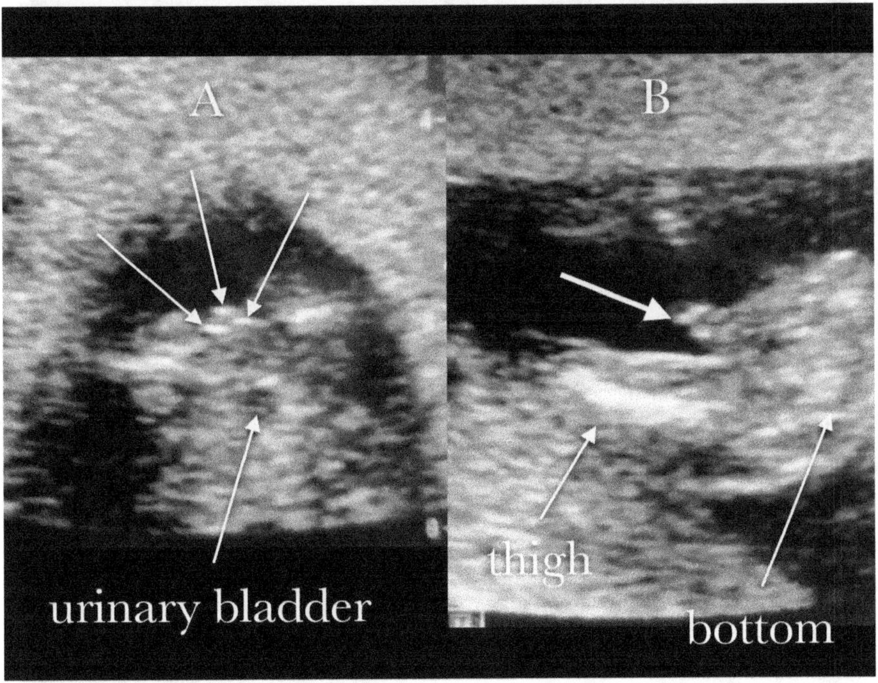

Figure 15.1: Week 15 ~ Dianne's Twins

Figure 15.2 through Figure 15.5 show more images of each twin. Cautiously optimistic, Baby A in Figure 15.3 still appeared very "girly." Notice the three lines that make up a female guess.

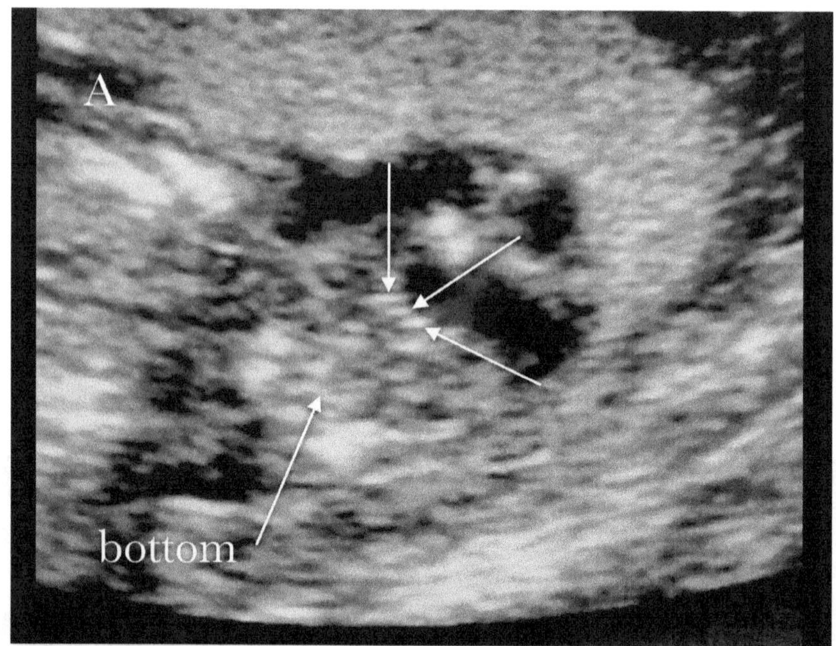

Figure 15.2: Week 15 ~ Baby A

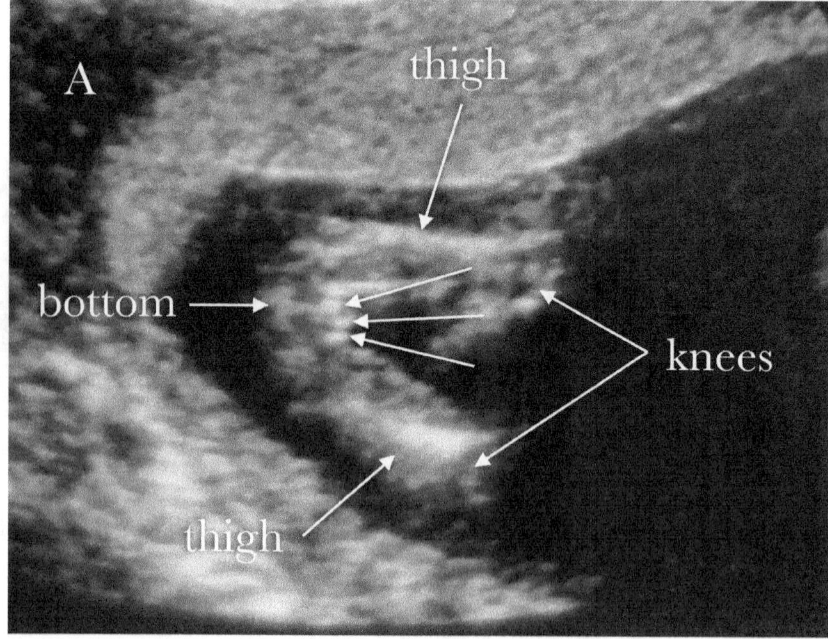

Figure 15.3: Week 15 ~ Baby A

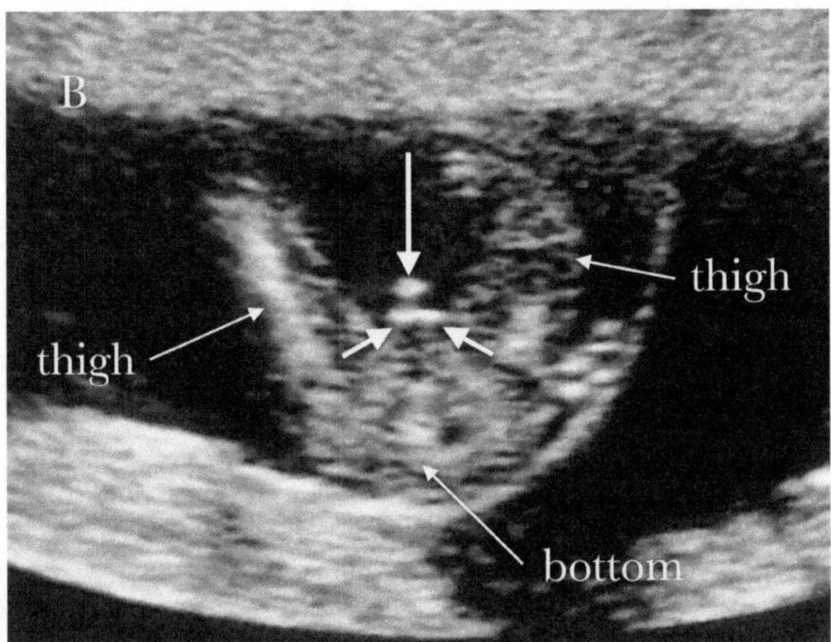

Figure 15.4: Week 15 ~ Baby B

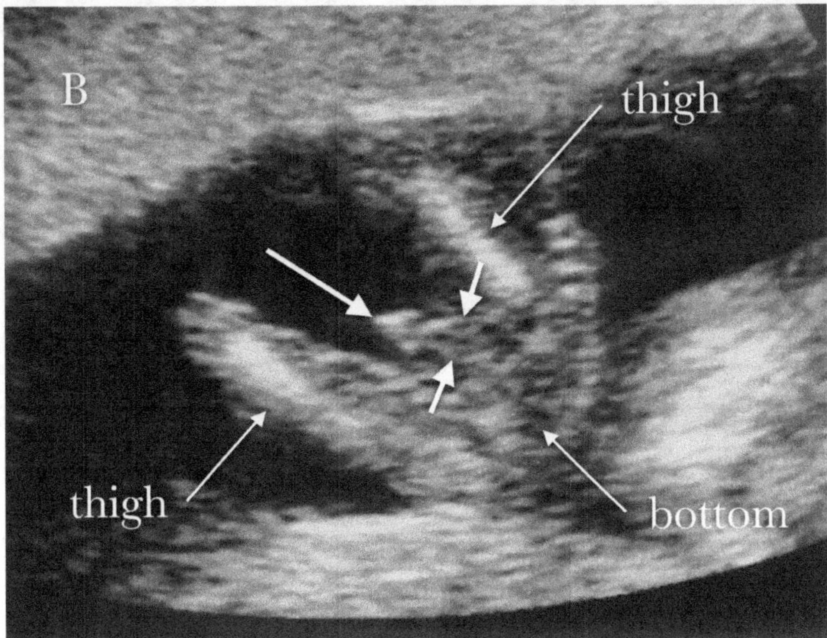

Figure 15.5: Week 15 ~ Baby B

Now for Baby B in Figures 15.4 and 15.5. In each image, the area suspected as a penis projects much further from the body than what we see in Baby A.

Additionally, we suspected the presence of a scrotal sac (smaller bold arrows). Though testicles within the sac cannot be seen until nearer to Week 28, the rounded appearance of the scrotal sac is strongly suggested in these images.

So, Week 14 provided a "very possibly one of each, but let's give it a little more time" kind of feeling. Week 15 reinforced Dianne's hopefulness for both a boy and girl. Would Week 16 reveal something different?

Even though Baby A presented a bit of a challenge with her low position, we still managed a pretty decent profile in Figure 15.6. So cute!

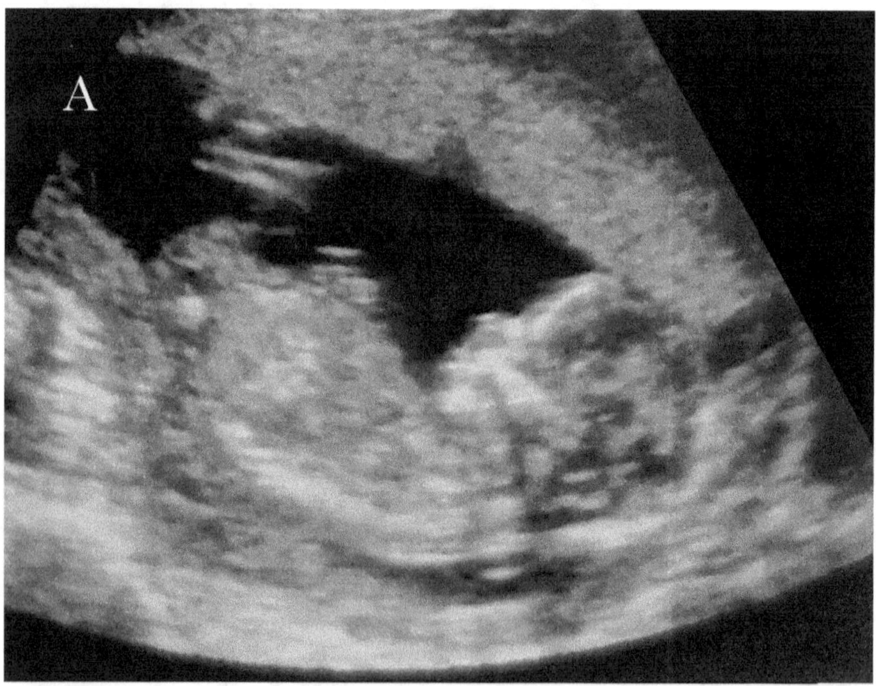

Figure 15.6: Week 15 ~ Baby A Profile

Figure 15.7 shows an image from a blog reader of a male fetus just beginning Week 15. This image might pose a problem for the new or inexperienced sonographer or parent-to-be. You've been told to look for three dots or lines to indicate a baby girl, right? But isn't that precisely what you see in this image?

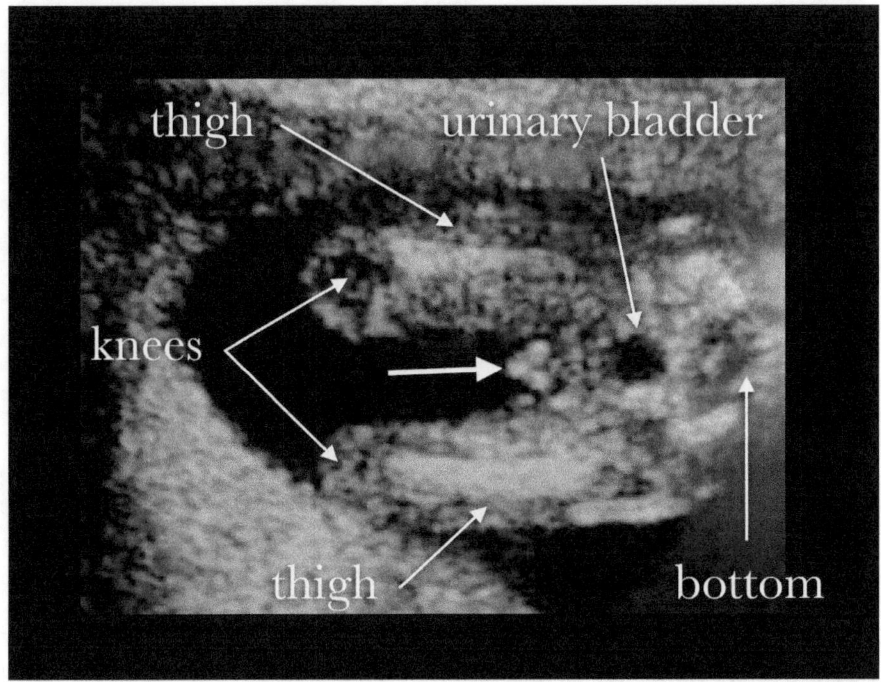

Figure 15.7: 15w0d ~ Male Fetus-1

Often the very tip of the penis can also appear as three dots or lines which is why we also look for the rounded appearance of a scrotal sac in the same image as the penis. We don't see that here, but why not? Part of the problem with this image is technical—meaning the sonographer's angle was off a bit. Instead, it included the penis and baby's urinary bladder which is a little higher in the pelvis than the scrotum. Without the scrotal sac in the image, it's difficult to say by this shot alone that this is a baby boy.

Enjoy a few other male gender images of Week 15 babies in Figures 15.8 and 15.9. These babies are closer to Week 16, and the penis appears a little more rounded. However, in both, we can identify the penis *and* scrotal sac. See the difference compared to Figure 15.7?

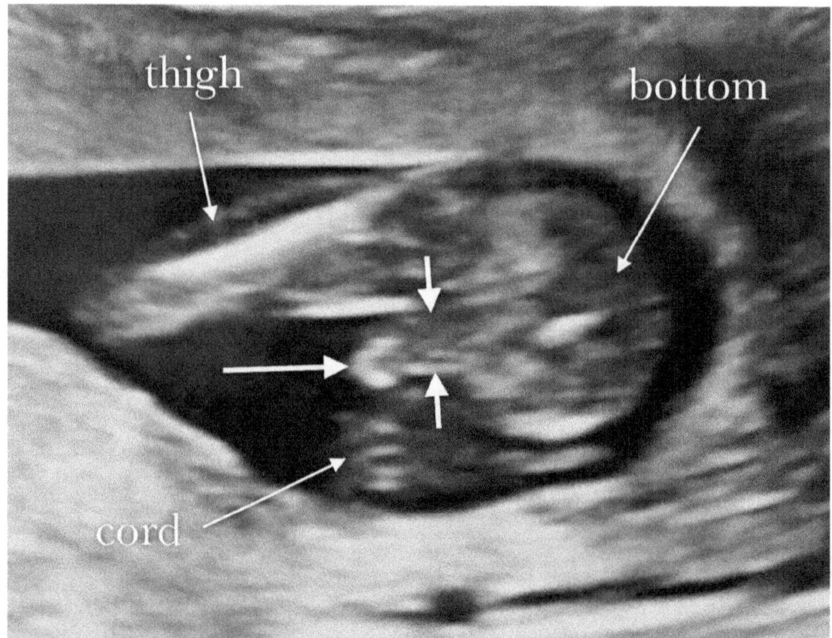

Figure 15.8: 15w5d ~ Male Fetus-2

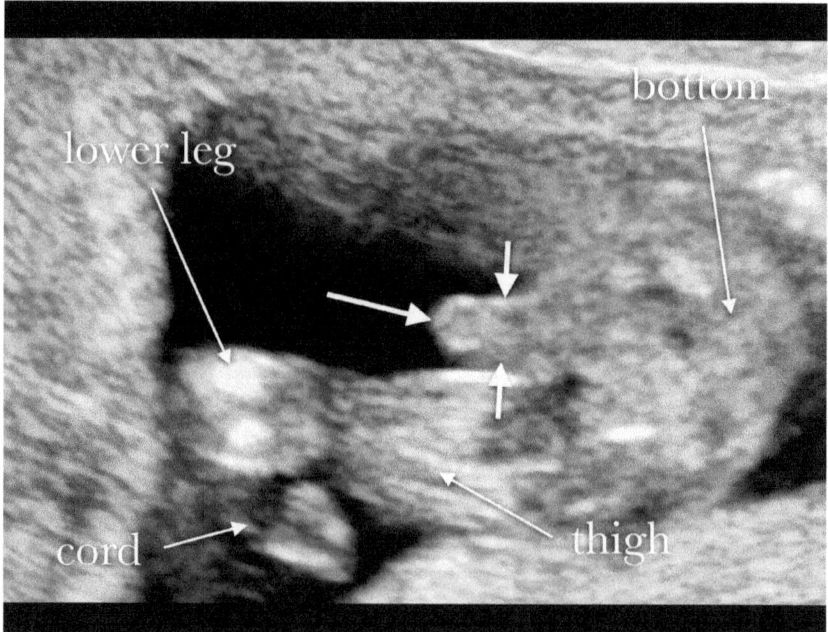

Figure 15.9: 15w6d ~ Male Fetus-3

Week 16

Week 16 begins with gender images of Baby A. Figure 16.1 is one of my favorite examples of textbook female genitalia at Week 16.

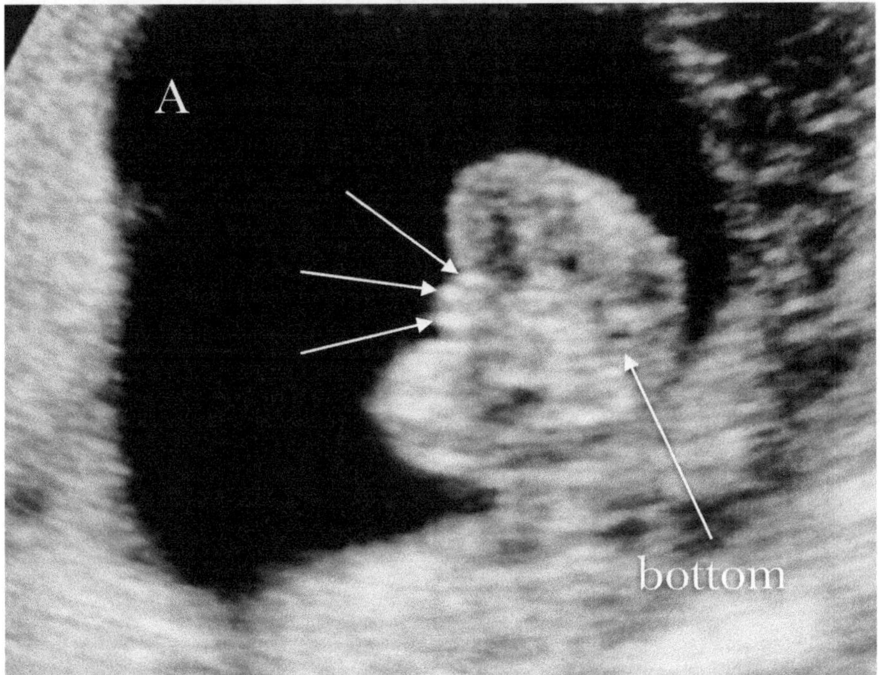

Figure 16.1: Week 16 ~ Baby A-1

Readers familiar with my blog know it's my go-to shot for this gestational age. We see here a bottom view with no legs in the image—imagine her feet pulled up to her face. If looking from below, only a bottom with no legs in the picture would be the view, right? And the three arrows clearly point out three white lines appearing close to Baby's body—the outer lines depicting the labia and the clitoris as the center dot.

Figures 16.2 and 16.3 are two more images of Baby A revealing a slightly different angle, but the same three lines can be appreciated in both. No gender opinion changes for Baby A in Week 16. We felt confident in our guess for a baby girl at this point. However, Week 19 will seal the deal.

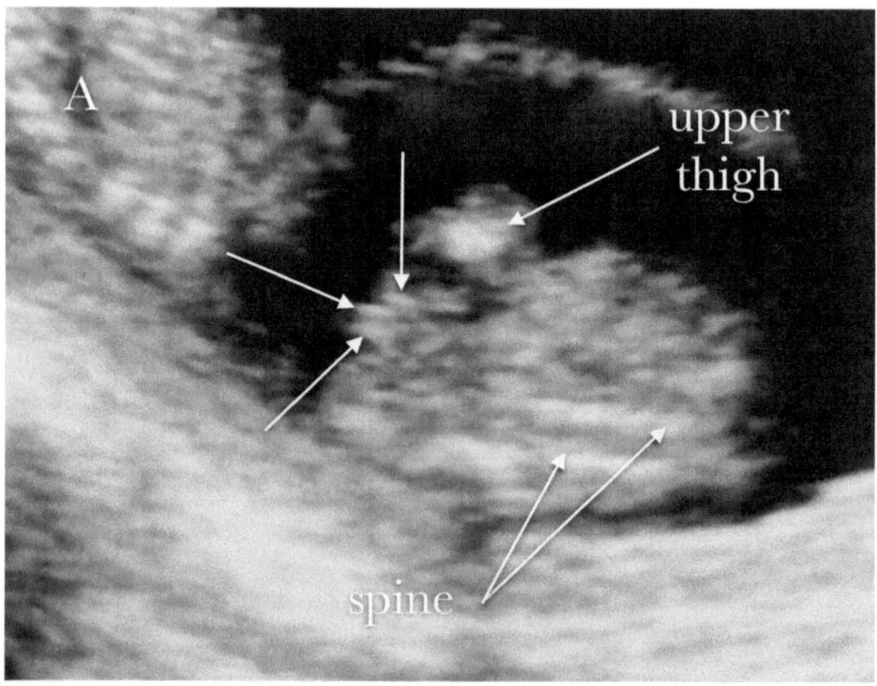

Figure 16.2: Week 16 ~ Baby A

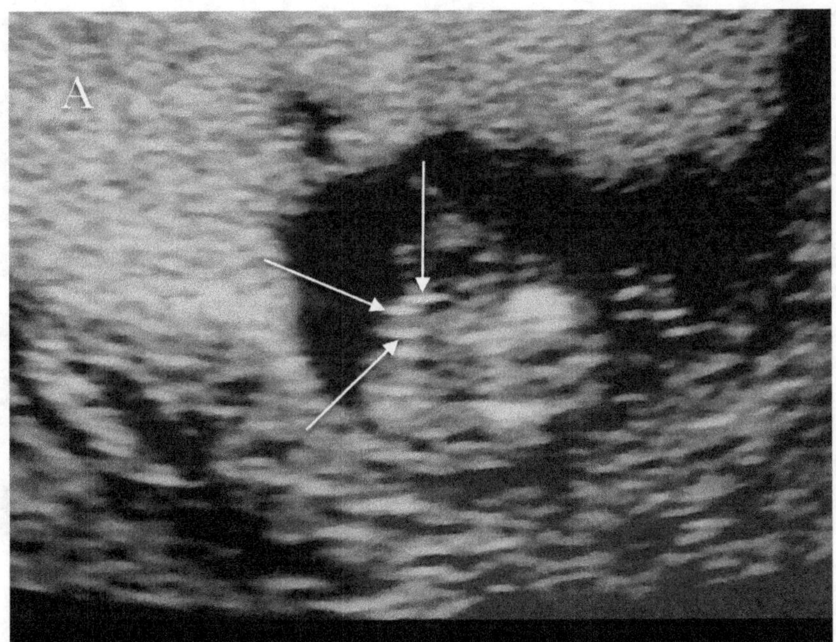

Figure 16.3: Week 16 ~ Baby A

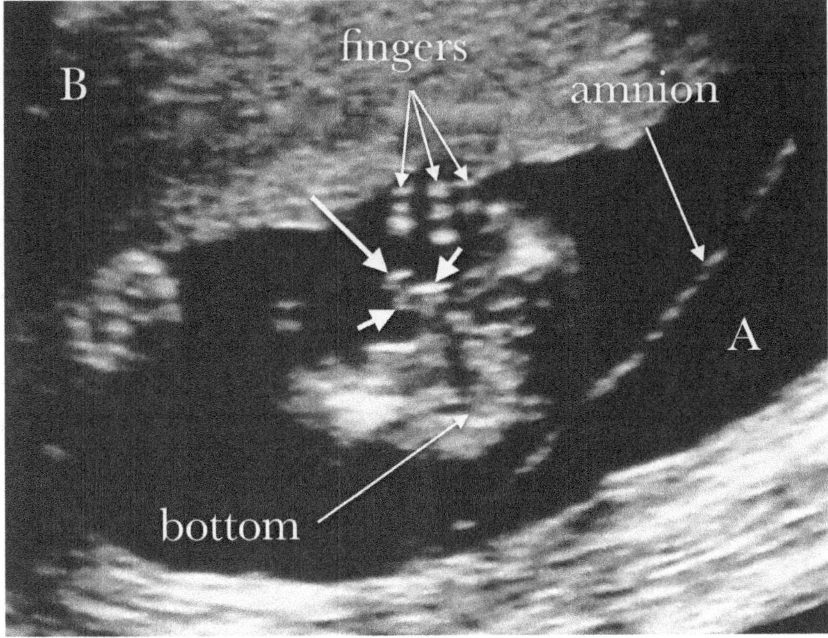

Figure 16.4: Week 16 ~ Baby B

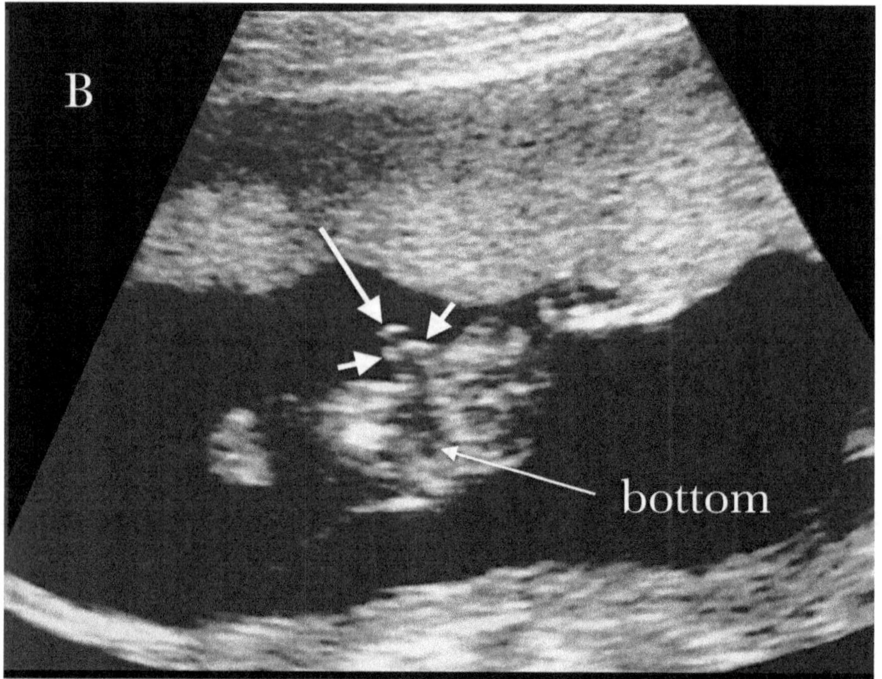

Figure 16.5: Week 16 ~ Baby B

What about Baby B? Take a look at Figures 16.4 and 16.5. How do these compare to Baby A's images?

No guess changes for Baby B, either. Anything could happen, but the imaging had been so good to this point that we were confidently optimistic. And the other sonographers agreed. We knew considering our optimal views that changes in genitalia going forward over the next couple of weeks would be minimal. How perfect! …Very possibly a boy and a girl for Dianne and just what she wanted.

Dianne felt content regarding the well-being of her babies at this point in pregnancy, so she relaxed on the scans for a few weeks. They were growing appropriately which truly was her greatest concern. Her next scan would come at Week 19 for her diagnostic anatomy screen.

Figure 16.6 is another of a female fetus. Can you appreciate how similar this image appears to that of Baby A in Figure 16.3?

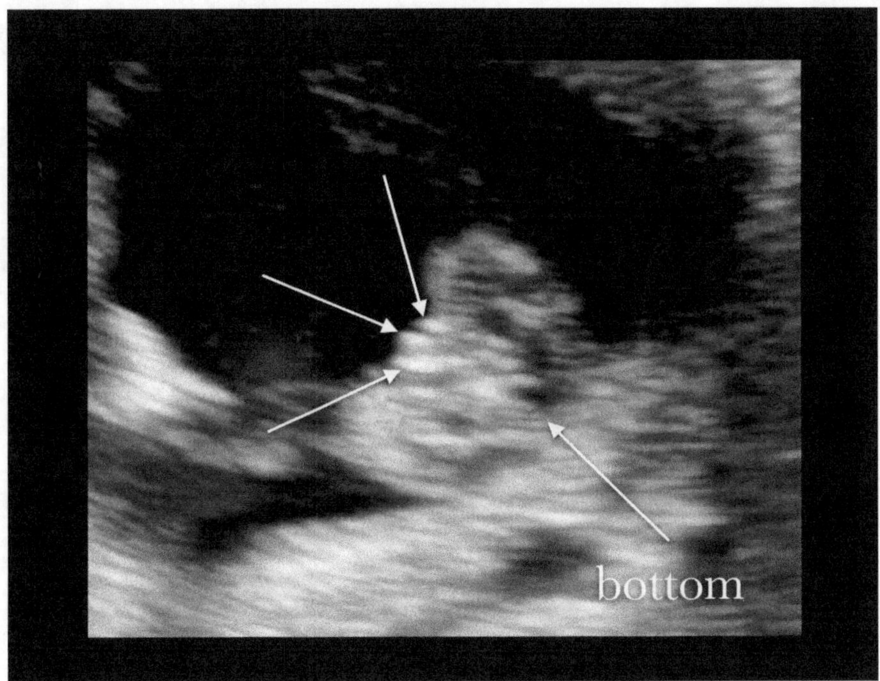

Figure 16.6: Week 16 ~ Female Gender

Next, take a look at male gender in Figures 16.7 and 16.8 on the following page. Both represent male babies, but you can probably appreciate how different they appear when comparing them.

In Figure 16.7, the penis may appear as three lines, but these lines project farther out from the body and the rounded area of the scrotal sac is very easy to see here. Even though the legs are not pictured, you may get the impression that they are spread open wide, allowing this great shot.

In Figure 16.8, male genitalia appears a bit different. The scrotal sac was not captured in the is image. It's also a bit too bright, making the penis look white. Sonographers can make images brighter or darker to achieve the right amount of "lightness," just the same as you can for your computer monitor or cell phone. This adjustment is subjective, but the overall image should be more gray than white or important details in the image become obliterated. Can you appreciate these differences when comparing both images now?

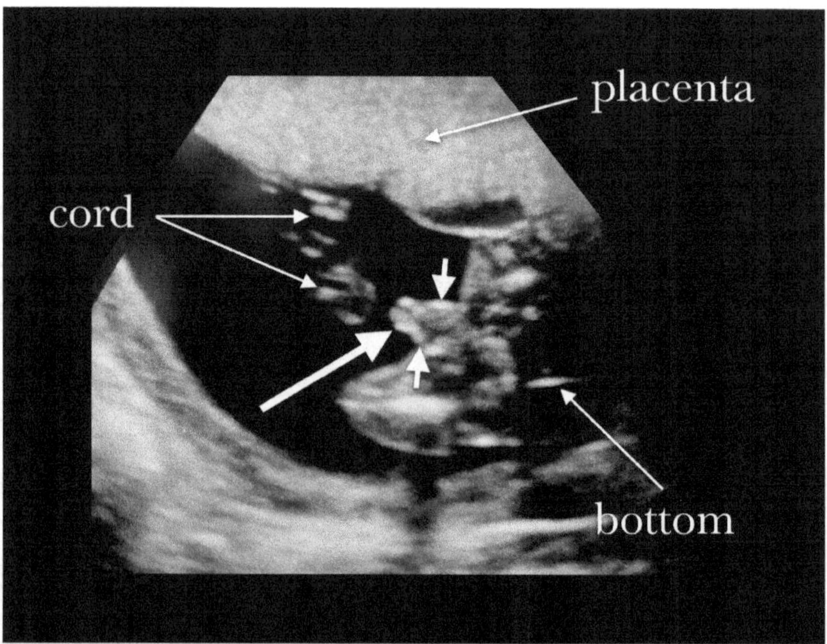

Figure 16.7: Week 16 ~ Male Gender-1

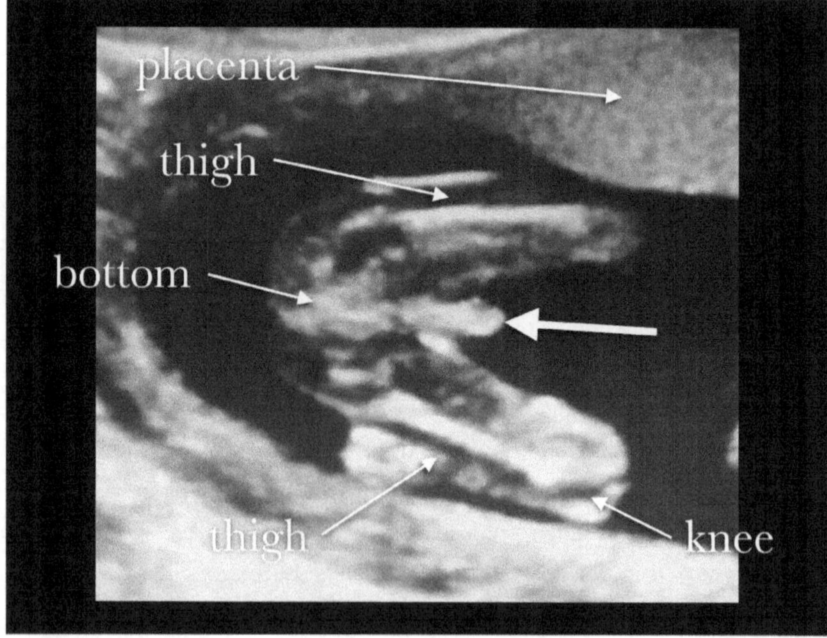

Figure 16.8: Week 16 ~ Male Gender-2

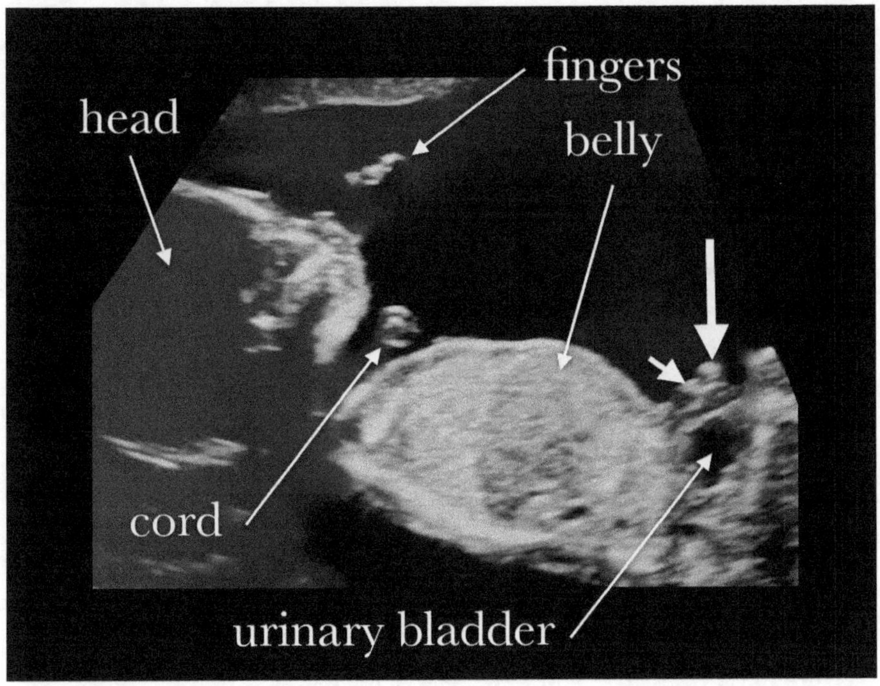

Figure 16.9: Week 16 ~ Side View, Male Gender-3

Figure 16.9 differs from the previous Week 16 images because here we see a side view of this male fetus, head and body, versus an underside shot.

Next, let's take a look at Figures 16.10 to 16.12, all of the same male fetus at 16w2d. Figure 16.10 represents a side view of Baby similar to Figure 16.9. The penis and scrotal sac are a bit more difficult to see, aren't they?

Figure 16.11 shows us a bottom view, but the legs are a bit close together and the cord is also seen here running between the legs—both present a problem in obtaining a clear view of genitalia.

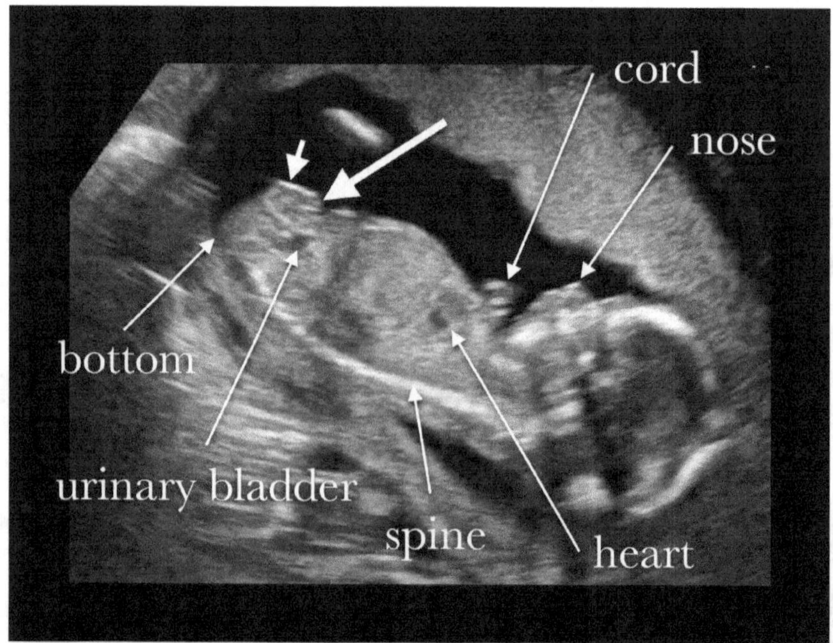

Figure 16.10: Week 16 ~ Side View, Male Gender-4

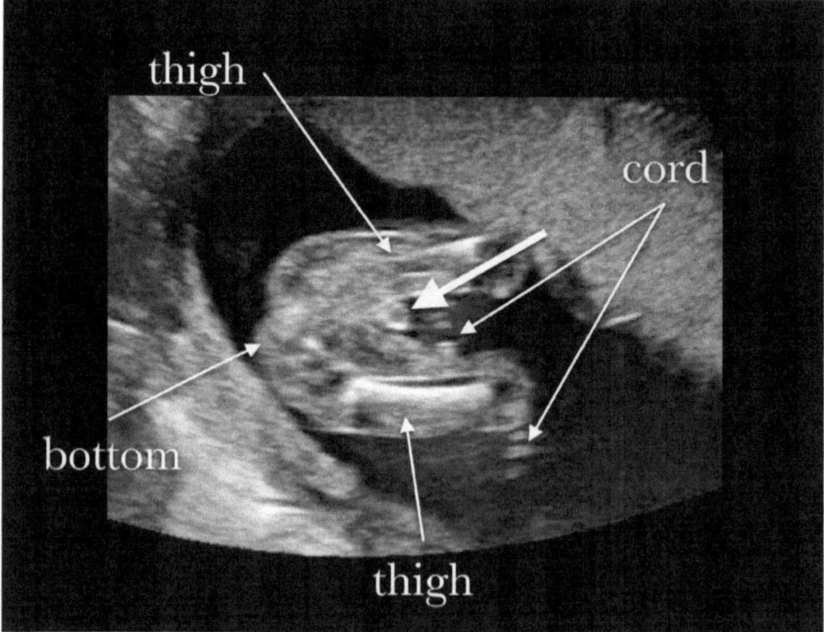

Figure 16.11: Week 16 ~ Male Gender-5

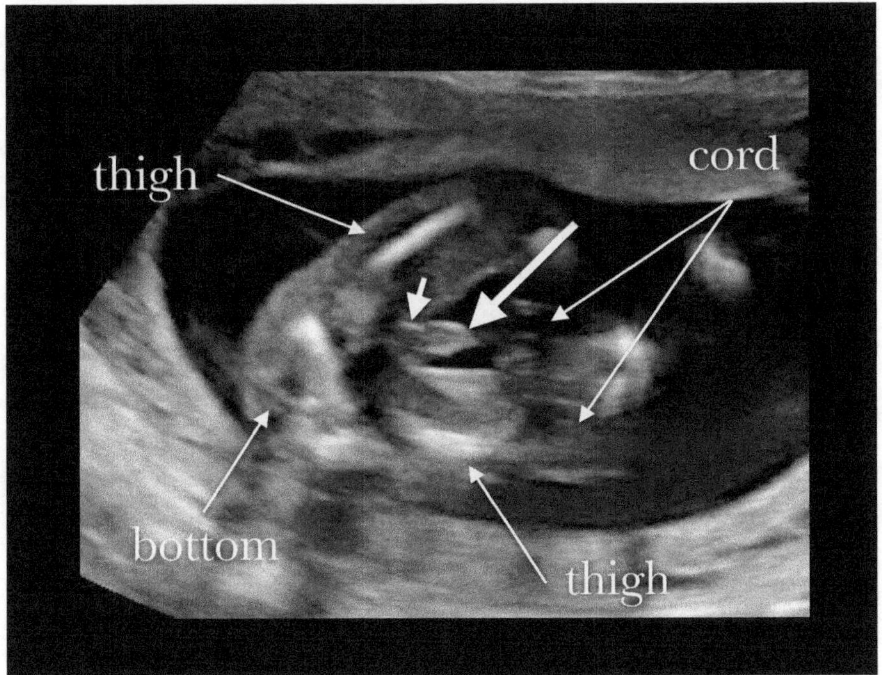

Figure 16.12: Week 16 ~ Male Gender-6

Figure 16.12 gives this mom the most reassuring shot so far. The legs are opened a little wider and the cord has moved away from the body enough to better see the penis and even a bit of the scrotal sac. What a difference a little shift in position and movement makes!

As I previously stated, we expected no future changes in the genders of Dianne's twins. We knew, however, that her next diagnostic scan in Week 19 could solidify our guesses and kick off the abundance of event planning that comes with every pregnancy, especially with two in tow—showers, the nursery, choosing names. Dianne was ready to dive in head-first…after her next scan. You'll find out, too, in Week 19. Did we get it right or get surprised?

Finally, in Figure 16.13, we have another great shot of twins at Week 16 and one of each gender. Here, you can easily see the difference between normally-developing male and female genitalia—a typical appearance for both. Such a great shot!

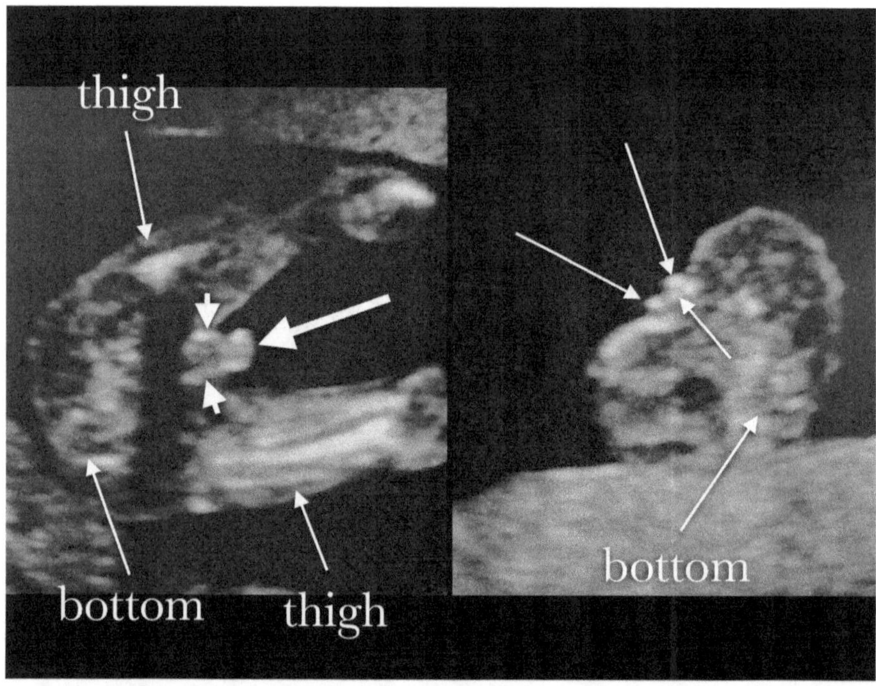

Figure 16.13: Week 16 ~ Another Set of Twins, Male & Female

Week 17

As I mentioned previously, Dianne's next scan will be addressed in Week 19. In the meantime, Figures 17.1 through 17.6 show us more gender images from 17 Weeks of gestation.

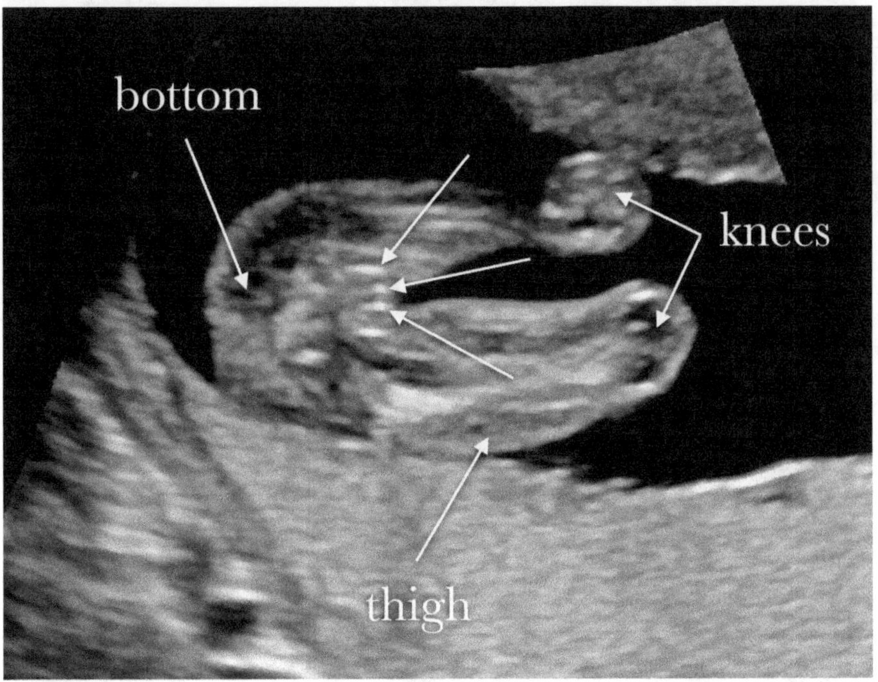

Figure 17.1: Week 17~ Female Gender-1

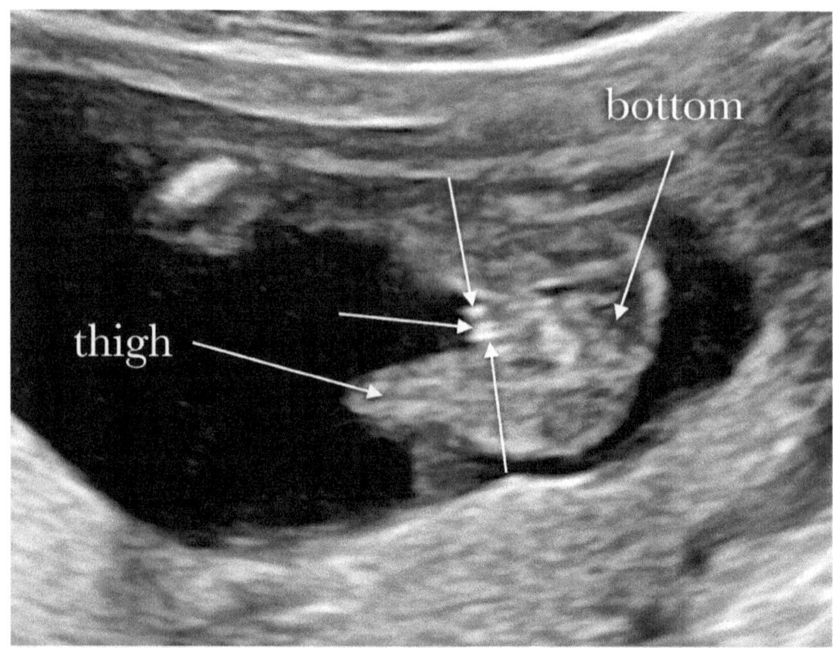

Figure 17.2: Week 17 ~ Female Gender-2

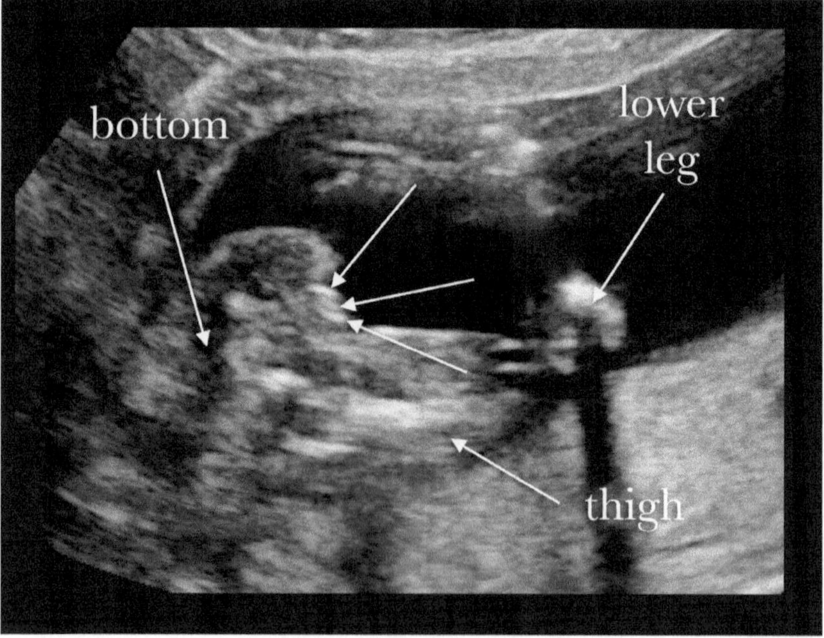

Figure 17.3: 17w3d ~ Female Gender-3

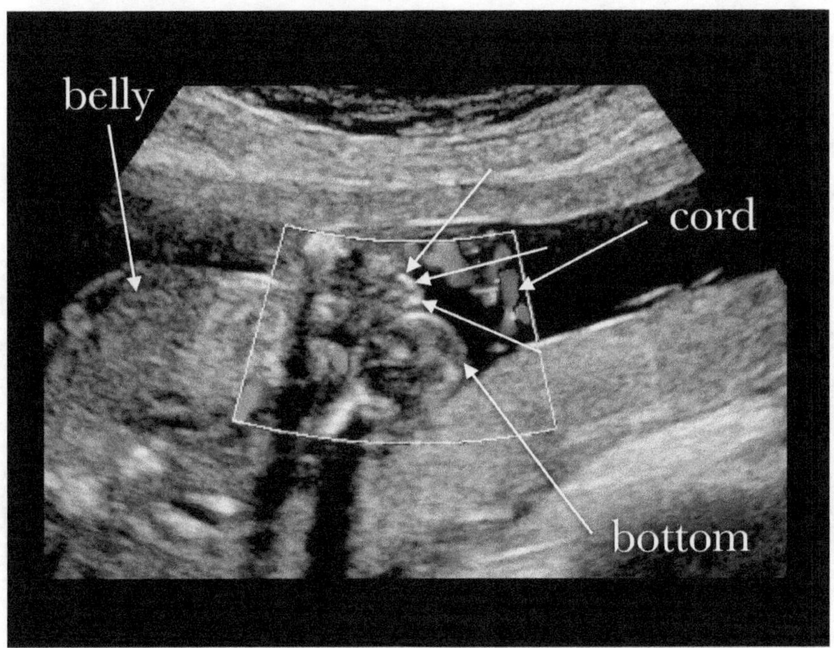

Figure 17.4: 17w3d ~ Female Gender-4

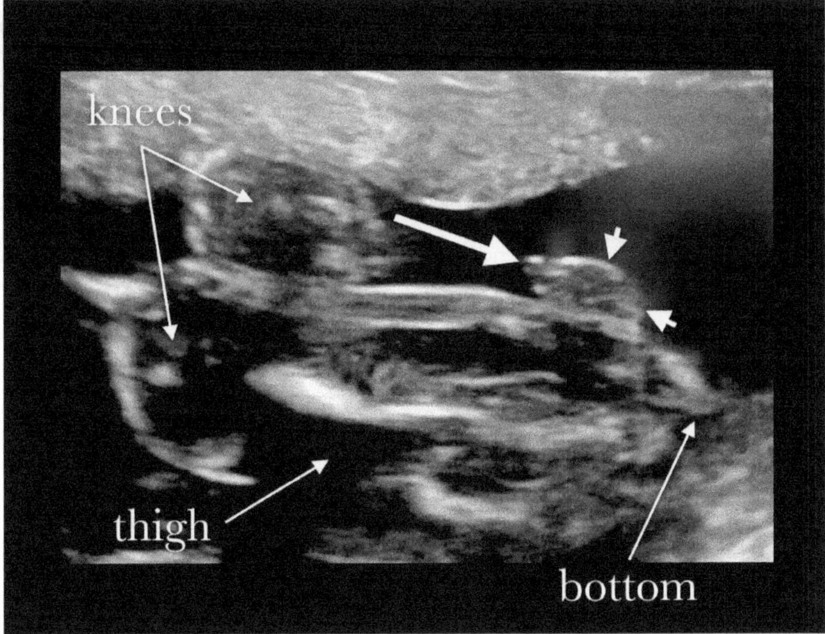

Figure 17.5: Week 17 ~ Male Gender-1

Figure 17.5 represents a side view of this male fetus. It's also why you cannot see both thighs in this view.

Figure 17.6 shows a great example of how even a small segment of the umbilical cord can interfere with determining gender. I feel we can easily appreciate the penis and scrotal sac in this otherwise great fetal position.

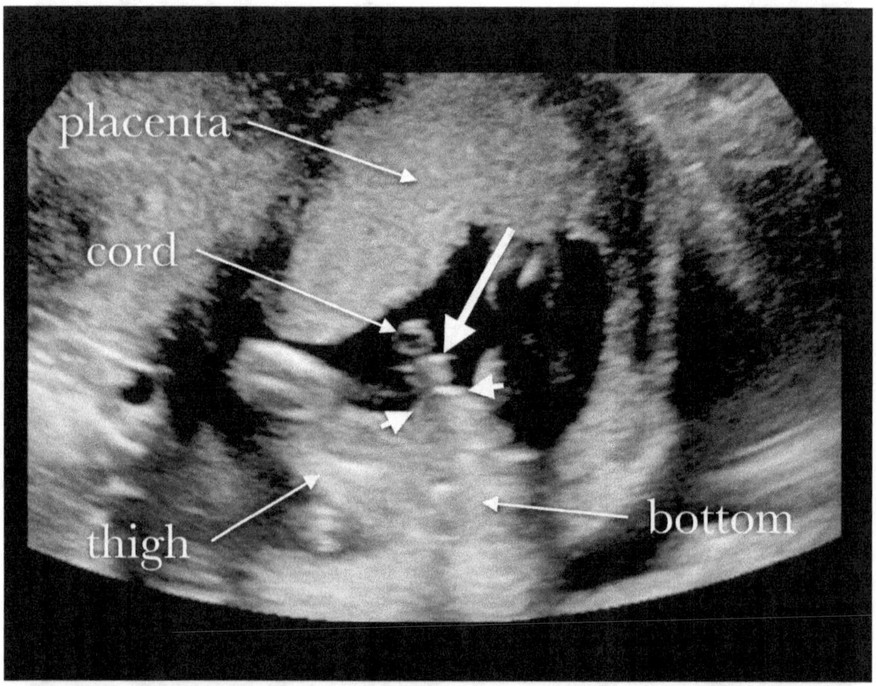

Figure 17.6: Week 17 ~ Male Gender-2

Week 18

Week 18 will reveal more of what we've seen in the previous week or two. The fetus will grow a little more each week, and genitalia will be easier and easier to see providing full fetal cooperation.

Figures 18.1 through 18.8 are more terrific examples of gender in Week 18.

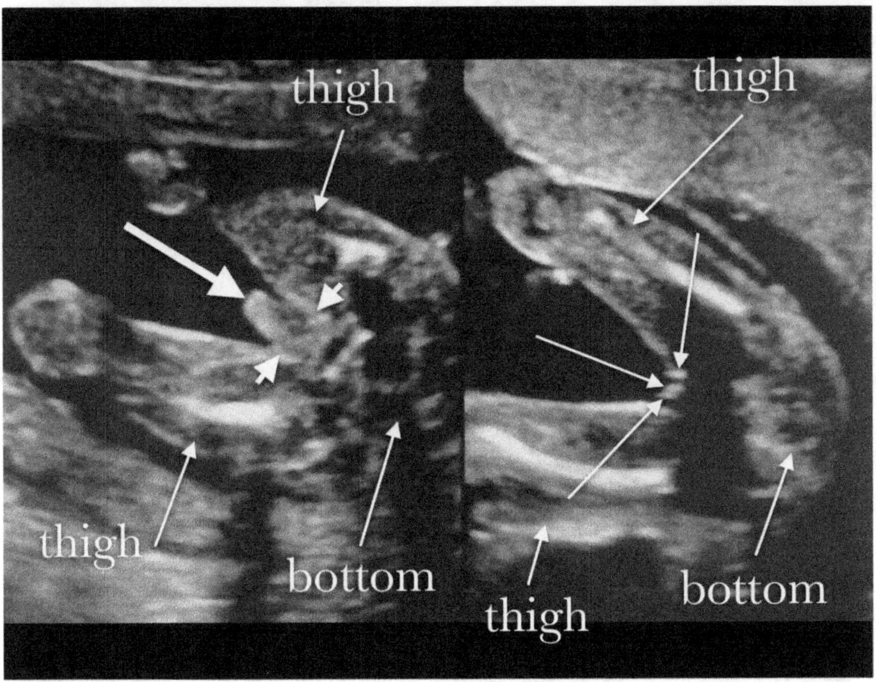

Figure 18.1: Week 18 ~ Male and Female Twin Gender

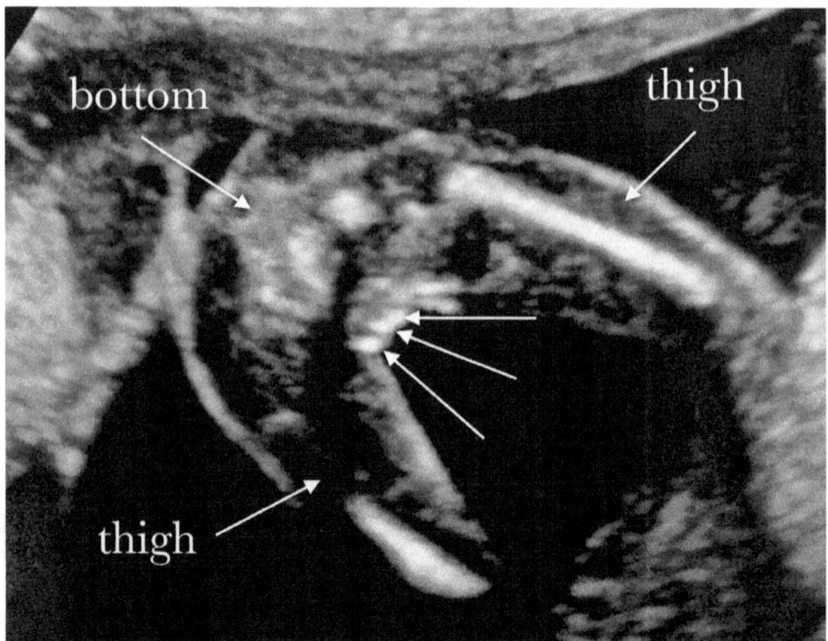

Figure 18.2: Week 18 ~ Female Gender-1

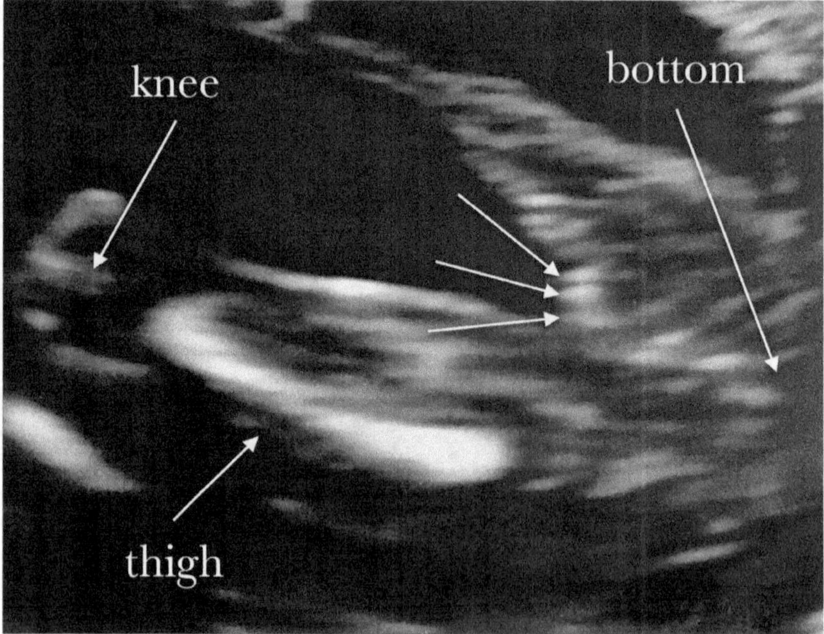

Figure 18.3: Week 18 ~ Female Gender-2

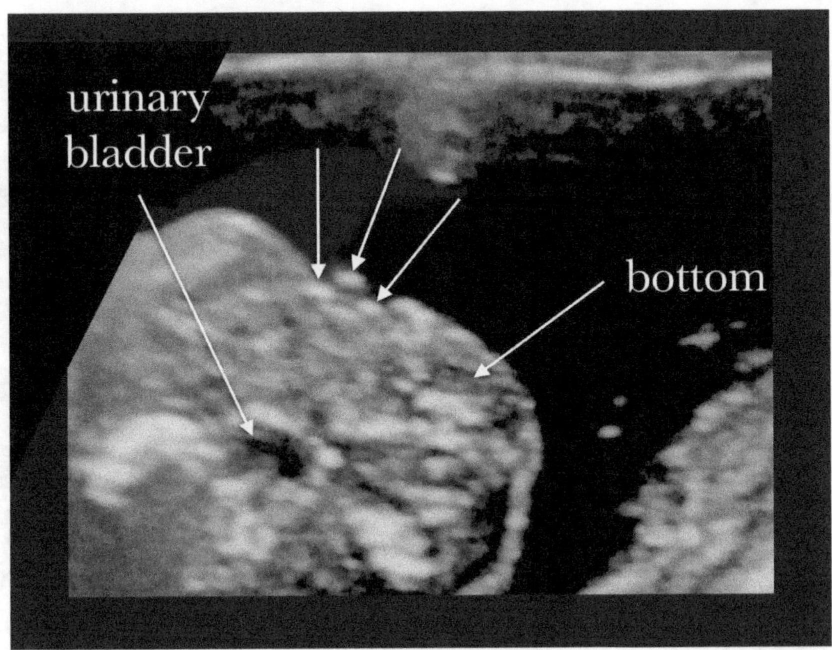

Figure 18.4: Week 18 ~ Female Gender-3

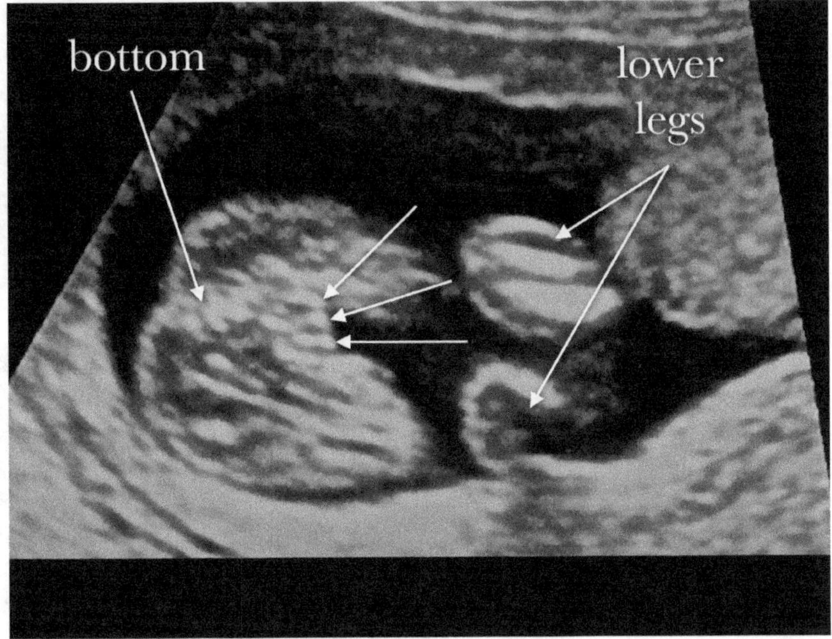

Figure 18.5: Week 18 ~ Female Gender-4

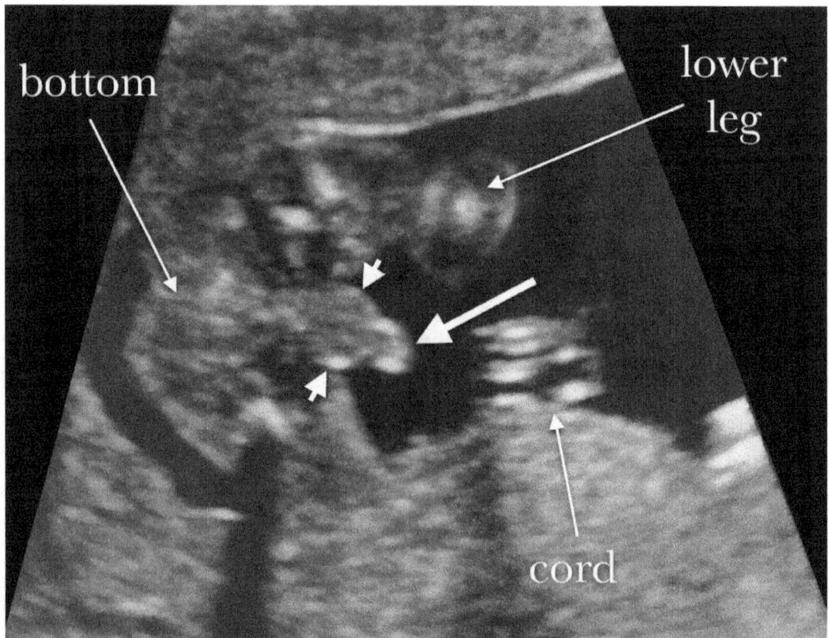

Figure 18.6: Week 18 ~ Male Gender-1

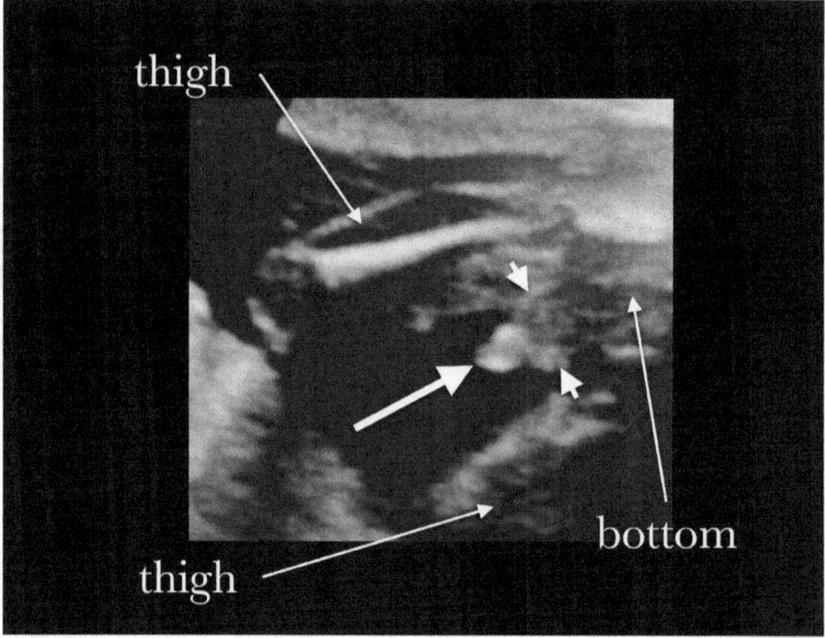

Figure 18.7: Week 18 ~ Male Gender-2

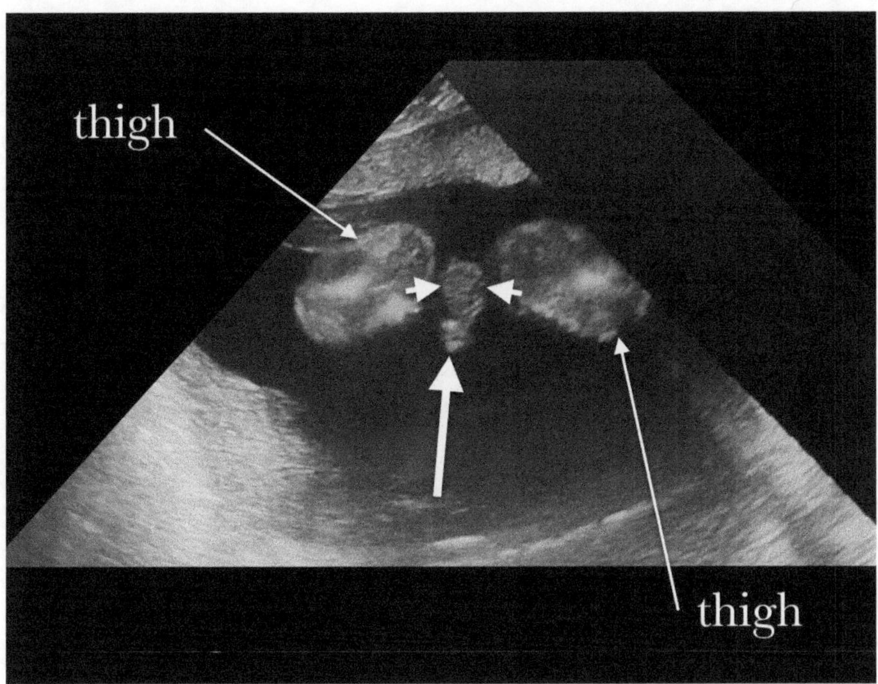

Figure 18.8: Week 18 ~ Male Gender-3

Week 19

The time had finally arrived for the twins' anatomical survey or anatomy screen. Can you guess what we checked first? We had begun attempting to distinguish gender five weeks prior, maintaining the same guesses all along. So, were we right or wrong? What's *your* guess?

AND THE VERDICT IIIIISSS...

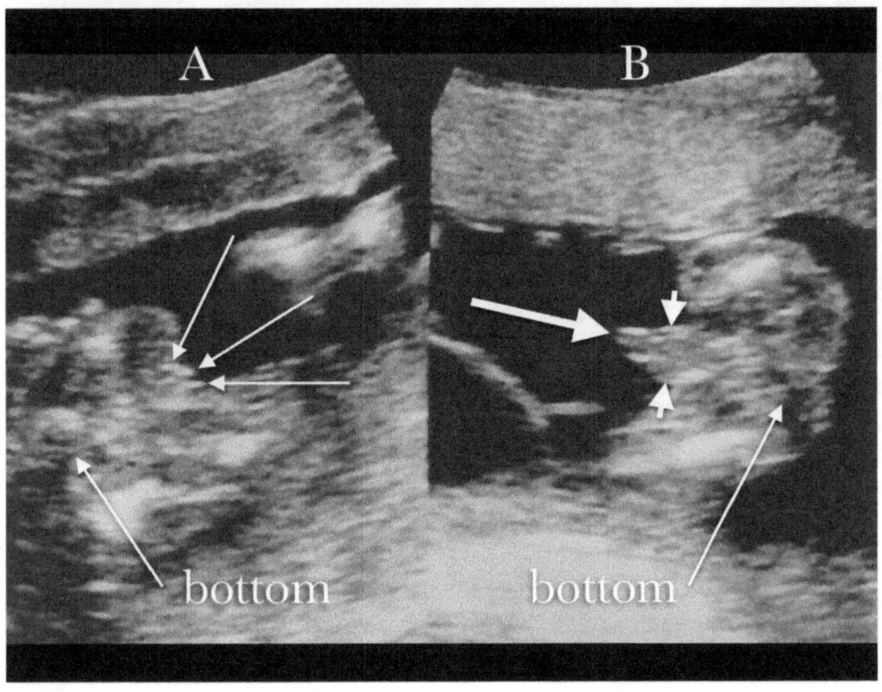

Figure 19.1: Week 19 ~ Dianne's Twins

ONE OF EACH!

Not surprised? Neither were we! Figure 19.1 shows Baby A's images on the left remained consistent with typical-appearing female genitalia and Baby B, still typical for a boy, indeed. With all the waiting behind her, Dianne was ecstatic to finally be able to dive right into all the mom shopping she'd been itching to begin. How exciting! And for our patients whom we know well, as friends or previous pregnancies we've helped care for, the experience is just as joyous for us!

Figure 19.2 is another image of Dianne's baby boy and girl.

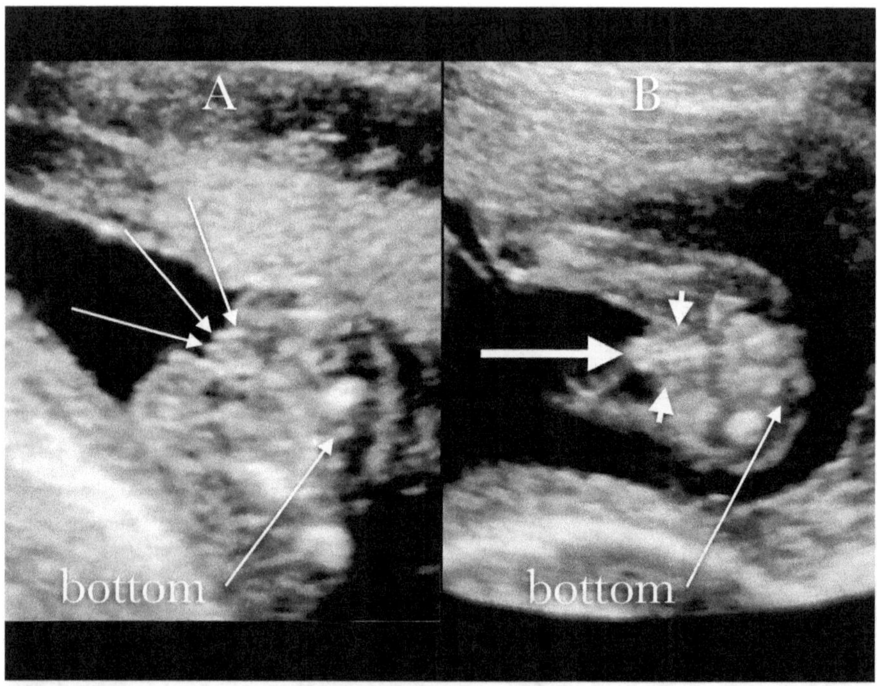

Figure 19.2: Week 19 ~ Dianne's Twins

On the left, three arrows point to the three lines or dots that make up labia and the clitoris for a baby girl. The right underside view shows Baby B's bottom, thigh, scrotal sac, and penis.

I'd like to point out here that there exists quite a large discrepancy in what we call "typical appearance" for male and female, especially in the Third Trimester. The size of the male penis will vary quite a bit, even now. The scrotal sac can be identified, but the testicles cannot yet be seen because they won't descend until somewhere around Week 27 or 28, generally.

A female fetus will maintain about the same appearance for a few more weeks until she starts to develop a little fat in her skin. The labia will then start to take on a slightly plumper appearance, what you'd expect to see of a newborn baby girl. You'll be able to see this in the upcoming images of female gender.

Just to demonstrate the flexibility of a fetus, Baby A more than happily showed off her acrobatic skills in Figure 19.3. Wouldn't it be great for yoga potential if we could all keep her degree of limber displayed in Figure 19.3?

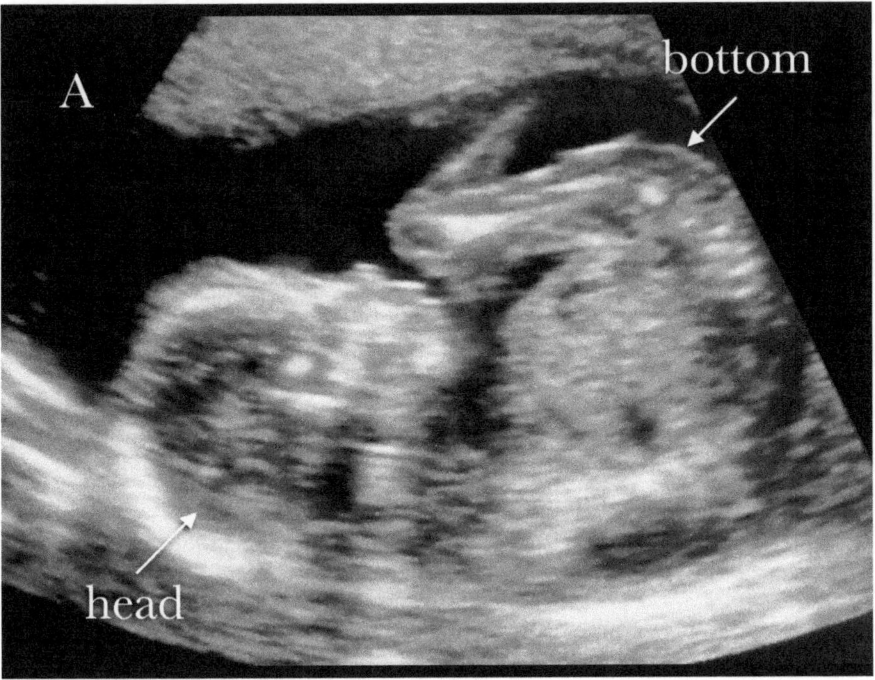

Figure 19.3: Week 19 ~ Baby A

You'll notice her knee right up to her face. And just look at that profile. Such distinct little nose and lips.

The twins' anatomy screen was quite normal, and the babies were growing concordantly. Fortunately, Dianne did better than expected for a twin pregnancy and only had a few more growth scans after this one. She was quite satisfied with her gender images at this point and needed no more convincing. Even though we looked again with each subsequent scan, she never asked for more images of gender and we didn't take any pains to document them. We'll revisit the twins one last time before delivery!

The Anatomy Screen

Because I'm not focused on diagnostic scans of the Second and Third Trimesters in this book, I'll not delve too deeply into this lengthy (especially for multiples) and detailed ultrasound examination. I do feel, however, that glossing over it entirely would minimize the importance of this scan and the benefits it provides. Instead, I'll highlight the general purpose of the test and what we attempt to document during your anatomy screen.

Most women receiving modern obstetric care may routinely undergo one ultrasound examination to confirm a pregnancy in the First Trimester and the detailed anatomy screen somewhere between Week 18 to 20 in the Second Trimester. As discussed in Week 12, an ultrasound study for the Nuchal Translucency may be performed if one elects early genetic testing. Otherwise, other scans are only predicated by certain complications of pregnancy which could arise.

The purpose of the anatomy screen is just that—to screen fetal development. We check for appropriate growth by measuring the head, abdomen, and femur. We document fetal limbs and ensure Baby's major organs are located in their proper positions, appear as expected, and are functioning normally. We may measure mom's cervix to rule out premature shortening or opening (which can lead to premature labor), to evaluate position of the placenta to confirm it isn't implanted too low to the cervix or covering it altogether (previa), and to assess amniotic fluid level.

All of this information is documented in a detailed report. If an organ is noted as "seen" and "normal in appearance," a representative image of that organ must support this documentation. Likewise, any abnormality or questionable concern is documented in the same way—with measurements, detailed descriptions, and images. We must also report whatever structures we could not see well. We cannot evaluate what we cannot visualize. And we cannot call "normal" what we cannot evaluate properly. Those structures might be labeled as "limited," along with the reason for the limitation (i.e., fetal position). Just as fetal position can hinder the determination of gender, it can also obscure important organs and structures, such as the heart or spine.

Your obstetrician, most other healthcare providers managing your pregnancy, and most expectant parents desire this information for obvious reasons. Again, the goal for any ultrasound exam is to detect an abnormality in advance of birth, to educate and counsel parents on the findings and extent of the problem, and to better manage your pregnancy for the healthiest and safest labor and delivery possible for mom and Baby.

Unfortunately, some providers who advocate natural pregnancy and delivery are vocal about their distaste for or distrust in ultrasound. They have a right to their opinion and to counsel their patients accordingly, usually those who desire the type of pregnancy and birth experience they offer. Parents have many options, and the ones you make during pregnancy are only the beginning of the many choices you'll make on behalf of your child over the course of his or her life. However, they should all be informed choices.

Anyone who blatantly and incorrectly refers to ultrasound as radiation or pushes a narrative of fetal harm from routine diagnostic testing is doing a disservice to the public they seek to influence. Baseless opinions should not set the foundation for any parent's decision to decline an ultrasound examination. To be sure, any parent has the *right* to decline. But in doing so, a parent must also fully comprehend and accept its consequences.

I've read the argument that the use of ultrasound does not improve the outcome of a normal pregnancy. This may be an easy conclusion to reach retrospectively. Yes, ultrasound can provide reassurance to expectant parents and medical providers alike when all appears normal. But ask any parent who learned of a genetic syndrome or fetal malformation in utero via ultrasound. How valuable then was ultrasound to them? And what lifesaving, educational, physical and emotional, and interventional measures did those ultrasound results provide? The benefits of ultrasound in cases where an abnormality *does* exist, where life-threatening conditions *can* be diagnosed and managed, and where high-risk management and intervention *are* required for a safer and healthier outcome should not be understated or undervalued.

No test can ever boast 100 percent accuracy, true. But I'm a proponent of educated ultrasound use because I've witnessed its benefits first-hand, from the perspective of the patient and the provider—even if I can only draw from my narrow experience.

Every provider in obstetrics has the responsibility to properly educate themselves and the parents they counsel. Only when armed with accurate information can parents decide for themselves and their own families what's important to them, what information they seek in advance, and what information they can live without.

Figures 19.4 through 19.11 are more images of gender at Week 19. Figure 19.6 depicts a side view of Baby. His head is not seen here but would be on the left side of this image. This is a side view of Baby's body with no legs in the image. Not only does it provide a great shot of male genitalia, it's also a fantastic view of the umbilical cord as it inserts into Baby's belly.

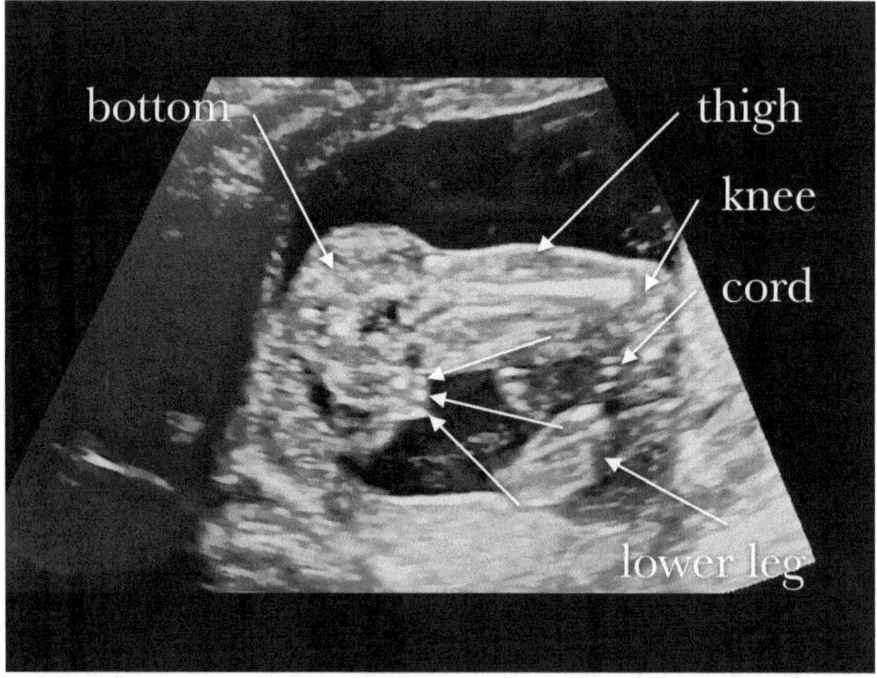

Figure 19.4: Week 19 ~ Female Gender

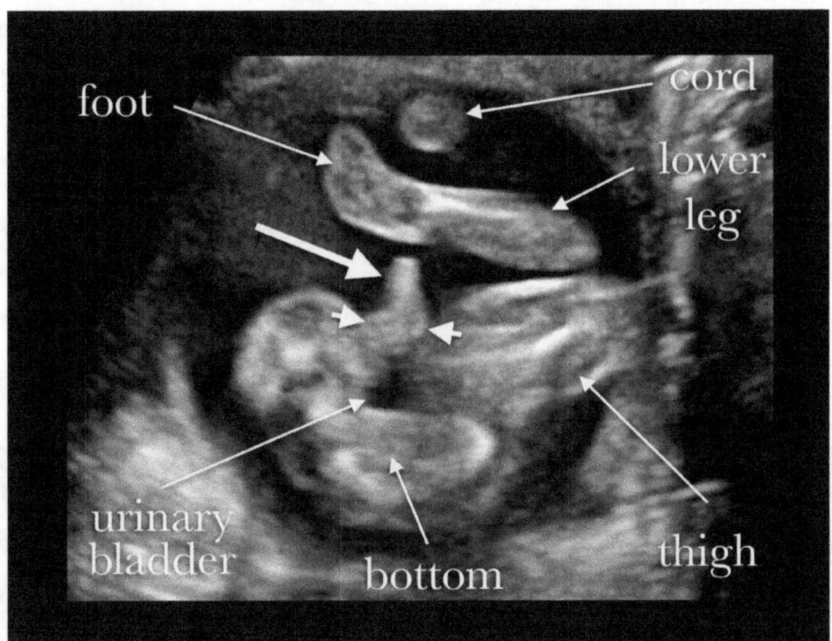

Figure 19.5: Week 19 ~ Male Gender-1

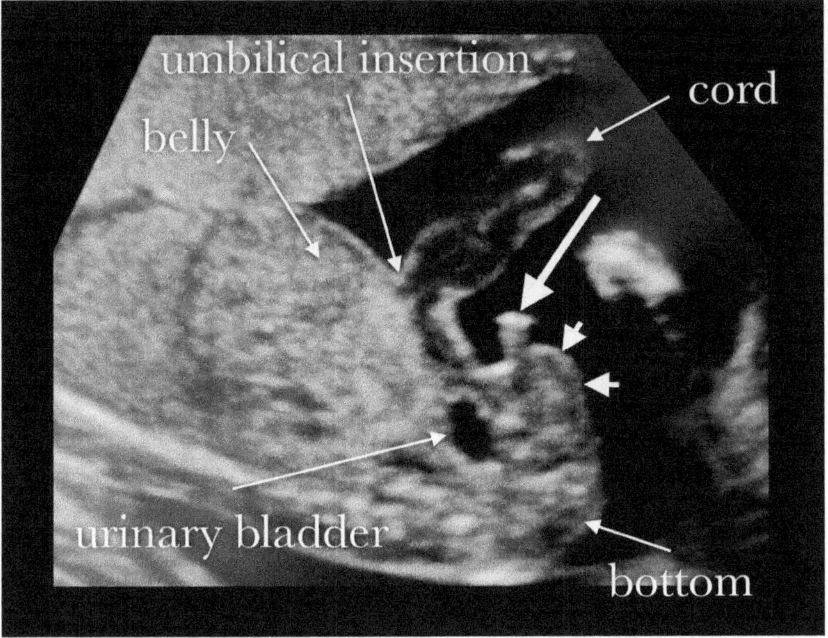

Figure 19.6: Week 19 ~ Male Gender-2

I've mentioned it before, but amniotic fluid is mostly made up of fetal urine which is recycled over and over. They drink and urinate. However, if this grosses you out, think of it this way—it's how we know your baby is doing some very important things in there like drinking and swallowing.

We know some pertinent organs are also doing their job—the stomach is filling and emptying and the kidneys are working by filtering the fluid. The urinary bladder is filling and releasing the urine. These are all great things to know about the normal development of your baby which are documented in your ultrasound exam. Figures 19.6 and 19.7 both demonstrate the fetal bladder well in these baby boys.

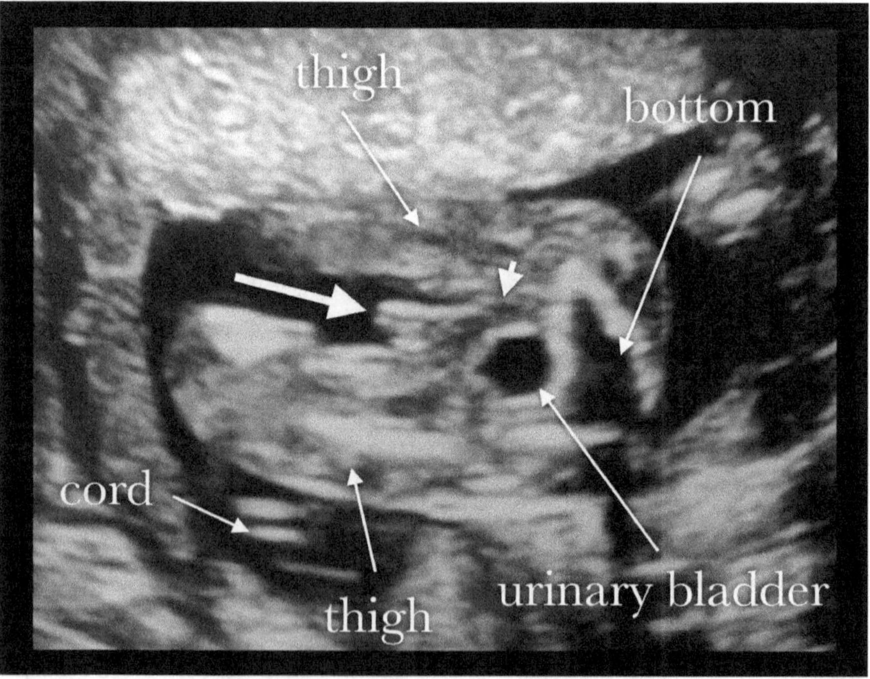

Figure 19.7: Week 19 ~ Male Gender-3

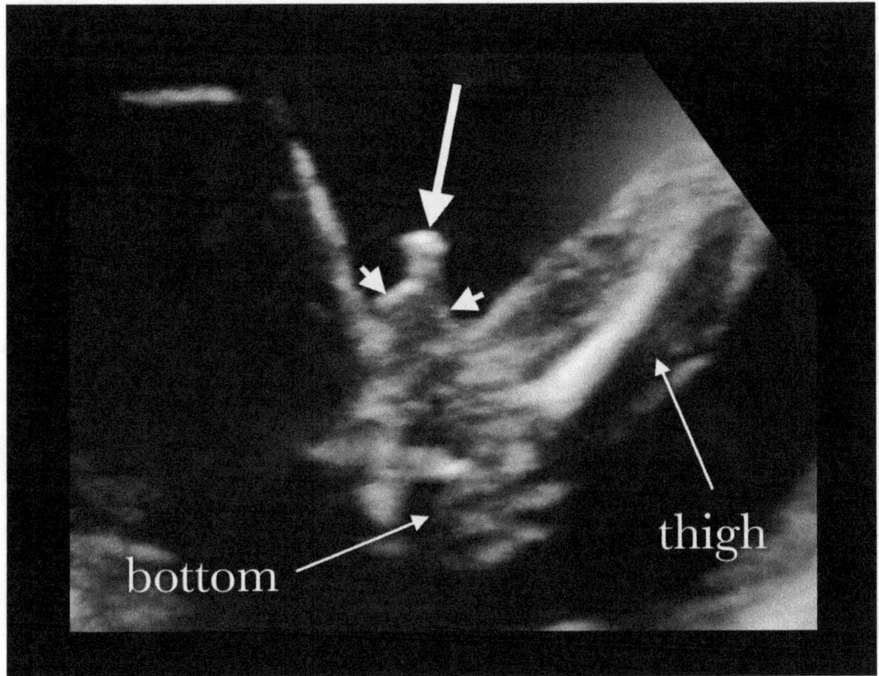

Figure 19.8: Week 19 ~ Male Gender-4

Figure 19.8 reveals one of those truly textbook shots for male gender. We'd typically respond to this image with a, "Wow, he's a proud one!" For some reason, dads would commonly comment on how they wanted this one for their wallets! Now, imagine mom's eye roll. Too funny.

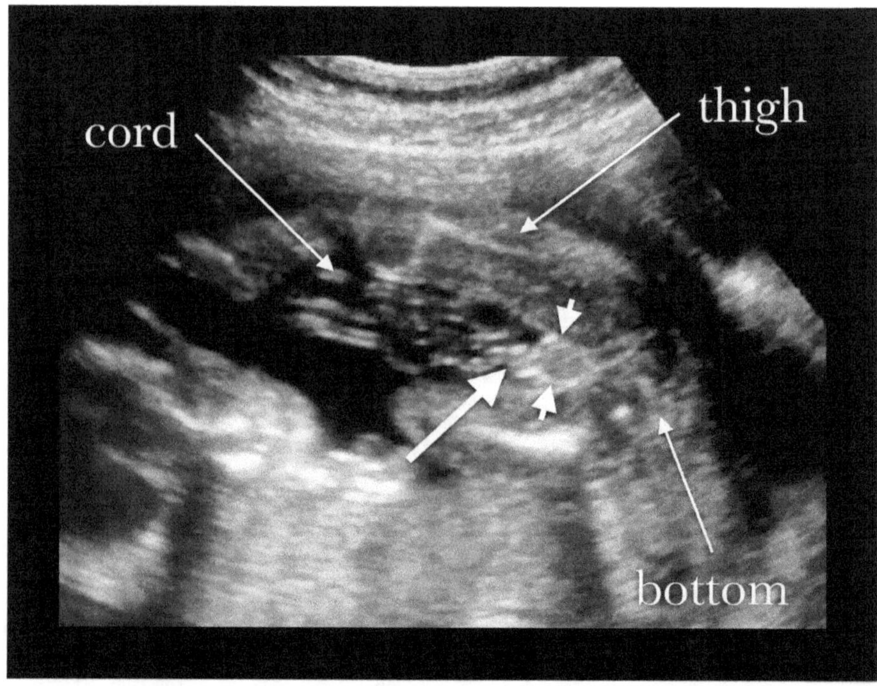

Figure 19.9: Week 19 ~ Male Gender-5, with Cord

Figure 19.9 shows a great example of just how a long stretch of cord can interfere with a gender guess. A reader of my blog emailed me concerned that her sonographer was wrong. She just could not see those "boy parts" very well and wanted my opinion. You may be able to appreciate her difficulty in the image she sent to me, Figure 19.9. With the labels in place, can you now separate the cord from the penis?

Sometimes, the cord makes its way between Baby's legs and up his/her backside, tightly against Baby's body. It's these sorts of scenarios which can make determining gender nearly impossible with no room for amniotic fluid between the cord and Baby's genitals. A good analogy might be like trying to guess the sex of a newborn wearing a diaper. You can't see what's covered up and neither can we.

Two more great images of male gender round out Week 19. In each image, you may be able to appreciate a clear bottom view with legs apart and plenty of amniotic fluid around the genitalia, helping to improve our view.

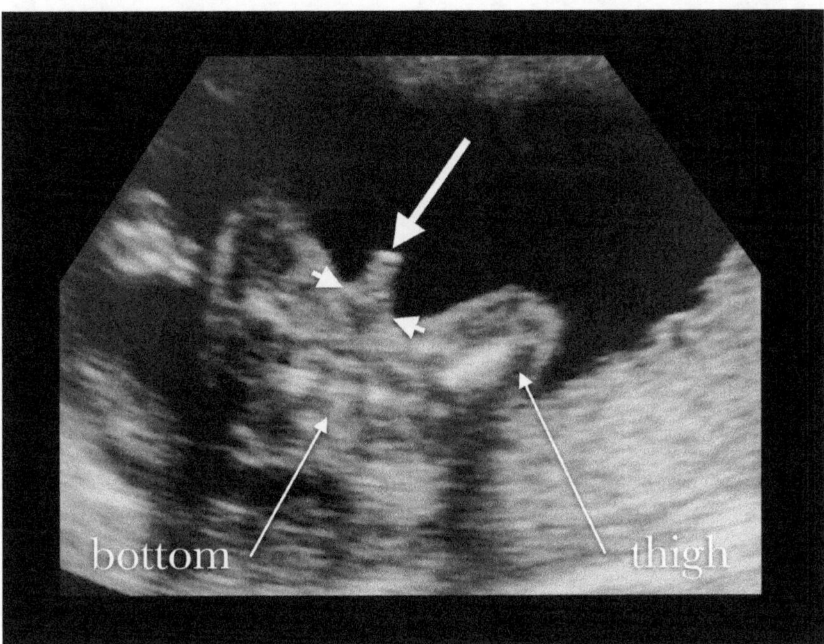

Figure 19.10: 19w6d, Male Gender-6

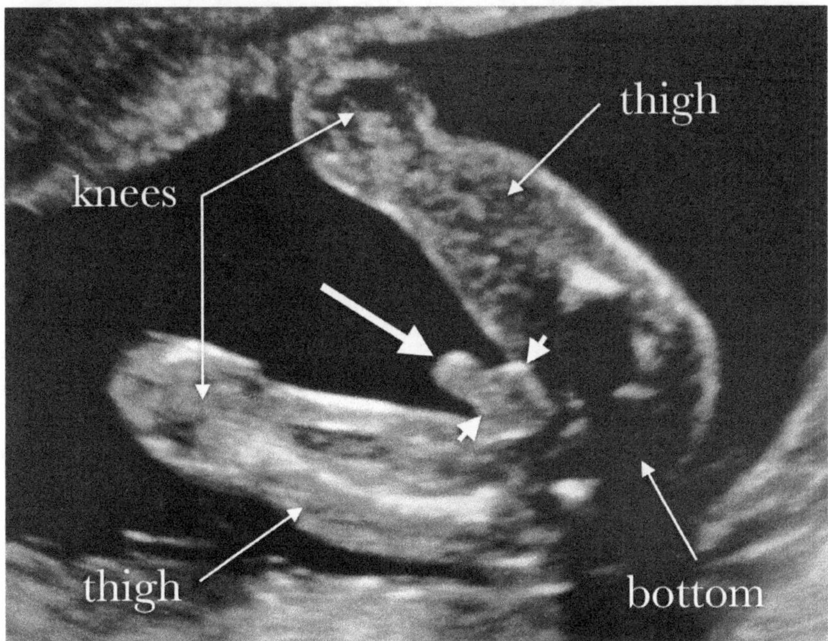

Figure 19.11: 19w6d, Male Gender-7

Week 20

Figures 20.1 to 20.6 are annotated images of gender scans for Week 20. I've just one image for female gender, but you can see her parts still appear relatively the same as in previous weeks—three white dots or lines, depending on the angle obtained.

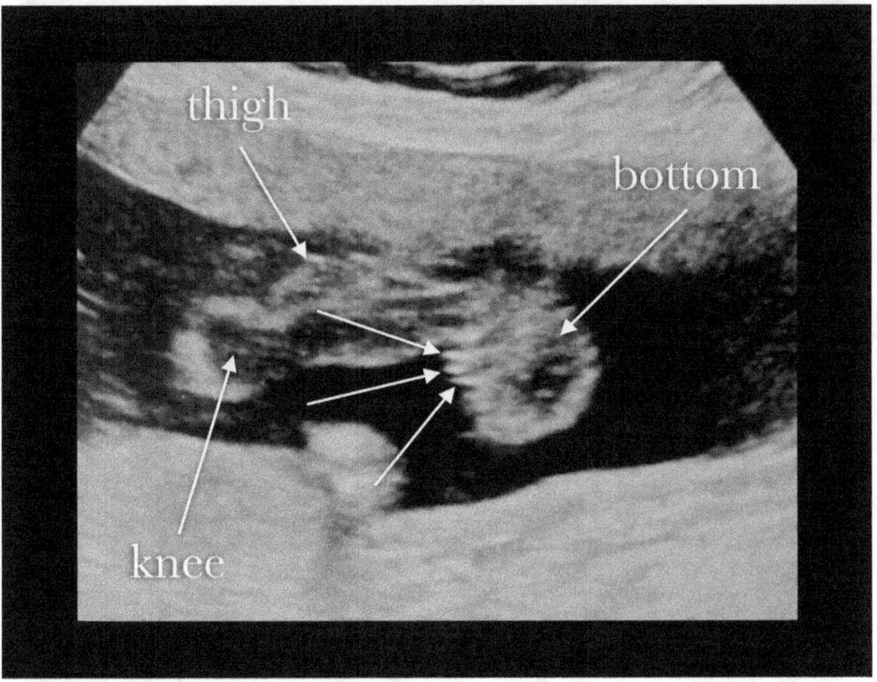

Figure 20.1: Week 20 ~ Female Gender

Next, in Figures 20.2 and 20.3, note that this is the same baby in both images. The only difference is the sonographer's slightly different angle. Only one thigh is visible in Figure 20.2; both are visible in Figure 20.3. The point is to show how varied external genitalia can appear from one second to the next in the very same pregnancy.

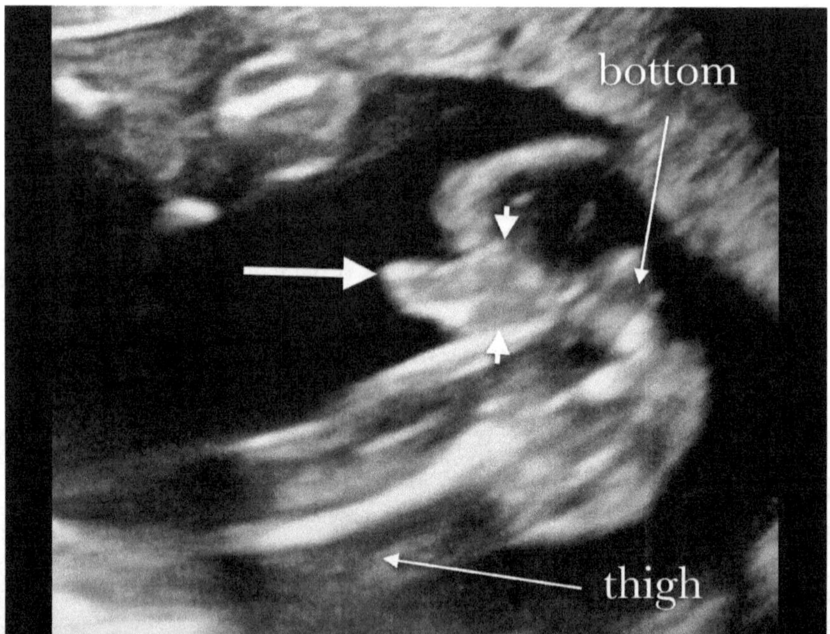

Figure 20.2: Week 20 ~ Male Gender-1

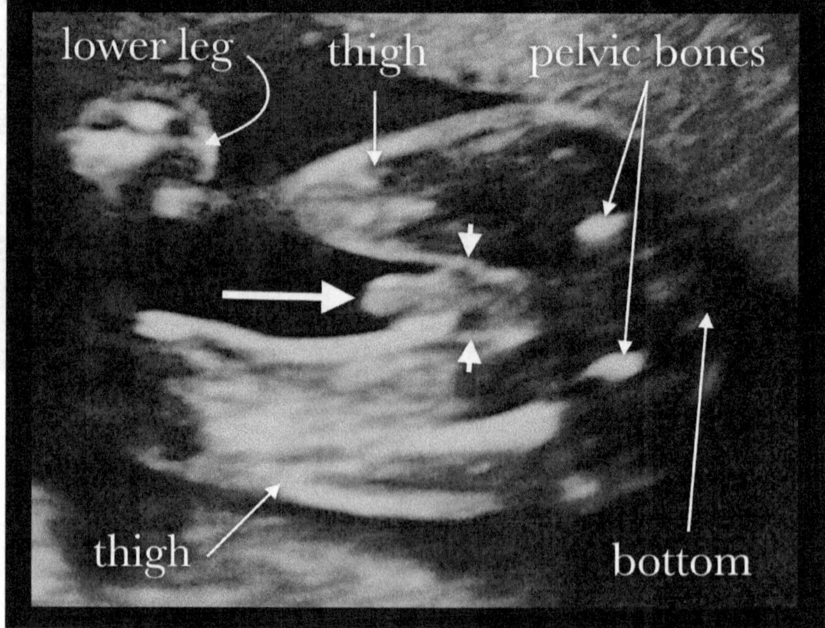

Figure 20.3: Week 20 ~ Male Gender-2

Figure 20.4 is another great example of how the cord can "get in the way." This cord lies just adjacent to the penis but does not cover it entirely.

As I've mentioned before, a good amount of fluid is needed around Baby's bottom to see genitalia well. If the cord runs between the legs, lies too close to the body or directly over external genitalia, a gender guess may be impossible. Since all fluid is black on ultrasound, we see just enough here in Figure 20.4 to discern that he's indeed male. Also, behind the penis you can see a rounded area for the scrotum. The testicles won't descend for a few more weeks. But when they do, we can see them, too!

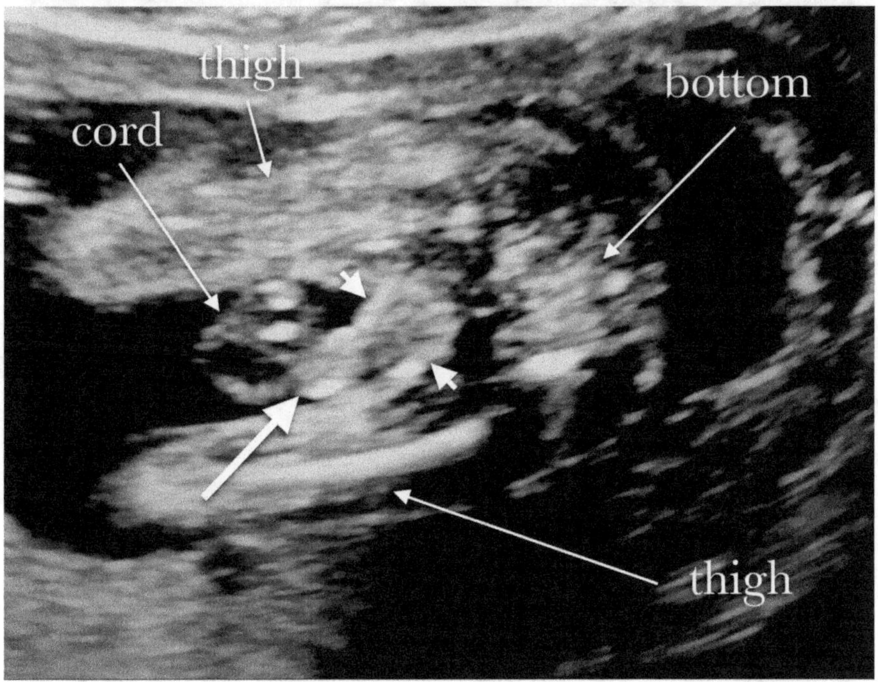

Figure 20.4: Week 20 ~ Male Gender-3

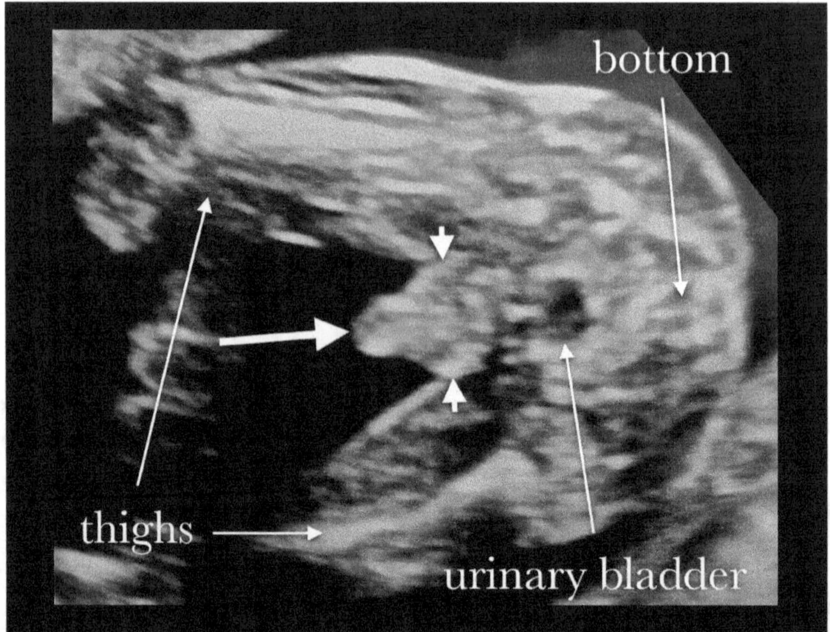

Figure 20.5: Week 20 ~ Male Gender-4

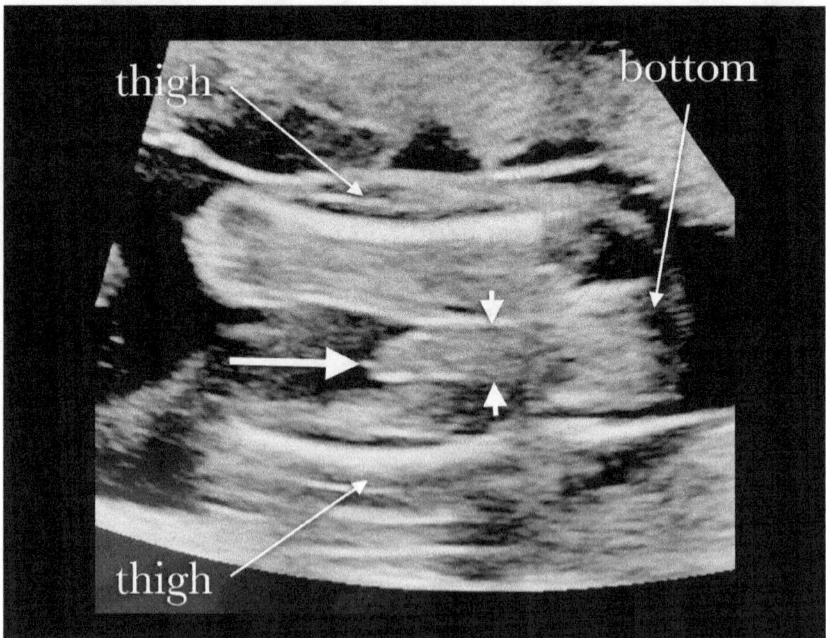

Figure 20.6: Week 20 ~ Male Gender-5

Can you note the differences here between Figures 20.5 and 20.6? Baby's legs in the first image appear to be spread out much wider than in the second, where his knees look much closer together. In Figure 20.6, we can still see the penis quite well, but the scrotal sac appears a bit compressed by the thighs. It's one of the reasons why gender can be difficult to determine if the legs are not positioned wide apart. Fetal position is everything in ultrasound!

Week 21

Figures 21.1 through 21.3 show the typical development common to both male and female at this GA.

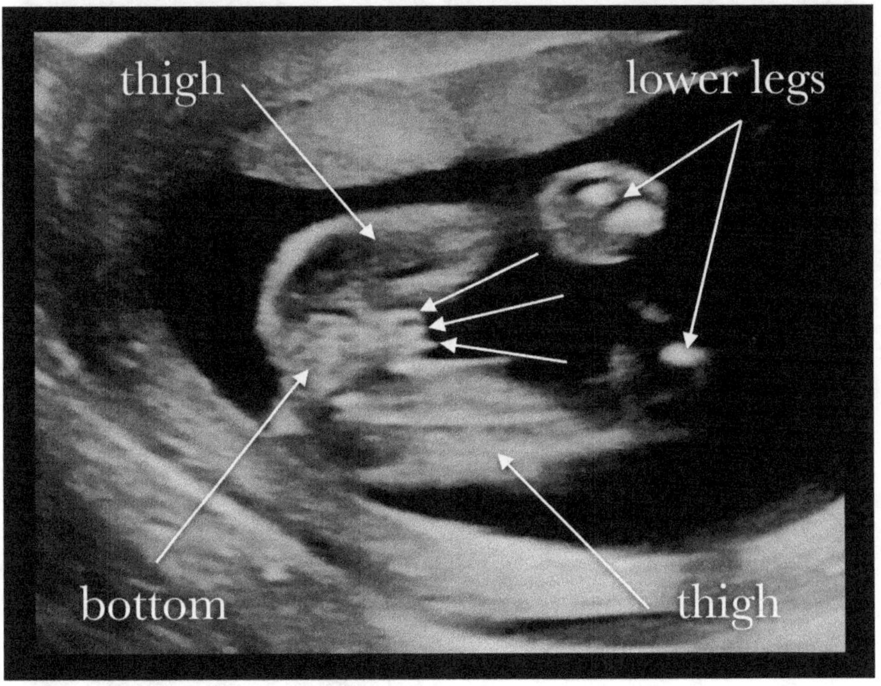

Figure 21.1: Week 21 ~ Female Gender

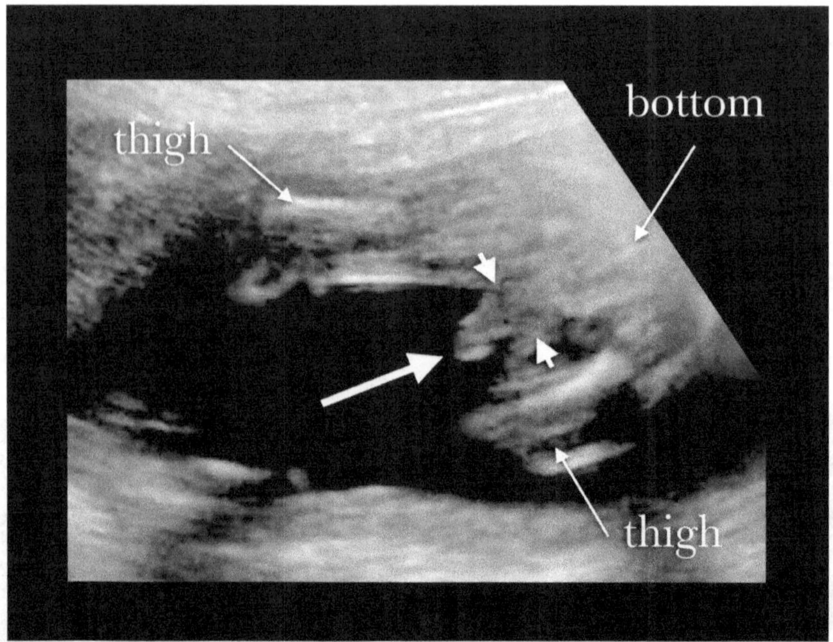

Figure 21.2: Week 21 ~ Male Gender-1

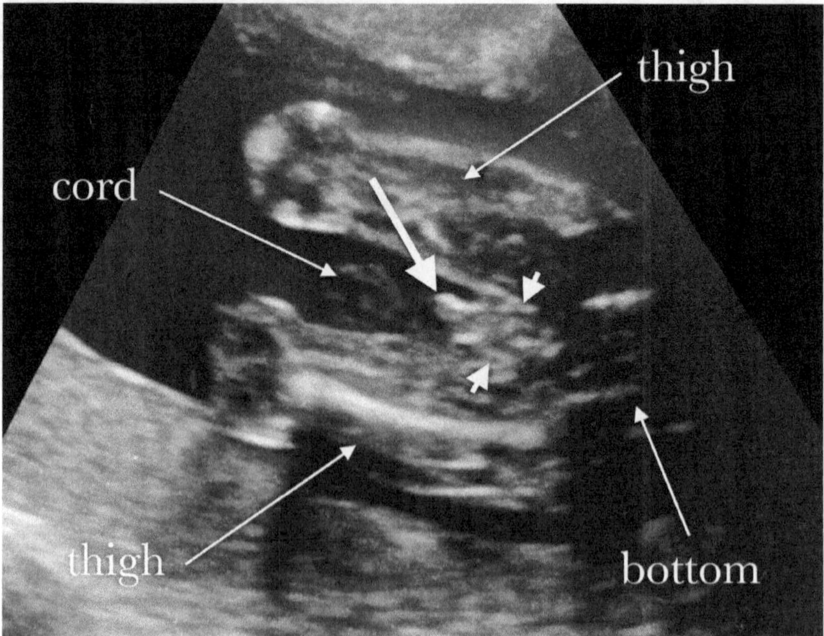

Figure 21.3: Week 21 ~ Male Gender-2

Week 22

igures 22.1 to 22.2 show little change of appearance in external genitalia for both sexes from the prior week of gestation.

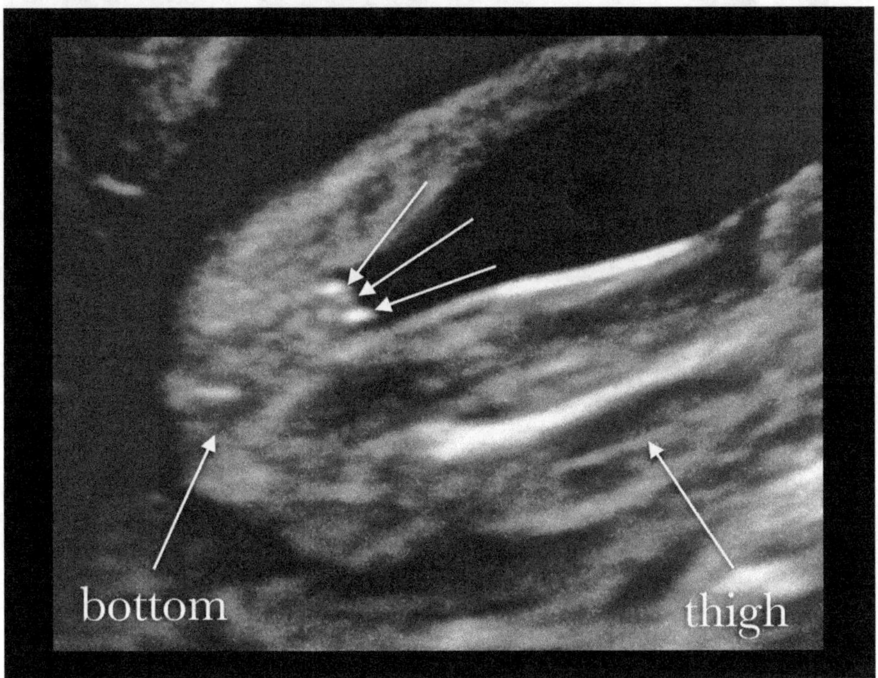

Figure 22.1: Week 22 ~ Female Gender-1

Figure 22.2 shows that this baby girl is developing some fat in her skin because her labia display a little "plumpness" here. Note this is not demonstrated in Figure 22.1. Even though the appearance between these two females differs slightly, there is nothing remotely close to a penis or scrotal sac to question a boy in either image.

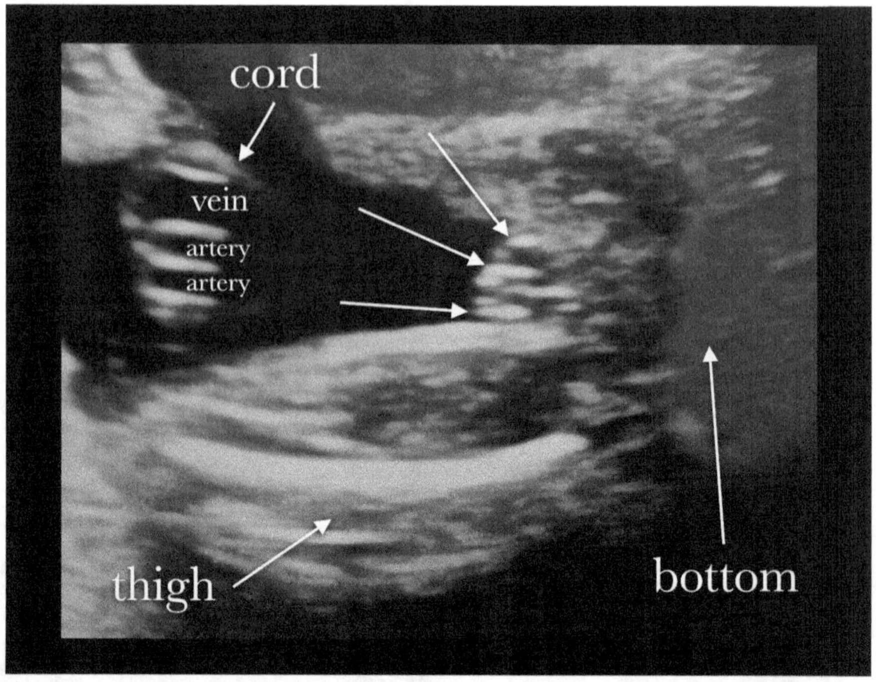

Figure 22.2: Week 22 ~ Female Gender-2

Week 23

Week 23 images show more and more fat in Baby's tissues, as we see here in Figure 23.1.

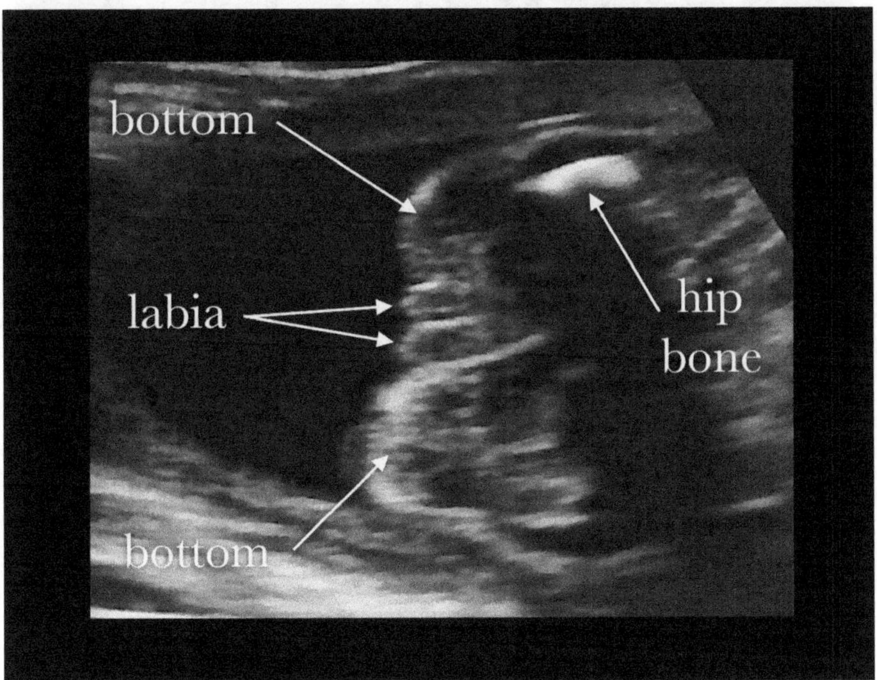

Figure 23.1: Week 23 ~ Female Gender-1

This is a prime example of the labia beginning to fill out, taking on the appearance which you'd expect of a newborn female. What a great shot of female parts here! Figures 23.2 through 23.4 show similar appearances for both male and female.

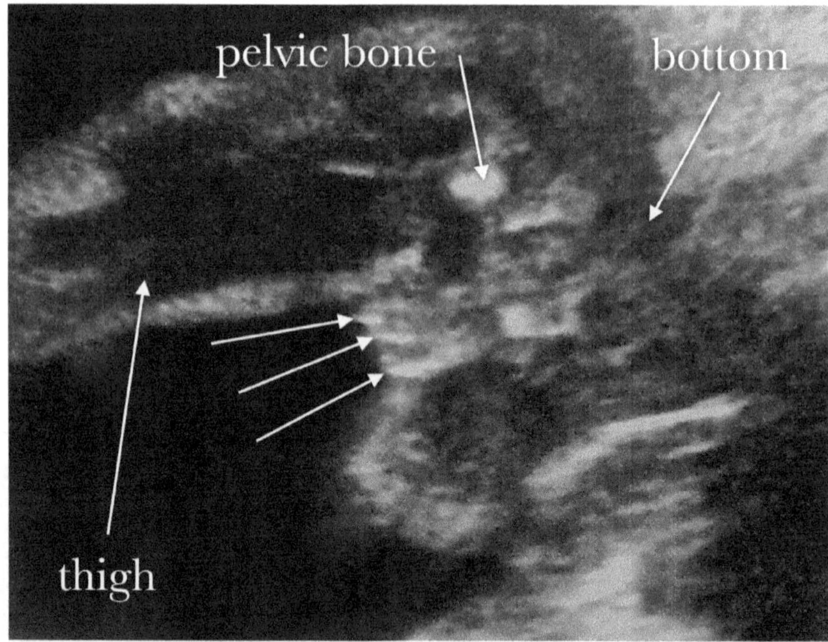

Figure 23.2: 23w6d ~ Female Gender-2

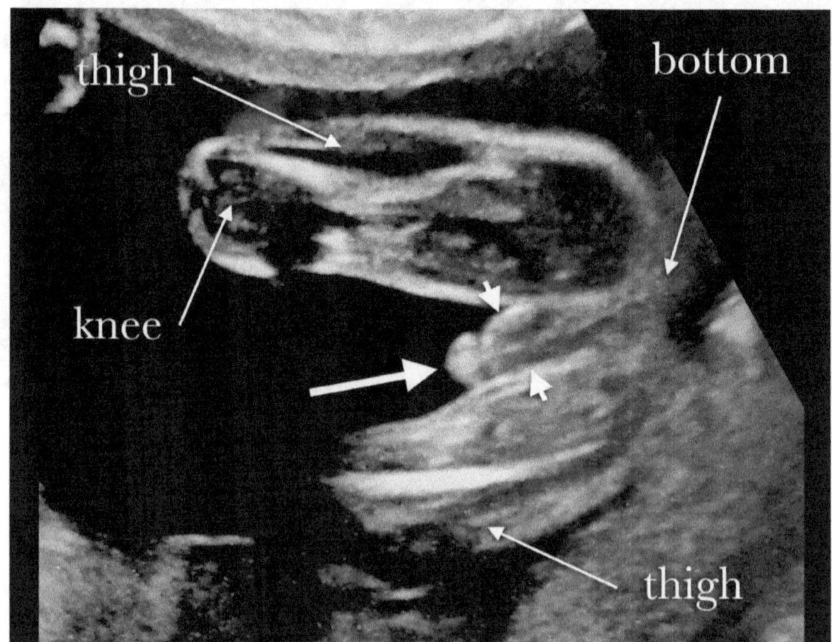

Figure 23.3: Week 23 ~ Male Gender-1

By now, you can probably characterize some of these differences without my help. I knew you'd be fast learners.

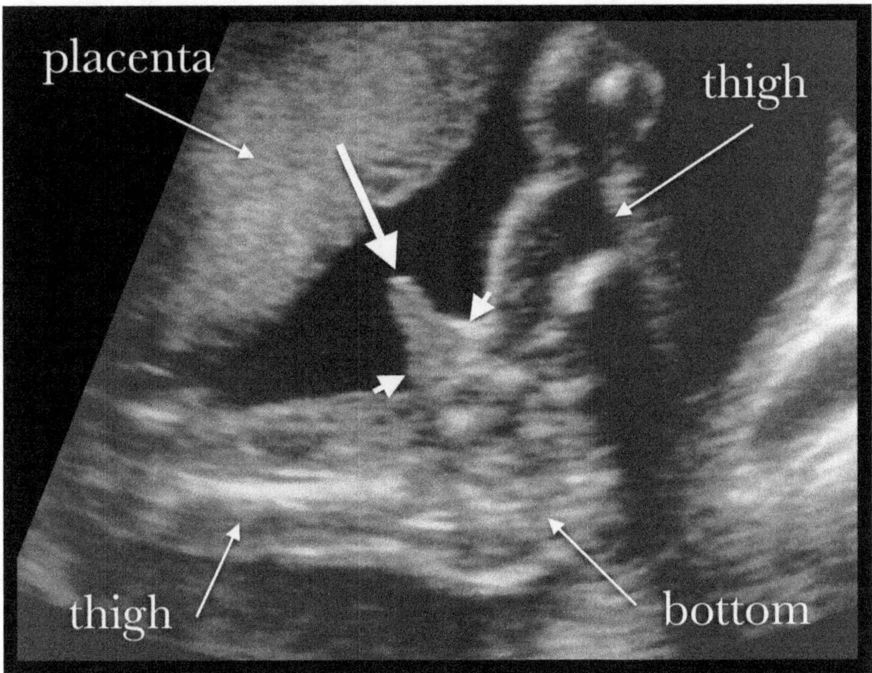

Figure 23.4: Week 23 ~ Male Gender-2

I ask you. Can we end out this chapter with any better shot than Figure 23.4? This is one proud little boy.

Week 24

igures 24.1 and 24.2 show typical development for both male and female at this GA.

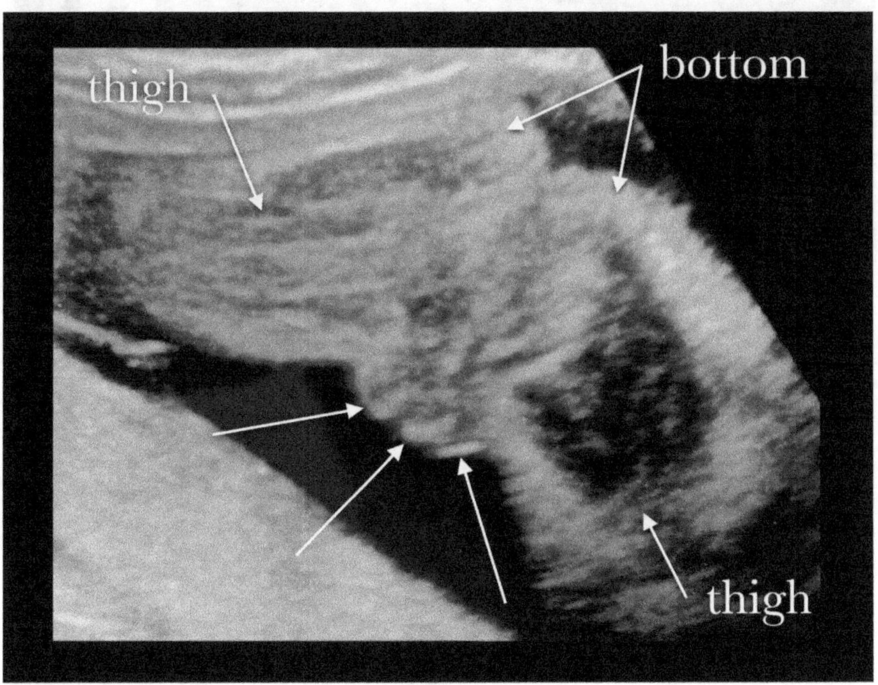

Figure 24.1: Week 24 ~ Female Gender

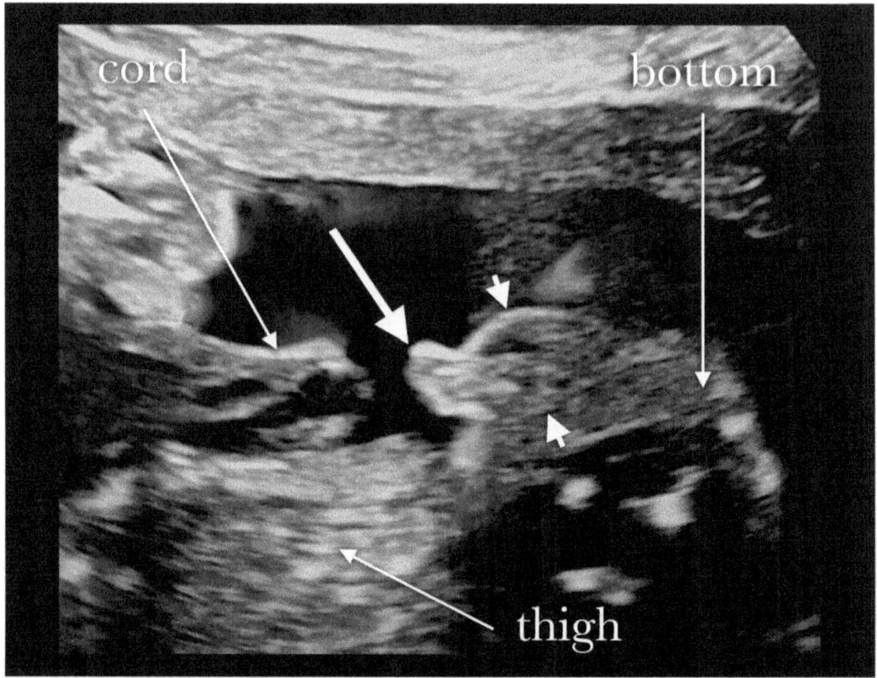

Figure 24.2: Week 24 ~ Male Gender

If Figure 24.2 isn't as obvious to you as some of the others, that's because it represents another side view rather than a bottom view with only part of one thigh pictured here. However, even with the cord nearby, male genitalia are easy to discern.

Week 25

igure 25.1, though a bit bright, shows the typical bottom-view shot of labia which we'd expect to see in Week 25.

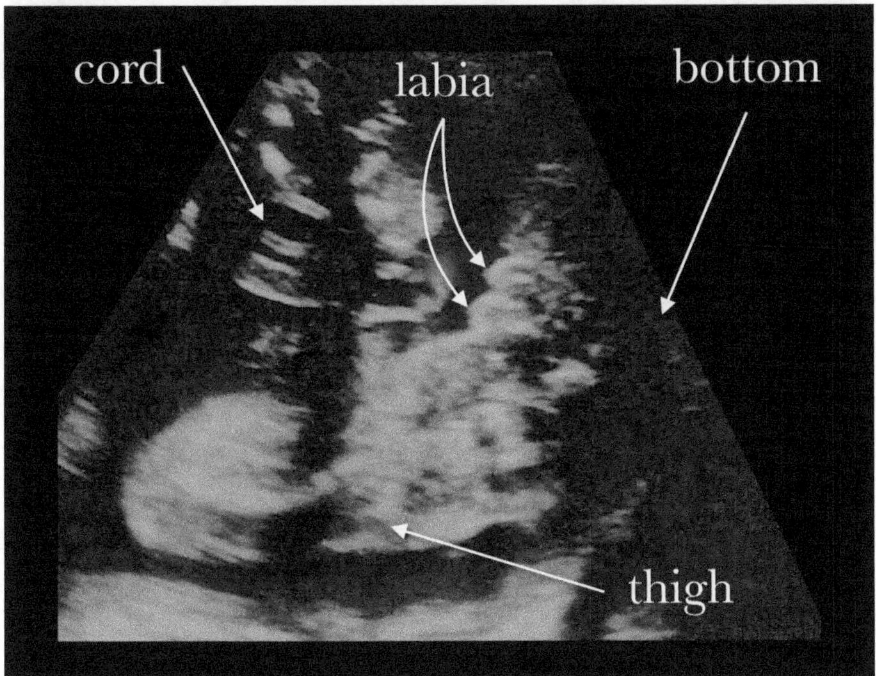

Figure 25.1: Week 25 ~ Female Gender-1

Finally, Figures 25.2 through 25.5 demonstrate female genitalia, but the appearance may be a bit of a departure compared to prior weeks' images. Part of the reason lies in fetal position. Where we normally view an underside or side view of Baby, what you see in both figures is a front view. I've included a graphic for each image to help orient you.

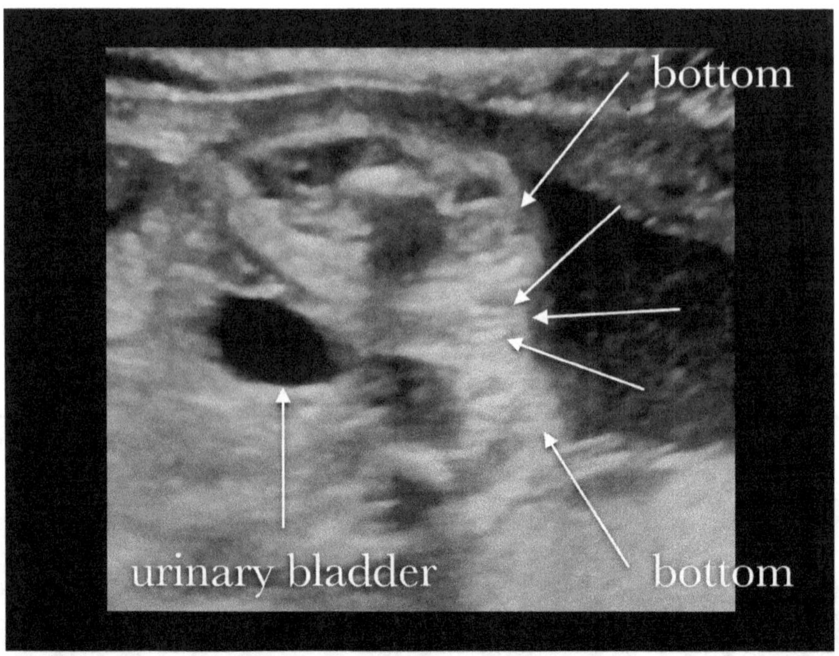

Figure 25.2: Week 25 ~ Female Gender-2

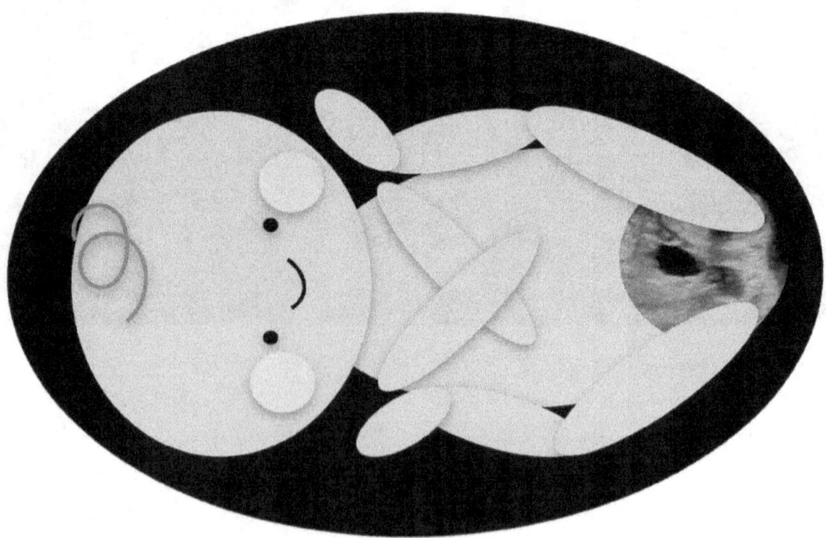

Figure 25.3: Week 25 ~ Female Gender-2 with Graphic

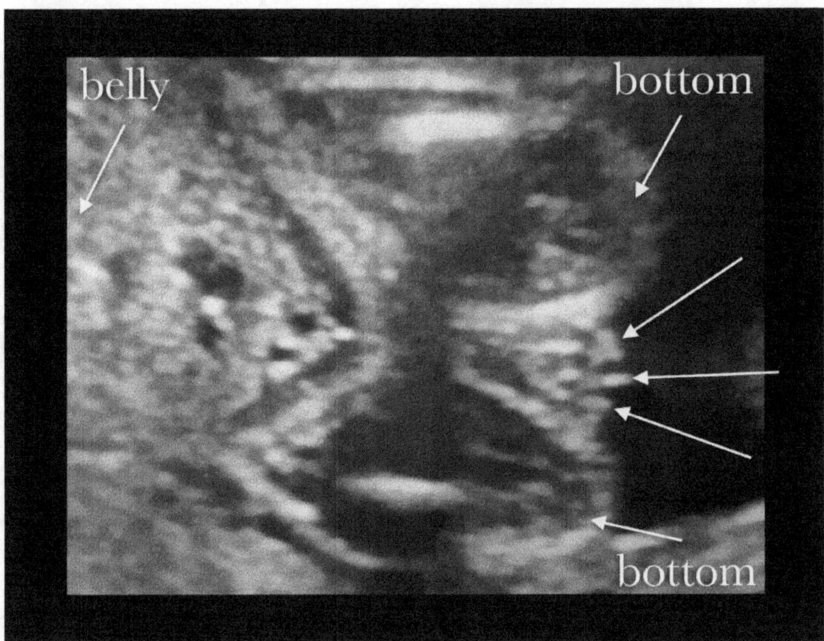

Figure 25.4: Week 25 ~ Female Gender-3

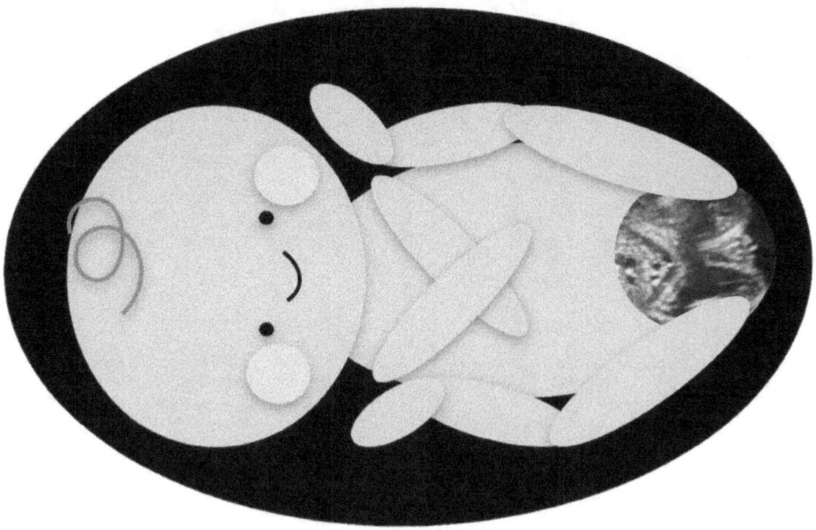

Figure 25.5: Week 25 ~ Female Gender-3 with Graphic

Let's close out this chapter with a great profile of Baby B at 25w5d.

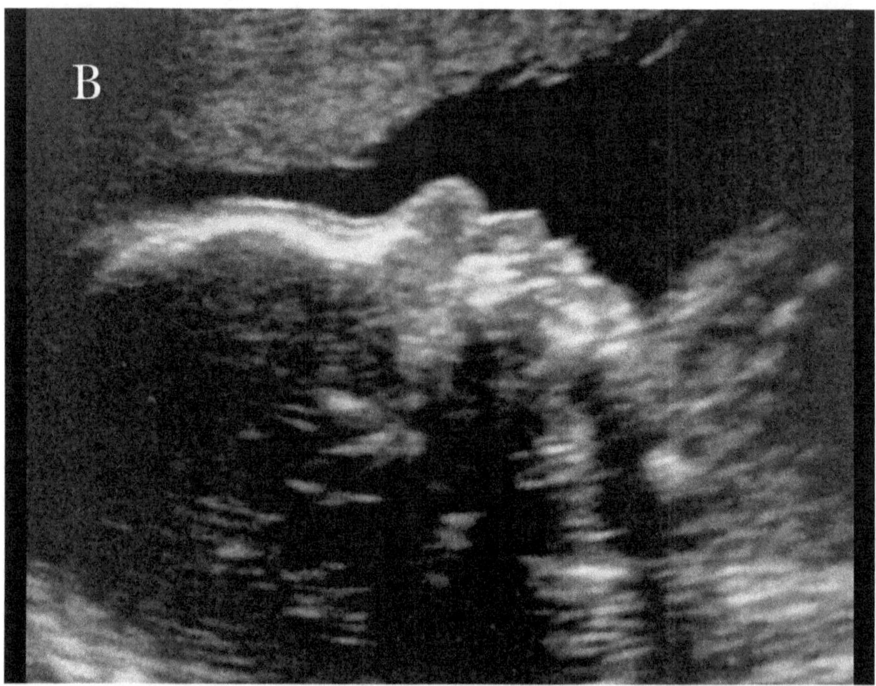

Figure 25.6: Baby B ~ 25w5d

Week 27

igures 27.1 through 27.3 show how normal female genitalia can appear a bit different depending on angle and, also, from fetus to fetus. Either way, labia are easily identifiable in the following images.

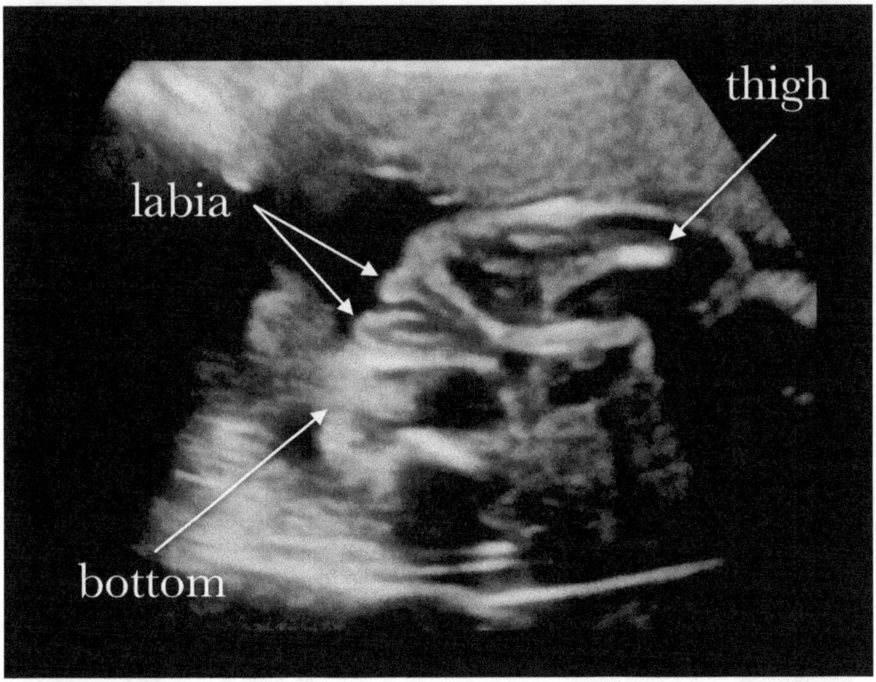

Figure 27.1: Week 27 ~ Female Gender-1

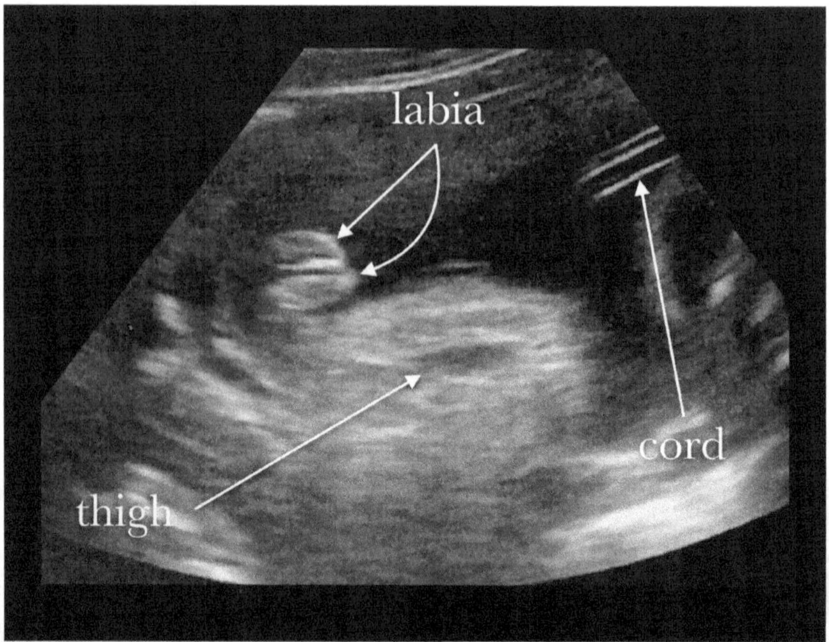

Figure 27.2: Week 27 ~ Female Gender-2

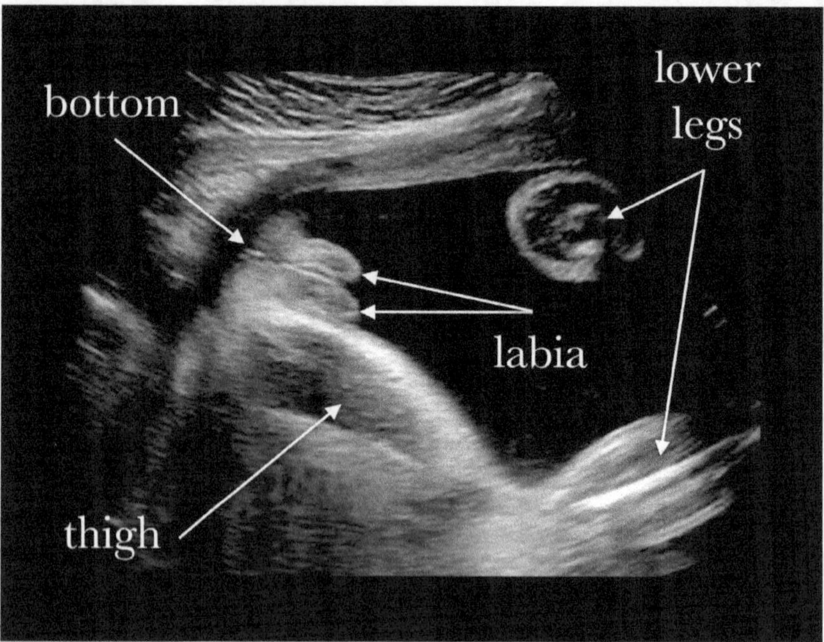

Figure 27.3: 27w5d ~ Female Gender-3

Week 28
Beginning the Third Trimester

Congratulations! You've officially made it to the start of the Third Trimester at Week 28. You may find that your doctor wants to monitor Baby's growth and well-being a bit more often here in the last trimester, most commonly after about Week 30. But this is only if it's been determined that your pregnancy has been complicated by any number of variables such as gestational diabetes, for example.

Last Peeks Begin at 28 Weeks

If all is going well with both mom and Baby, your physician may not feel the need to order another ultrasound scan. Quite often, obstetricians may order another at some point before delivery for an estimation of weight. If smooth sailing applies to you, congratulations! Enjoy getting all the things ready for Little Bit to make his or her big debut.

On to more gender images in the Third Trimester. If you are scanned during this period, you may find that your baby is becoming more and more difficult to see. They gain the most weight as you approach the final weeks, occupying more space and leaving less room for amniotic fluid—the stuff that helps us see well. With all the crowding, getting a good look at external genitalia may not happen. As babies gain more weight and fill the space, the less room to roll around and flip as they did in earlier weeks. Often, once they find a position they like, they're usually comfortable to stay that way! That means if a cord or leg is in the way of seeing gender, all the poking and prodding on your belly may not move Baby very much.

On the other hand, if Baby is positioned well and you have plenty of fluid to spare, seeing these parts may be better than ever. A great view in these last several weeks can leave you with all the confidence you needed to snuff out the naysayers in your family who doubted your earlier gender images! This is always fun, isn't it?

I have fewer Third Trimester gender images to share, so note that I've skipped weeks for which I have no images. Even though we all look a little different from one another, you'll see that the criteria for male and female parts are not drastically changing any longer, since those mid-Second Trimester images.

Figures 28.1 and 28.2 both show a great representation of male genitalia here. The penis and scrotal sac, but not testicles, are seen in these great shots.

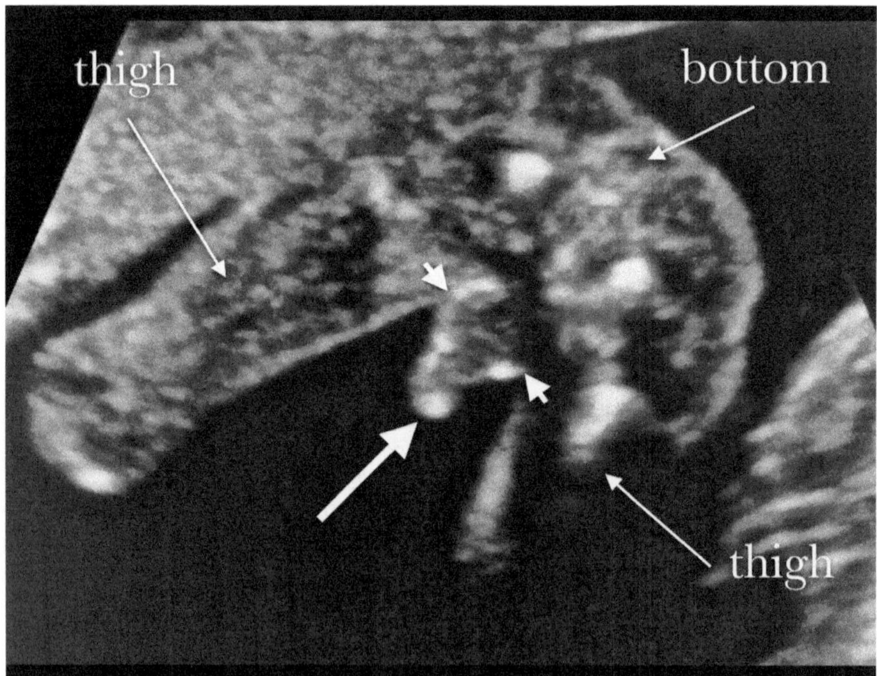

Figure 28.1: Week 28 ~ Male Gender-1

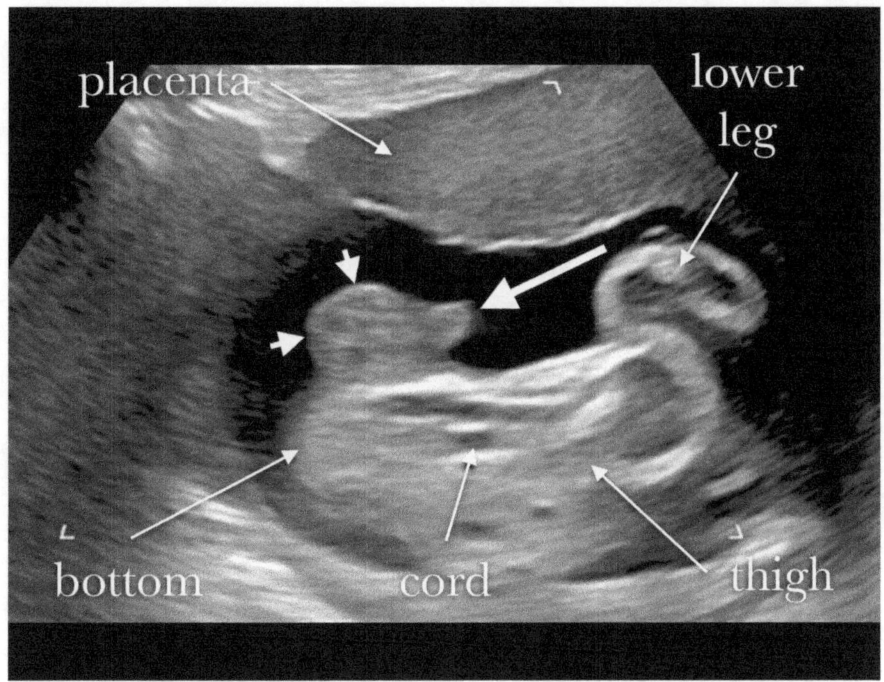

Figure 28.2: Week 28 ~ Male Gender-2

Week 30

Figures 30.1 and 30.2 show again how female gender can appear different depending on the angle obtained and how many other parts crowd the shot. Most of you will probably say that the second photo here makes it much harder to appreciate girly parts. Limbs, the placenta, and cord all take up space here, but the small pocket of fluid around the genitalia make the image possible at all.

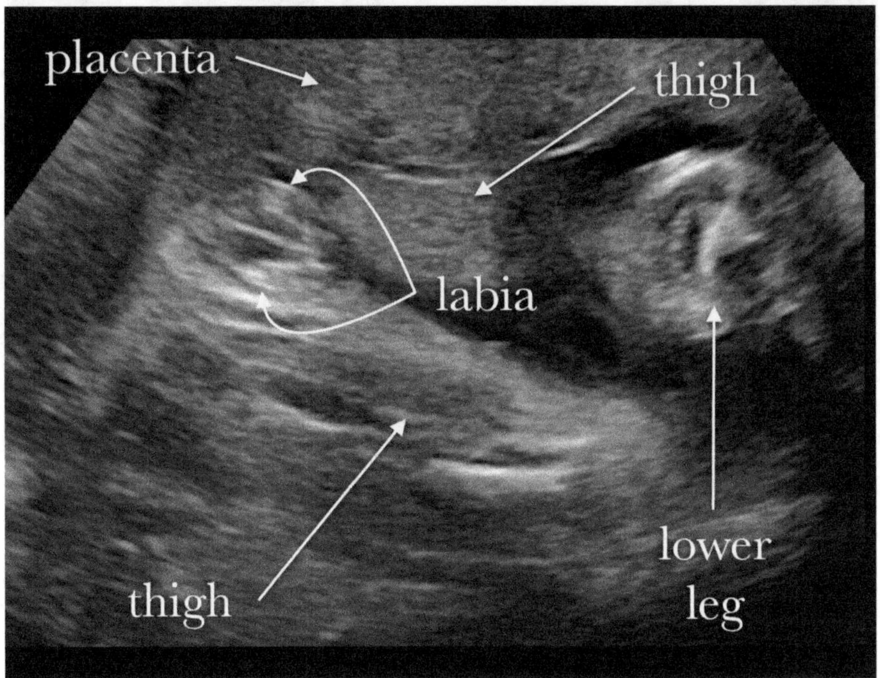

Figure 30.1: 30w1d ~ Female Gender-1

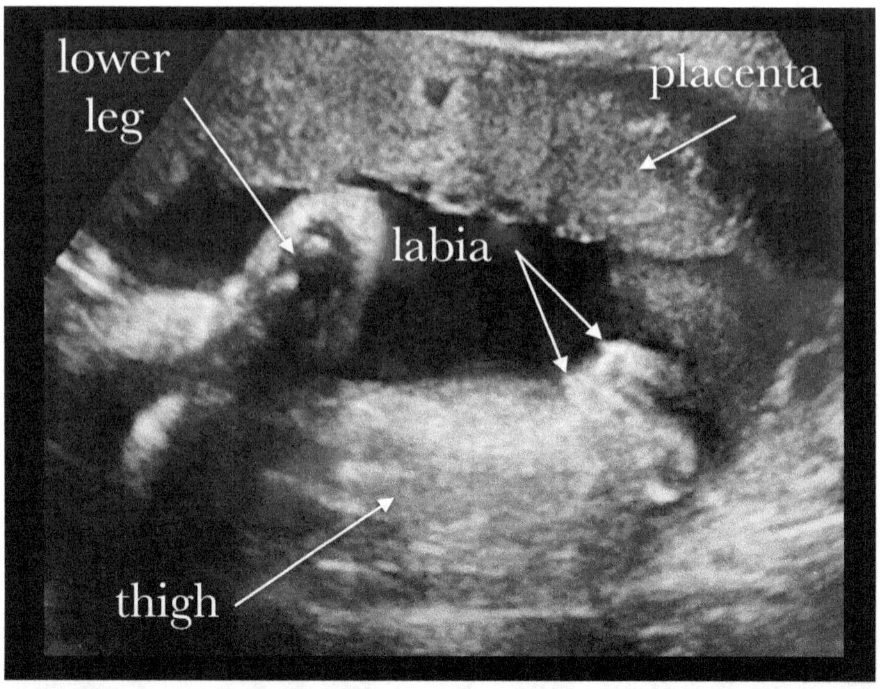

Figure 30.2: Week 30 ~ Female Gender-2

Week 32

My sole image for Week 32 is this proud little boy you see here in Figure 32.1. We can't identify a bottom and only part of his legs. However, male genitalia is easily seen—even one of the testicles can be visualized. Even though she reached out for my opinion, there wasn't really much guesswork here for this mom.

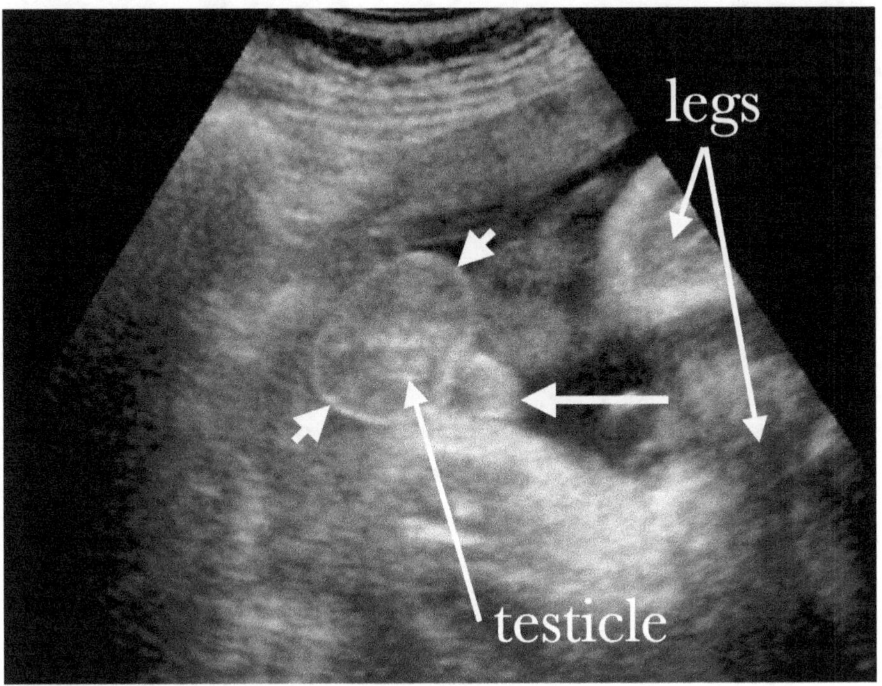

Figure 32.1: Week 32 ~ Male Gender

Week 33

igure 33.1 shows us a very magnified image of female labia and one of the best I've seen. Note a comparison between this one and the two photos from Week 30, Figures 30.1 and 30.2.

Compared, they are a great representation of how little girls can look different from one baby to another. Here we see only labia. Figures 30.1 and 30.2 demonstrate smaller labia and visualization of the clitoris.

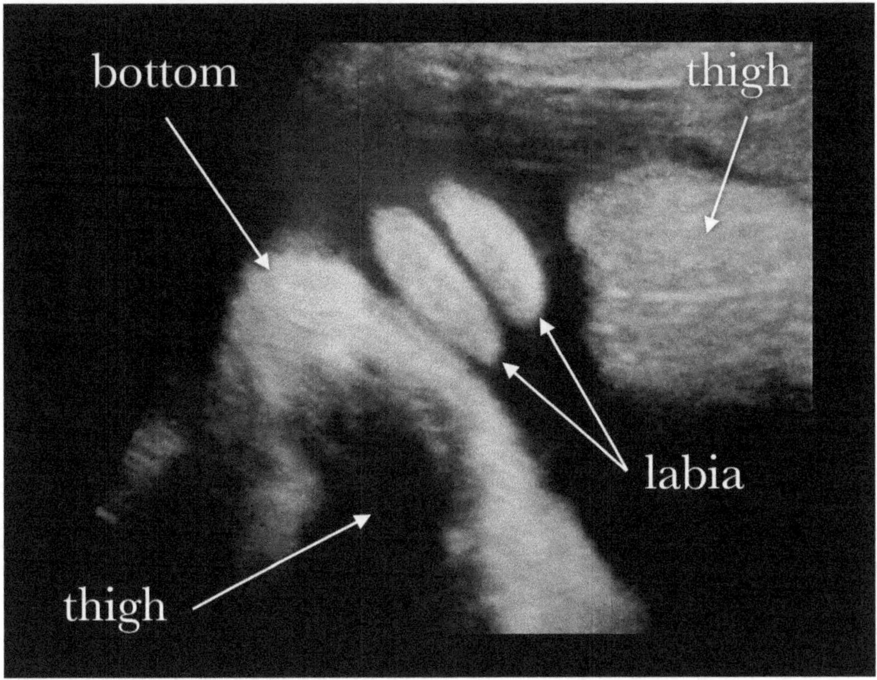

Figure 33.1: Week 33 ~ Female Gender

Week 36

created Week 36 for the sole purpose of featuring the last great facial profile I have of Baby A at 36w5d. It's one of my favorites. Facial profiles prove so very difficult to obtain later in the Third Trimester, especially with twins. Typically, as one can imagine, the space is cramped and fluid is normally slightly diminished. However, Baby A made this an usually easy shot and one worth the showcase. It won't be long now before the twins make their debut.

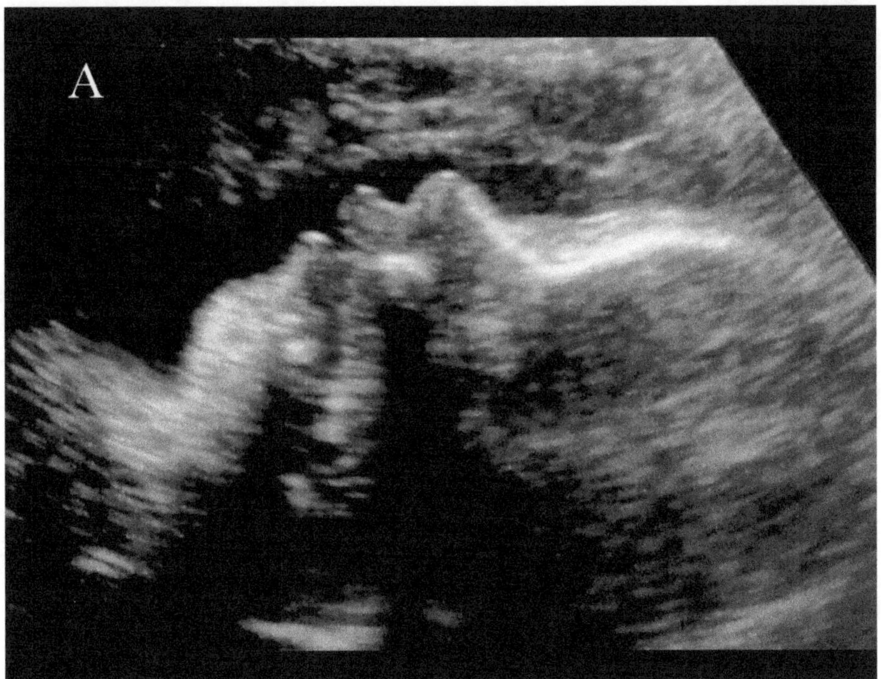

Figure 36.1: Baby A ~ 36w5d

Week 37

Figure 37.1 probably represents the best of all male genitalia images in my possession. This is an image from the side and here you can easily see the penis, scrotal sac, and even a very well-defined testicle, as well. Such a great shot!

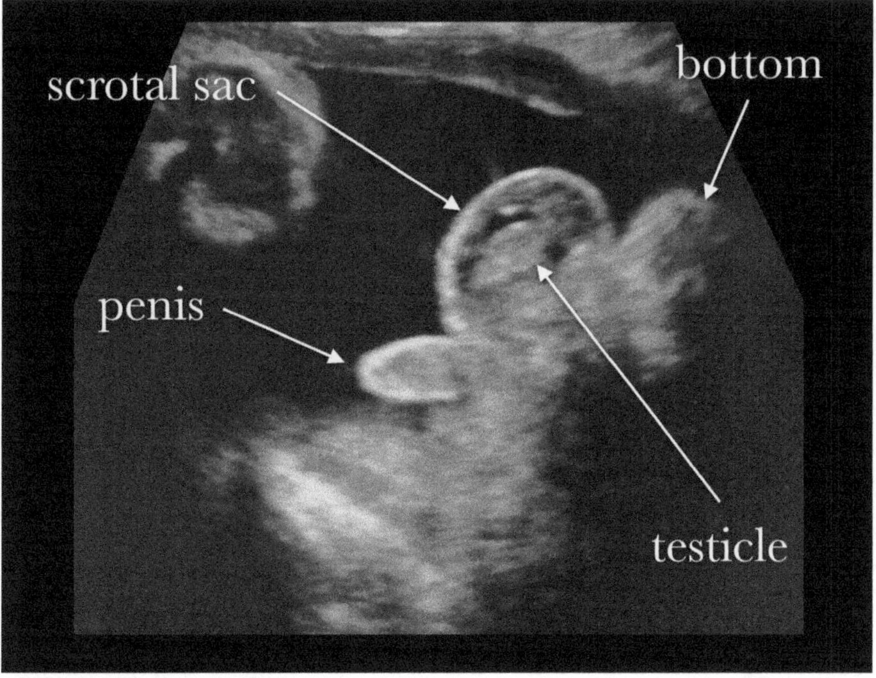

Figure 37.1: Week 37 ~ Male Gender

Week 38

ere's one last baby girl image to round out the bunch at 38 Weeks. This is the same female fetus as in Figure 33.1! Her little bottom was positioned a bit more firmly against the uterine wall this day, making the image at 33 Weeks just a bit clearer.

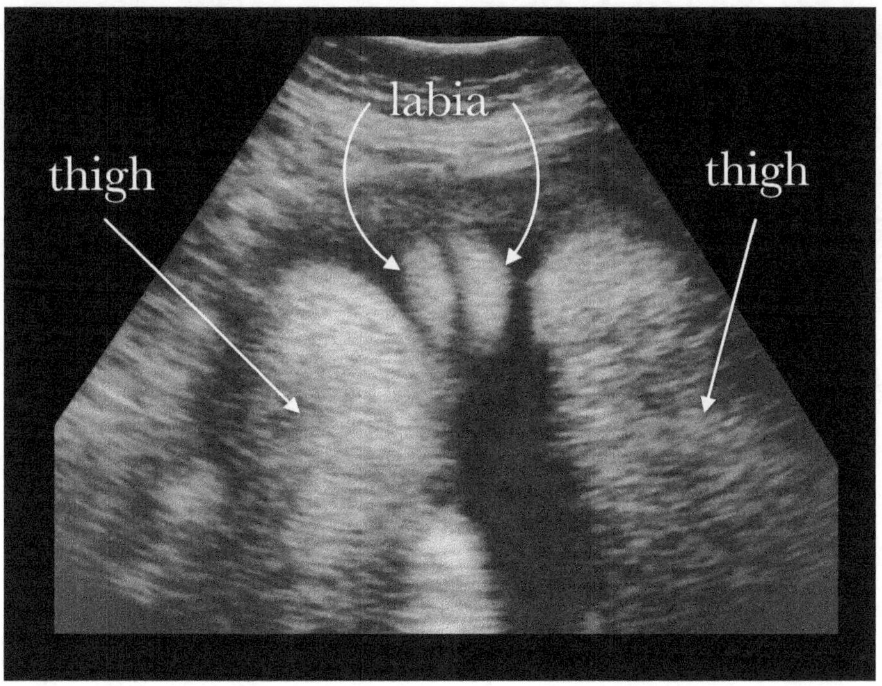

Figure 38.1: 38w5d ~ Female Gender

With our exploration through fetal gender complete, I hope it gave you a clearer understanding of not only the differences in development between male and female but also the differences we see in the *same* gender compared to one another in varying stages of gestational age. Hopefully, these images provided a broader pictorial view of the challenges presented which can make fetal sex determination very difficult—and sometimes impossible. Last but not least, I hope Part Three provided you with the foundation to better comprehend your own gender images a little better.

Won't it be fun to put yourself to the test with your next sonogram? I'd love to know if you pass!

Conclusion

Dianne and her twins hope you have enjoyed following them on their journey through the early crucial weeks of life in utero, watching them grow, and discovering their genders. Fascinating exploration, wasn't it?

Please meet Dianne's twins!

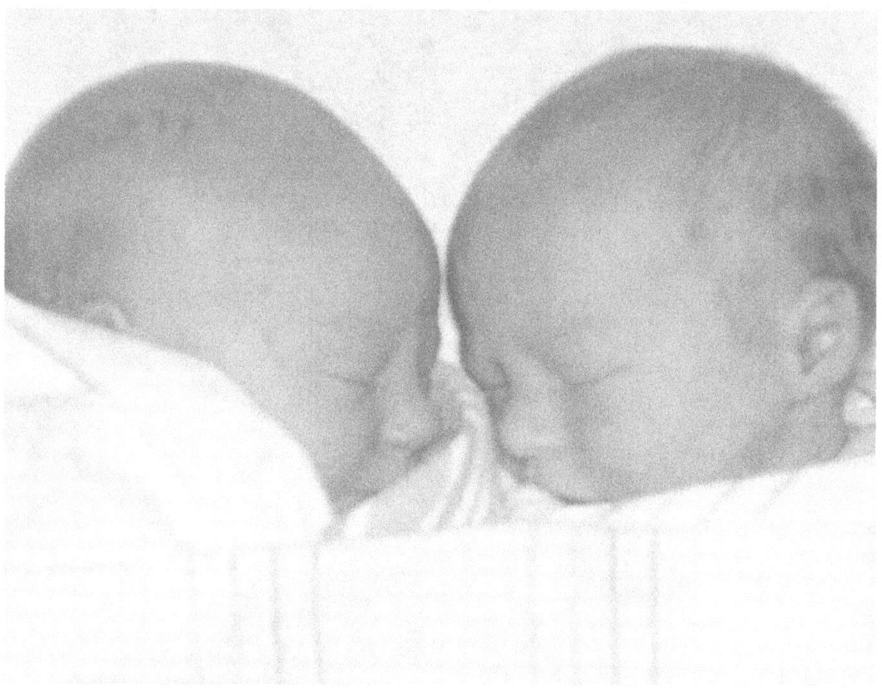

Babies A and B

Baby A officially became Megan.

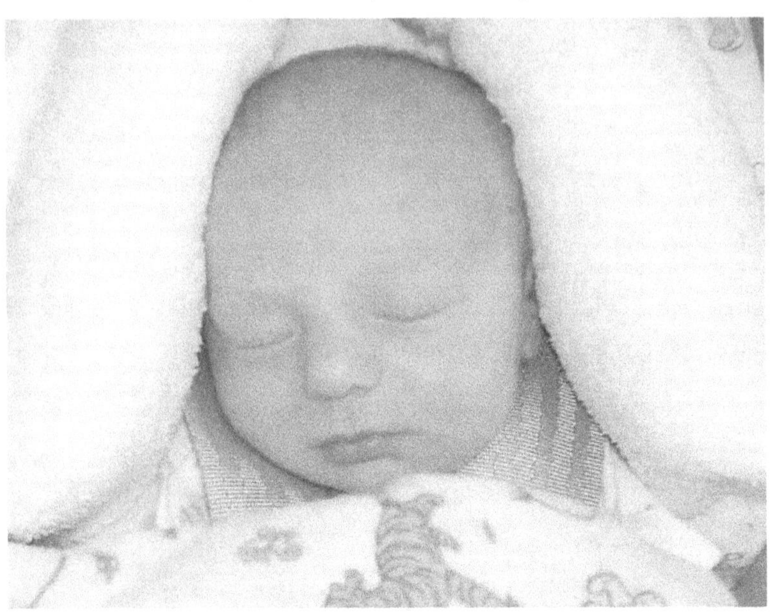

Meet Megan, Baby A

Baby B officially became Patrick.

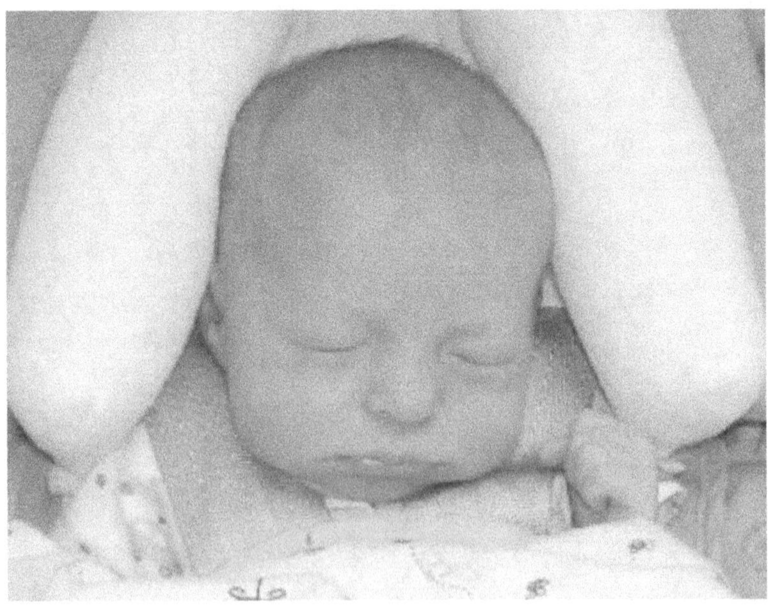

Meet Patrick, Baby B

Megan and Patrick were born very healthy babies at 37w6d. Megan weighed 5 pounds, 8 ounces. Patrick weighed 5 pounds, 13 ounces. They are now both very healthy pre-teens who also had a baby sister added to the mix just a couple of years later. I still look forward to receiving their Christmas card and picture every year. Our babies grow up so fast!

It's my sincere wish that you've enjoyed the pregnancy journey from a sonographer's perspective. I was so privileged to be a part of this extraordinary journey in Dianne's life. Even though I scanned tens of thousands of patients at various weeks of pregnancy for years, to witness all the changes in the *same* pregnancy from so early on (and twins, at that!) proved an exceptional educational experience for us both. It's not every day that a sonographer *or* patient is presented with such a unique opportunity. In fact, this was the *only* occasion in my entire career for such an experience. I am honored and sincerely grateful to have played an integral role in the adventure.

More than anything, I hope you found this book an informative and illuminating discovery into pregnancy through the eyes of ultrasound. And I hope also that I have imparted a bit of insight into understanding your images, as well as, the fascinating week-by-week transformation of your baby's growth.

Perhaps you might even surprise yourself during your own future sonogram. You're caught up in the excitement of meeting this life you carry inside you for the very first time. Your heart beats fast in anticipation, somewhere between anxiety and fear. The moment is surreal. This is *your* baby, the child you've dreamed of your whole life. You hold your breath, for just a moment, and then you see the flutter of that tiny beating machine. You relax, though still mesmerized by the movie playing out before you.

And then it happens, in the midst of your examination, as you watch in utter amazement, a light bulb goes off...an epiphany! A "Hey, I know that view!" moment. It's the revelation when you actually recognize fetal anatomy on the monitor. Maybe it looks curiously familiar to the images you've pored over in this book. If so, congratulations! You're a great student. Every one of us who has studied this technology recall that reaction, the giddy excitement that comes with the accomplishment of recognition. But beware. The feeling is addictive. And you may end up like many of us—who call ourselves sonographer. I should know.

I wish every expectant parent, couple, and family out there a very healthy and uneventful pregnancy. Congratulations on the start of your incredible adventure called Parenthood. If you're as blessed as I am, it will be the greatest love you know.

"in dolce attesa"
(in sweet waiting)

~ *the end* ~

Q & A

May I send you an email?

Of course! You can email me at UltrasoundUnwrapped@gmail.com with your questions. You can upload images and short video clips there, too.

May I send you a personal question about my pregnancy?

See the email address above. Remember, however, I am not a physician nor am I your sonographer. This means I do not have all the information about your case and may not be able to provide the answer you seek. But I'll do my best to give you as complete a response as I can.

Can my baby hear the sound waves?

No. Ultrasound utilizes sound waves that exceed far beyond human hearing.

Can my baby feel the sound waves?

No. However, Baby does tend to react to pushing or pressure on the belly, but not always. At times they will not budge despite lots of pushing or having mom perform head stands; being "difficult" can start at a very early age!

Why can't I video my ultrasound?

We get this one a lot. In fact, I've probably heard it almost as much as the question of fetal sex, but there's very good reason behind this policy. Yes, it's your baby, but the ultrasound examination belongs to the medical practice performing it. Your diagnostic ultrasound is firstly a medical examination on you and your baby. That examination is not complete until it is read and signed off on by a physician.

So, in short, most medical facilities do not want unread images or video flying about the Internet in this age of social media. Unfortunately, and much to the chagrin of most patients and family, this has become a necessary protection for many medical practices. If it's your wish to record, be sure to inquire about the policies where your ultrasound will be performed!

I am interested in a career in Ultrasound. Can you give me some basic information?

Absolutely! The main certifying body for sonographers in the United States can provide some helpful information, ARDMS or The American Registry for Diagnostic Medical Sonography. (https://www.ardms.org/discover-ardms/students/resources-for-sonography-students/)

Additionally, the CAAHEP, Commission on Accreditation of Allied Health Education Programs, can provide a list of accredited programs within the United States. Search Profession Name "Diagnostic Medical Sonography" and select degree/credential of interest to find many programs by city and state. (https://www.caahep.org)

I am happy to provide you with some personal insight into the blood, sweat, and thick skin required on the path to a career in sonography as well as a little about what a busy workday was like for me in OB/GYN. Good luck in all your efforts! Just see the posts below on my site, UltrasoundUnwrapped.com:

Becoming a Sonographer—Is it for You?
(https://ultrasoundunwrapped.com/becoming-a-sonographer/)

Sonographer Education and Training
(https://ultrasoundunwrapped.com/sonographer-education/)

New Sonographer Advice for the Newbie
(https://ultrasoundunwrapped.com/new-sonographer-ultrasound-advice/)

Unwrapping A Sonographer's Work
(https://ultrasoundunwrapped.com/sonographers-work/)

An OB Sonographer's Day
(https://ultrasoundunwrapped.com/day-life-ob-sonographer/)

Thanks for Reading!

I invite you to email me at UltrasoundUnwrapped@gmail.com to share your questions, thoughts, and reactions. If you finish this book feeling enlightened, comforted, hopeful, or entertained, my efforts in writing it have been worth every second.

Meet the Author

Sandra M. Minck, RDMS is a Registered Diagnostic Medical Sonographer of 29 years. She dedicated most of her career to a private OB/GYN practice specializing in women's healthcare where she performed obstetric studies in all weeks of pregnancy as well as gynecologic sonography. *Ultrasound Unwrapped: A Week-by-Week Pregnancy Image Guide* is her first book.

She is the creator and author of UltrasoundUnwrapped.com and @ultrasound_unwrapped on Instagram, both credible sources of information for expectant parents. She enjoys translating clinical knowledge into easy-to-understand material, key to quality patient communication and awareness. She is currently pursuing an interest in Health Communication Writing and most recently contributed blog health content for AIUM's, *The Scan.*

Sandra is a devoted mother of two grown daughters and especially loves international travel with her family. She enjoys painting and the arts, and her favorite place in the world is a beautiful beach anywhere. Sandra lives in south Florida with her husband, Jeff, and fur baby, Gus, where she takes every opportunity to dig her toes in the sand.